IVAN LENDL

THE MAN WHO MADE MURRAY

IVAN LENDL

THE MAN WHO MADE MURRAY

MARK HODGKINSON

Aurum
Press

First published in Great Britain
2014 by Aurum Press Ltd
74–77 White Lion Street
Islington
London N1 9PF
www.aurumpress.co.uk

A catalogue record for this book is available from the British Library.

ISBN 978 1 78131 290 2

1 3 5 7 9 10 8 6 4 2
2014 2016 2018 2017 2015

Typeset in ITC New Baskerville by SX Composing DTP, Rayleigh Essex
Printed and bound by CPI Group (UK) Ltd, Croydon, CR0 4YY

For Amy, Molly and Rosie

CONTENTS

PROLOGUE

Others invented the tie-break, the titanium racket and the Hawk-Eye line-calling technology; Ivan Lendl created the Fuck You Forehand. He would happily smash a tennis ball into your face. Among Lendl's legacies to the sport, this is where tennis crosses over into psychological violence; he would be looking to leave psychic bruises as well as raspberry-coloured welts on your skin. Jimmy Connors gave you the finger and John McEnroe had his foaming furies; Lendl launched the ball at your head, and started a revolution.

'If you watch tennis now, everyone is doing it, but Ivan was the first,' Mats Wilander, who contested five grand slam finals against Lendl, told me. 'Ivan would come at you, hitting the ball so hard that you couldn't get out of the way, and, in those days, when he was the first to use that tactic, that wasn't seen as being very sporting. We would all be thinking, "Oh, Ivan, that's a bit strange". Ivan was a pioneer in other ways, like the way he worked out, and the way he prepared for matches, but he was also a pioneer in the way he hit people.' Several tennis generations later, just a few days out from the 2013 Wimbledon Championships, and during a charity doubles match opposite Andy Murray at London's Queen's Club it became clear just how Lendl's invention had been turned against him. This was the most violent of Sunday afternoons in West Kensington: after all those years of unloading forehands at others, now Lendl was the one experiencing the sting of a tennis ball exploding on his flesh, and it was Murray who had thrashed hard in his direction.

On the Cold War-era tennis tour, there were no disarmament conferences or marches, nothing that Lendl's rivals could do to nullify the destructive, atomic power of his forehand. It was tennis's first great forehand, a shot struck with such force that the watching Arthur Ashe believed that Lendl was deforming tennis balls, the late American novelist David Foster Wallace thought that the man from the East was playing a kind of brutal art, and Lendl himself was publishing instructional books with titles such as *Hitting Hot* and *Power Tennis*. You wouldn't buy those to add subtlety to your game. Lendl's forehand was terrifying enough when he was ripping the ball through the court for winners, with the felt-covered missiles bouncing and then thudding into the backstop; there was a whole new level of brutality and terror when Lendl aimed at his opponent, pressing fire on one of those head-seeking, hellfire forehands. Here was a shot designed to cause maximum damage to your opponent's mental wellbeing; clobber someone with a forehand and you're telling him, as well as all those watching, who's alpha and who's beta.

Just look at what Lendl started. Before Lendl, tennis wasn't a contact sport; its ethos was still that of the country club and not far off that of the vicarage lawn. In today's tennis-speak, or language of the locker-room, these deliberate and provocative acts are known as 'tagging', 'tubing' or 'drilling' – you're clumping the ball with all the power your racket arm can generate, and you're hoping, where possible, to take your opponent's head off. And you're not going to apologise. You certainly never whisper a 'sorry' or raise a hand in silent apology after striking your opponent – you could, as Lendl did once after knocking McEnroe to the ground, just spin around and prepare for the next point, not bothering to look back at your battered, floored opponent. Remorse was for wimps. To apologise would have been to lose much of the impact of assaulting your opponent in the first place.

There's only one problem with this analysis, with this idea that Lendl was looking to use a direct hit to gain a psychological edge over his adversary, and that's that it's simply not based in reality. As we shall discover, over the years a mythology has built up around many parts of Lendl's tennis life, and one of the many Lendl myths concerns those forehand zingers. And Lendl hadn't always worked hard to correct the myths that suited his cause. If everyone had come to believe that Lendl was using his racket to blast holes in an opponent's psyche, if they imagined he was so determined to win tennis matches that he would behave like that, well, he wasn't going to tell them any differently. As one former player who was on the tour with Lendl said to me, the Czech-born player was hardly going to mind a reputation for psychological violence that helped to 'strengthen his locker-room aura', so why bother addressing this untruth about himself? And, thirty years on from Lendl winning his first slam – at Roland Garros in the

spring of 1984 – it's a character trait that people keep returning to and glorifying, just like his supposed inability to smile,
which is another of the great Lendl myths.

It's undeniably true that Lendl was the first to regularly take
deliberate aim at the poor saps opposite him. And he did so on
the practice court as well as in the stadium. Almost everyone
from the 1980s that Murray had spoken to about his former
coach has an anecdote about being stung by Lendl's bomb of
a forehand. Lendl became known for it. Playing a duff shot
against Lendl, and then standing there at the net believing
that he wouldn't be gunning for your forehead, was an idiocy;
you had effectively turned yourself into a firing-range silhou-
ette dressed up in tennis togs. You should have known better
than to do that; in all likelihood, you were going to end up
with the ball manufacturer's logo imprinted on your skin.

So Lendl hadn't done much to correct this myth. But the
sense is that Lendl believes that others, and the soft-headed
media especially, sometimes made too much of a big deal
about when his forehand connected with an opponent's
face or upper body. However, that wouldn't be the first or
last time that he thought that commentators had psychoanalysed something to death. The truth appears to be that Lendl
hit this shot because of practical, rather than psychological,
considerations. And that's a view supported by comments he
made in his book *Power Tennis*, which was published in the
1980s – if his opponent was at the net, it was often the right
play. In the early years of his career, Lendl felt as though he
was losing too many close-range exchanges – essentially, those
points would come down to guesses, with the opponent having to decide whether Lendl was going to go for a passing
shot down the line or cross-court. If the opponent made a

correct guess, Lendl would generally lose the point. Okay, you could play a lob, but what if your opponent was responding well to those, too? What were your options? A practical solution, and it was one he found by accident on the day he mistimed a forehand which ended up going down the middle of the court, was to whack the ball directly at his opponent – if he was able to put enough oomph into the shot, it was more than likely he would come off best. And winning the point was what mattered. Nailing McEnroe, or a missile at Vitas Gerulaitis' forehead – those are the two most celebrated occasions he went after his opponent – would have counted for nothing if he hadn't won the points.

Just one successful strike could make life easier for the rest of the match; Lendl found that his opponents would then stand a step or two further back from the net, a consequence of which was that Lendl would then have bigger angles, and more court, to aim for when going for passing shots. Doubtless Lendl's belligerent nature brought him a few free points every week. But it just wasn't true, Lendl has suggested, that he would put his cross-hairs on an opponent's head. The target, as he noted in his manual *Power Tennis*, was the right side of the stomach, as a ball hit with pace into that area would 'jam' his opponent. 'Contrary to what cynics say, I'm not aiming for the head. It sometimes looks that way because any ball hit hard [in the right side of the stomach] causes an extremely awkward reflex. Try it and you'll see that your foe may fall down trying to get out of the way.' Lendl's view was that he hadn't invited his opponent to approach the net, so if his 'foe' chose to venture into the service box he was doing so at his own risk. Why should he feel any remorse for cutting a man down at the net?

And, anyway, wasn't this just cartoon violence, worthy of nothing more than a Batman-style 'Kapow!' bubble? Who was ever seriously hurt, let alone hospitalised, after being hit by one of Lendl's forehands? A Lendl kill shot could cause you no more pain than a paintball splat. Talk to some of those who travelled the tennis trail with Lendl and they don't exactly seem to have been mentally tormented by his forehand. Once the locker-room had got over their initial surprise, there was an almost universal acceptance that the shot was an entirely legitimate play. And, as Pat Cash said when interviewed for this book, if Lendl was able to hit you in the head with his forehand you must have played a 'pretty crappy shot', so you would have deserved the pain. Another player who used to practise with Lendl spoke of 'suffering the consequences' for playing a poor shot against him. So opponents didn't want to be hit, which was why some of them backed off the net a little bit, but that wasn't to say that they were terrified or intimidated by Lendl.

What if Lendl was motivated by laughter? Lendl liked to hit his opponents because he thought it was funny, because it appealed to his sadistic, cruel sense of humour. That time he scored a direct hit on McEnroe and immediately turned his back on his battered, floored opponent? It was because he was already laughing. That was about the happiest Lendl ever looked on a tennis court. 'Who wants a robot as the world number one?' McEnroe had once asked, but that was to believe that Lendl was a communist caricature – grey, and completely bloodless and artless. When Lendl was firing balls at his opponents, he was being bold, confrontational and more than a little mischievous. Most of the time, Lendl kept his emotions and his personality hidden away on court – you could say that thc times he hit opponents were about the only moments he ever displayed his true character during matches. Hitting McEnroe would have been a particularly pleasurable moment, as Lendl knew just how much the New Yorker hated coming under bombardment. At heart, Lendl has always been a provocateur, someone who likes causing trouble. So knowing that McEnroe hated being pelted with tennis balls would hardly have discouraged Lendl from doing it again – he once threatened to swing his forehand to administer some corporal punishment on McEnroe for whining about line calls. But don't let's imagine this was primarily about vengeance – he would slam a forehand at his opponent for two main reasons: to win the point and to amuse himself.

There were times when Lendl couldn't hide his amusement from his victim; if it happened in practice, he rarely bothered to disguise the pleasure such a shot had brought him. Mark Philippoussis, for instance, has recalled a practice session when he fed Lendl a vanilla forehand, and pointed at the sky to signal he wanted his training partner to float up some soft lobs for him to smash away. 'Instead, Lendl just came in and smashed the ball at me as hard as he could,' the Australian has said. 'That was Ivan's way of joking, his sense of humour.'

As with all the other Lendl myths, it's not the reality that matters but the perception. So old contemporaries such as Brad Gilbert recall: 'There was no act – the guy was rough.' And most still contend that Lendl was a psychological menace. The idea persists that Lendl was going after his opponents' minds. And there are some in tennis who seem to be saying that Lendl wouldn't have been Lendl without those Fuck You Forehands (forgive the profanity, but Lendl doesn't mind the occasional obscenity, so let's talk his language). Could Lendl have won eight grand slam singles titles, and held the world number one ranking for 270 weeks – more than anyone but Roger Federer and Pete Sampras – if he hadn't had the Fuck You Forehand in his repertoire?

And from the very start of Murray's coaching relationship with Lendl – announced on New Year's Eve 2011 – there was immediate interest in whether Murray would soon be aiming his forehand at the unsuspecting faces of Rafa Nadal, Novak Djokovic, Federer and others. It was as if some of Lendl's other skills and attributes had faded into the background. Who exactly had Murray hired here? The Marquis de Sade with a tennis racket? Naturally, Murray had seen the clips of his coach attacking his contemporaries from the 1980s, when the 'ball had popped up on top of the net, and his aim was just to absolutely nail them'.

From the off, it sounded as though Murray's new coach was as interested as anyone else in seeing the Scot launching Lendlesque forehands. Mostly, Murray has disclosed, that was because Lendl found the idea funny, because he would have got off on the mayhem. 'As soon as this guy comes to net,' Lendl would urge Murray, 'just try to hit him.' 'That's Ivan's sense of humour,' Murray once said, a remark that seems to confirm the view that, back in the 1980s, Lendl didn't clock opponents because he was going after their psyches. And Lendl also didn't mind coming under fire himself. 'If he gets hit with a ball his reaction is not: "Ow, that's sore". It's to laugh. That's what gets him going, I guess, weird things like that.' Sometimes Lendl would go for Murray on the training court, but that was Lendl's way of showing affection; the more Lendl smacked the ball at Murray, the fonder he must have been feeling towards his employer. Lendl has been overheard trying to incite something between Murray and Dani Vallverdu, his Venezuelan assistant coach, who had been playing a game of mini-tennis: 'Come on, bury him. He's talking shit about how slow you are. Make him suffer.'

Generally, though, Murray wanted to make anyone who shared a court with him suffer in other ways – he hoped to produce tennis of such exceptional quality that opponents were left feeling both physically and mentally incapable. Murray, not being as confrontational or as shameless as his coach, has never attacked players as Lendl once did. He always thought he had other ways of winning points than 'absolutely nailing' his opponent. Murray had hit a few opponents, 'but not like the way Ivan hit them'. Sure, the summer before, when playing Jo-Wilfried Tsonga in the semi-finals of the 2012 Wimbledon Championships, Murray had struck his opponent in the Slazengers, and the Frenchman had curled up in a ball on the grass. But Murray hadn't set out to hurt Tsonga, and certainly hadn't taken any pleasure from it. Still, there was one person whom Murray had great interest in assaulting, and that was the tennis grandee he had hired to help him win grand slams. Which brings us to the summer of 2013 and the charity Rally Against Cancer exhibition match at the Queen's Club, organised by one of Murray's close friends, the British doubles player Ross Hutchins, who was having treatment for Hodgkin's lymphoma.

As soon as it was confirmed that Murray and Lendl were to be on opposite sides of the net during the exhibition match – with Murray to partner Tim Henman and Lendl paired with Czech Tomas Berdych – they spent many a spare moment discussing how they wanted to smack the other with a tennis ball. 'They had been talking about that match for months, about hitting each other,' Henman recalled, and it's the Englishman's view that Murray will never hit again a body shot like the one he landed on Lendl, a forehand swing volley that slammed into his coach's flesh. 'Andy has been playing tennis for years, and I promise you that he would never have hit a shot like that before in his career. And he will probably never hit one like that again. For Andy to actually make contact with Lendl, that really was a once-in-a-lifetime moment. You saw by Andy's reaction just how much it meant to him. And there wasn't much comeback for Lendl, not when he was live on the BBC, and playing in front of a crowd of a few thousand people.'

So Murray, who had lost his footing while playing his response to Lendl's looping volley, jumped up on seeing he had struck Lendl, and then whirled and bounced around the lawn, almost dancing. 'You could see the absolute delight on Andy's face when he tagged Ivan,' Murray's mother, Judy, told me. Wanting to prolong the pleasure later, he watched it all back on video.

Walloping Lendl was more than just an instant YouTube classic on Murray's phone; it was loaded with greater significance than that. This was the occasion, just eight days from the start of that summer's Wimbledon fortnight, when it became clear that Murray was fully Lendl-ised. The moment that Murray's forehand collided with Lendl – his coach had tried to twist his body out of the way – was confirmation of how Lendl had made Murray rethink his approach to tennis. Roughing up his opponents had never previously been Murray's style. True, this was *only* an exhibition match, and the ball was aimed at his coach, and not at one of his rivals, but it wouldn't be going too far to say that this stinging forehand from Murray's racket demonstrated the extent of Lendl's influence. Pre-Lendl, Murray would never have known that causing pain could be so enjoyable.

This book tells Lendl's story, on and off the court, but it's also the tale of how Lendl transformed his Scottish employer, how he enabled Murray to become the first British man wearing shorts to win Wimbledon. And what better sign could there have been of the player and coach's unity, and of the dynamic at the heart of the Lendl–Murray project, than the sight of Murray attempting to hurt Lendl in public? Consider Lendl's reaction to being hit in the chest; he was far from unhappy. He didn't even bother pretending to scowl. Instead the Queen's Club galleries were treated to what is supposedly one of the rarest sights in tennis, that combination of Czech gums and big-dollar American dentistry: the Lendl Smile.

CHAPTER ONE

CODENAME IVAN: ENEMY OF THE STATE?

For some Westerners, this tale from behind the Iron Curtain will read like the plot of a John le Carré tennis novel, one called *Biffer Basher Bully Spy*, or perhaps *The Baseliner Who Came in from the Cold*. It's disturbing to consider that the All England Club's summer garden party – with its pink fizz and elegantly crumpled linen suits, its sprinklers, ivy and hanging baskets – was potentially also a place of Cold War fear, paranoia and espionage. So Ivan Lendl never made it on to the list that mattered so much to him, the one recording every All England Club Single-Handed Champion of the World. And yet, as he played and lost in Wimbledon finals, his name already featured somewhere considerably more sinister – he was among the 'monitored persons' who were being trailed, investigated and spied on by Státní bezpečnost (the StB), communist Czechoslovakia's state secret police.

And I would suggest that the darkest part of this story is the identity of these 'tajný spolupracovník', or 'secret collaborators', who were informing on Lendl. Such was the Socialist Republic's interest in the tennis player's affairs, the spooks had recruited some of his family's closest friends as moles codenamed 'Olga' and 'Marek'; those the Lendls trusted with sensitive and personal information were delivering it straight to the StB's agents. As the StB's officers warned in the final paragraphs of the intelligence reports on Lendl that were circulated internally: 'If a non-tactical usage of stated information is applied there is a threat of disclosure of both secret collaborators, as they are confidential friends of the Lendl family.' There were also StB informants at Lendl's first tennis club, as well as in his neighbourhood, in his parents' workplaces and on the international tennis tour, in addition to the collaborators who had infiltrated the Czech emigrant communities. For Lendl and his parents, picking up the telephone, or posting a letter, was to risk every word and thought being captured and analysed by the country's security services.

Just like its Soviet equivalent the KGB, or East Germany's Stasi, the StB was known for its brutality, for going far beyond just snooping on its citizens; it kidnapped, intimidated, interrogated, blackmailed, suppressed, drugged, tortured and imprisoned those considered to be enemies of the state, confined them to mental institutions, or had them executed or assassinated, depending on whether they went to the bother of organising a show trial or not. It was in late 1981, so just a few months after Lendl had appeared in his first grand slam final at Roland Garros when he was the runner-up to Björn Borg, and also the year he moved from Czechoslovakia to America, that the state's security apparatus first did a 'check' on Lendl and his family. Not long after that, on 16 January 1982, an StB division chief in Prague signed a document approving the opening of a personal file on Lendl, with the 'Czechoslovak tennis representative to be examined with regards to his connections with adversary persons in the field of professional sport and connections in KS [Komunistická strana, or communist party]'. There in the StB's files, among 'Satan', 'Twist' and others – among the other monitored persons and those suspected of being subversives, dissidents or, in some other way, enemies of the state – I found 'Ivan'. Just plain 'Ivan'. In the world of Eastern Bloc espionage, Lendl's first name also served as his codename.

Lendl once said he hated living in the past, as he prefers to live in the present and plan for the future. But critical to understanding Lendl, and to understanding Lendl's player–coach relationship with Andy Murray, the most successful partnership in modern British tennis history, is to know something of his and Czechoslovakia's past. John McEnroe and Jimmy Connors were for ever making snide remarks about Lendl, never appreciating what he had accomplished by making it from this Socialist Republic all the way to the international tennis tour. The intelligence reports and other papers I have seen demonstrated that Lendl was under extremely close surveillance; the index in his file listed his known associates, as well as dozens of separate documents containing material on him sourced directly from agents or gathered from a network of informants. And the StB's X Division, responsible for 'the counter-intelligence against internal enemies', wasn't just interested in Lendl's character ('an ambitious and strong-willed person whose main priority is tennis'), his mother and father's personalities and the dynamic of his parents' marriage; they also made it their business to know how much money Lendl was making, as well as who he was talking to, and especially whether he was in contact with any Czech émigrés. The state even knew the identity of the people Lendl was selling dogs to; on one occasion, a 'collaborator' alerted them to the fact that Lendl had sold a puppy to someone under suspicion of wanting to emigrate. Also included in Ivan's file was information that the state's spies had gathered on where a young Lendl liked to spend his leisure time – in discos and cinemas, apparently – and also details of his sex life, with one of the intelligence reports claiming: 'He has a very good relationship with women. He has reportedly begun a close friendship with a Miss New Zealand. Moreover, Ivan allegedly has a woman in every city he plays in, since he has money, which is attractive to women. He himself has mentioned a number of times that he knows many women around the world who are willing to spend time with him.'

When we met in London, I volunteered to show Lendl his StB file, but he passed on the offer, saying he had already seen it and had no desire to look again. 'I don't know how you got hold of those documents – somebody's going to be in trouble, as I don't think you're supposed to have them – but to anyone who knows what that regime was like, this shouldn't be a surprise,' Lendl told me, and he added that he had been aware in the 1980s that he was under surveillance: 'I knew at the time that this was going on.'

Born on 7 March 1960 in Ostrava, 'The Black City of Europe', somewhere that was for ever breathing in the industrial flatulence from its coalmines and metalworks, Lendl has said that those who grew up in the West will never be able fully to comprehend what it was like as a boy and a young man behind the Iron Curtain. How can those who come from sun-buttered, hopeful places such as California ever possibly understand what it would have been like living in a totalitarian state that, among its many other sins, wasn't above trailing and humiliating its athletes, or anyone else considered to be an enemy of the state? As someone with expert knowledge of Czechoslovakia's secret police said, 'Sportsmen attracted the attention of the StB because they were a substitute for the aristocrats who were so sorely lacking in a communist society. Like other nations, they have always yearned for inspiration. We all hope to find in others the greatness that we know we lack. So for the missing aristocrats, they substituted great industrialists or movie stars or writers or indeed great athletes.' And any public figure who spent a lot of time in the West – as all professional tennis players had to if they were going to compete internationally – was in danger of attracting the attentions of the StB.

But there was one reason why the secret police were so interested in Lendl, and that reason was Martina Navratilova. Her surname may be translated as 'The One Who Came Back', but that was exactly what she *didn't* do, with her defection to the United States an international embarrassment for Czechoslovakia. It's no exaggeration to say that one of the key moments of Lendl's life – he was only fifteen at the time and an ocean away – came on the day during the 1975 US Open when Navratilova took a cab to Manhattan's Lower West Side and walked into the offices of the Immigration and Naturalization Service (INS). What Prague didn't want was for Lendl to go the same way as Navratilova, dropping Marxism-Leninism for the pursuit of grand slam titles. 'That's why,' one source said, 'they would have wanted to have known Lendl's views and whether he was likely to follow in Navratilova's path.' The documents confirm that: the StB were determined to discover whether Lendl was considering defecting.

Tennis players could never escape the reality that it was in the state's power to destroy their careers, to have their ambitions filed away in some bureaucrat's drawer. Sometimes, the officials thought they had to remind the players of that. 'They threatened that they could make or break me,' Navratilova observed in her autobiography. 'And I never liked threats. We already had plenty of those from the Russians: who needed threats from a fellow countryman?' The communists thought that Navratilova was too Americanised, that she was always more interested in going out for dinner with Chris Evert and Billie Jean King than she was in sharing a table with officials from the Czechoslovak Tennis Federation. They also thought she was becoming too powerful, and called her 'nose in the air'. In communist Czechoslovakia, wanting to pick your own friends was an act of insubordination. 'The Czech government just couldn't deal with a Czech being a bigshot on the women's tour, and starting to get ideas of her own. They wanted total control, but the more I won, the less they could control me. They were willing to sacrifice my tennis career in order to control me. And I wasn't going to stand for that.'

Between trips, tennis players' passports were kept in safes, and the athletes had to sweat on whether or not they would receive exit permits for their next tournaments. In addition, they couldn't set their own schedules and were forbidden from owning property or keeping currency outside the country. Also banned was having foreign currencies loaded on to bankcards. 'The whole problem,' Jan Kodeš, the 1973 Wimbledon champion, has said, 'was that the state wanted to demonstrate its power over the people – everything was directed by some kind of violence.' Low-level officials could show their power over an athlete, as well as ingratiate themselves to their superiors, by being obstructive, or by writing reports that dressed up the pettiest of transgressions as crimes against the state.

These state-versus-athletes tensions were never higher than when a teenage Navratilova announced in New York City that she had sought political asylum in the United States. To Navratilova's mind, the state's control over her had been such that it hadn't been far off telling her when and where she could go to the lavatory. There had also been strict financial controls. In the early days, Navratilova had been forced to accept turning all her winnings over to the federation; all she received for her efforts was a tiny daily allowance, to cover her food expenses, plus the possibility of small and occasional bonuses. During her last few months playing for the Republic, she had been allowed to keep a little more, but was still handing over around 80 per cent of her earnings. Had the state stopped at low-level harassment, and grouching that she was spending too much time with foreigners and had become too 'Americanised', Navratilova probably could have coped and stayed; what she wouldn't tolerate was the constant threat of having 'my tennis ambitions crushed'. An increasingly concerned and frustrated Navratilova was never certain she would be granted an exit permit to compete at international tournaments. So off she went to America, a country that, ever since she was a little girl, she had thought of as a magical place.

When she defected, first Prague trashed Navratilova's reputation in the state media, with the tennis federation announcing in a statement that she had 'suffered a defeat in the face of our proletarian public – Czechoslovakia offered her the means for her development, but she gave preference to a doubtful career of a professional and a fat bank account'. The newspapers reported – there has to be some doubt as to whether this was fact or communist fiction – that a mob angry at her defection had registered their revulsion by smashing windows, throwing stones and uprooting the apple tree that she had sat under as a child. Prague's next move was to turn this enemy of the state into a non-person – she was redacted from public life.

Lendl has sometimes been critical of Navratilova's politics – he has derided her for being a 'limousine liberal' – but there can be no doubt that he benefited hugely from someone who for many years didn't officially exist. In a counterfactual history of modern tennis, in which Navratilova didn't defect, and didn't drive around America in a silver Mercedes with a personalised number plate 'X-Czech', Lendl almost certainly wouldn't have been the same player. There was no historical inevitability that he would win eight grand slam titles and hold the number one ranking; his career could have been decimated. Lendl has acknowledged he owes a great debt to Navratilova, that he wouldn't have had the opportunities he did if she hadn't fled to the West: 'Without her, I don't think I could have pulled off what I did.'

At first, as Czechoslovakia considered this post-Navratilova world, they tightened controls over their players. But that was only because they were acting on instinct. After a little thought, they concluded that if they were to avoid another high-profile defection, they would have to give their tennis players more, not less, freedom. The financial arrangements would also have to be looked at: there was to be a great reduction in the percentage of the prize money players had to give to the state. Under the new arrangements, Lendl had to pay around 20 per cent of his cash to Czechoslovakia; given the high taxes levied on his Western colleagues, he may well have ended up with a better financial deal than many of those around him in the locker-room. Thanks to Navratilova eating hamburgers in America, Lendl was able to become, as some would snidely describe it, 'a paper Czech'. If Navratilova had done as she was told, she said, 'you would probably have never heard of me'. And you would probably never have heard of Ivan Lendl either.

In the minds of the Czechoslovak Tennis Federation, the political classes and the StB, the West had stolen Navratilova, and so there was concern at the highest levels of society that America was going to pinch another tennis asset. As one of the StB's intelligence reports on Lendl in the early 1980s observed: 'Considering his character, it cannot be ruled out that, under the influence of people who have a hostile relationship to the CSSR [the Czechoslovak Socialist Republic], he could be convinced to emigrate.'

Go in search of Lendl and you find yourself on a grim slalom through some of the bleakest times in the country's history. Lendl couldn't just get on with competing and trying to win grand slams; not when there was so much propaganda value attached to tennis players, not even every forehand winner was potentially doing a little bit to promote the glory of the Politburo. Among the documents I found in Ivan's file was a five-page letter that Lendl wrote to 'Comrade' Minister of the Interior Vratislav Vajnar in 1984, the contents of which showed he was scared of the power that the state had over him. Lendl knew that just one caustic memo could have seen his passport destroyed, which would also have meant the obliteration of his international tennis career. The reason he had been avoiding Czechoslovakia, and had instead been spending his time at foreign tournaments or at his American base, was because of 'my worry that I may not be allowed to travel again'. For Lendl, who won his first grand slam title just a few months after he sent that letter, when he came from two sets down to defeat John McEnroe at Roland Garros, there was always the fear of being silenced or purged from public life, of seeing the state's tank turrets swivel in his direction. Hitting tennis balls against a background of fear and suspicion is always going to inform any player's character; in order to be successful, Lendl became colder and harder, at least on the outside. And, later in Lendl's life, if Murray ever encountered any off-court problems that threatened to distract him, there was no one who could give him wiser counsel than his coach.

International glory as an athlete was no protection from a paranoid and vengeful state. Lendl would have been aware of how the government had burned the great Emil Zatopek, a long-distance runner who had won three gold medals at the 1952 Helsinki Olympics, in the 5,000 metres, 10,000 metres and the marathon. In retirement from running, Zatopek made trouble for himself by being on the democratic wing of the communist party. In 1968, an eight-year-old Lendl watched as Soviet tanks rolled across Czechoslovakia, flattening the Prague Spring and squashing under their tracks any hopes of liberal reforms and the promised 'socialism with a human face'; Zatopek was on the wrong side of history. During the Moscow-led reprisals and repressions that followed, Zatopek was punished and degraded for the crime of 'lacking understanding of the fundamental problems of the development of our socialist society, and the need to defend it on the basis of the principles of Marxism-Leninism and proletarian inter-nationalism'. He was given dirty and dangerous work: he was made to clean lavatories, dig wells, empty bins and toil in a uranium mine. And the communists didn't find it so hard to make tennis players vanish, to turn them from champions into non-persons. To become, as Lendl would put it, 'blacked out'. No wonder Lendl was fearful.

There's something almost mundane about the StB choos-ing his first name, Ivan, as their code for Lendl's personal file and all checks and investigations. This was a society that felt as though it was under constant surveillance. Even when you weren't being watched, you usually imagined that you were. The population was living, some thought, in a state of existential terror, for ever concerned about what the StB had on them at their Bartolomějská headquarters in Prague, or at their Ostrava base, or across the country. In the words of Václav Havel, the dissident playwright who would go on to become post-communist Czechoslovakia's first President, the StB was a 'hideous spider whose invisible web runs right through the whole of society'. One estimate of the StB's reach suggested that, at one stage, one-tenth of the country's popu-lation was either directly employed by the secret service or had been recruited as collaborators.

Until 1989, when the Velvet Revolution brought about the bloodless collapse of communism, and when Lendl was nearly thirty, this was the only Czechoslovakia that the tennis player knew. The years between 1968 and 1989 saw the transforma-tion of Lendl from a frightened little boy into one of the most successful players in tennis history; they were also what became known as the 'Normalisation Period' in Czechoslovakia's history, a repressive time when the state exerted strict controls over the population. During the bleak 1970s and 1980s, there was much twitching of the Iron Curtain in everyone's street or tower block; the reach and the power of the StB created an atmosphere of such suspicion and betrayal that some ordinary citizens thought the only way to survive was to get their denunciations in first – friends informed on friends and neighbours on each other, often for such seemingly trivial matters as complaining about a long queue outside a shop. No one could be trusted, not even that young couple pushing a pram in the street – one StB ruse was to have agents pose as new parents, with a camera instead of a baby under the hood. Cameras were also hidden in parked cars, radios, briefcases, handbags and tobacco pouches, anywhere that allowed Big Brother to snoop and pry. Lendl's file was evidence of this betrayal: his family shouldn't have trusted some of their closest friends, or even those they encountered at the local tennis club in Ostrava.

On at least one occasion during Lendl's career – and appropriately enough for this Orwellian tale, this was in 1984 – Lendl had proof he was being bugged by the state. Lendl and his Davis Cup team-mates had been preparing for a home tie against France, to be played in the city of Hradec Králové, when they had their suspicions aroused. Having requested that they would like to move from the first floor to a higher level – the noise from the street was keeping them awake – they were told that they had to stay in the rooms they had been given. Kodeš, the 1973 Wimbledon champion, who at that time was captain of the Davis Cup team, said he wasn't at all surprised that the rooms were bugged. According to Kodeš, Lendl tried to make light of the discovery of the bugs, saying: 'So, they are going to listen to the sounds in my room if I have a girl here, right?' But it's possible Lendl could have been using humour to try to defuse any anxiety; team-mate Tomáš Šmid was absolutely horrified by what they had found, as just the night before he had been critical of the Russians.

No state ever spied on its tennis players like the Czechoslovak Socialist Republic did. 'Everybody in tennis was under surveillance, everybody. Everyone was being watched,' Šmid, a Wimbledon and Australian Open singles quarter-finalist in the 1980s, as well as a former doubles world number one, told me. 'The StB seemed to know everything, and I don't know how. They were trying to control the people.' I also found Šmid's name in the StB's files, codenamed 'Tenis', while Kodeš was there, too, known to the spooks as 'Vitez', meaning 'winner'. And Navratilova was under surveillance; Czechoslovak tennis was being closely watched.

Spying on tennis players was more of a challenge for the StB than snooping on those who played team sports. The first move from the StB playbook, when spying on athletes in teams, was to coerce colleagues into informing on each other, and, if pressure needed to be applied, it could often be applied on their families, if not by blackmailing the athlete. However, Lendl and other tennis players were rarely part of a team: only for a few weeks of the year, when they were representing their country in the Davis Cup, or the women's equivalent the Fed Cup, did they compete as part of a collective. But the StB found a way. On the Czechoslovak tennis scene there was the suspicion that it was the coaches and the officials from the tennis federation who were supplying information to the StB. Players who competed at foreign tournaments tended to travel with federation chaperones, and those minders would often be sending memos – detailing who the athletes were mixing with, and what was being discussed – back to the StB. And when players were given permission to travel to minor tournaments without a minder, they often had to sign statements before they left, promising to report anything of interest.

'I know that some people from our federation were passing reports on us,' Kodeš told me, 'but we mostly knew who was part of the StB, who could be that person passing on information, so we watched out not to give ourselves problems.' Šmid recalled how there was 'always someone watching you'. 'When you went to tournaments outside the country, there would be a guy travelling with you, and when you got back, you suspected that he would be reporting back on who you had spoken to,' he said. He also recalled occasions when he returned from international tournaments and he would be searched at Prague airport or the StB would take him in for questioning. 'This was when I was a junior. I would come back to Prague and they would search me for propaganda material. They would take me into a room and search me, and I would have nothing, of course. Other times, I would return home and the StB would question me at their headquarters, and ask me who I had been talking to, and whether I had met with any Czech émigrés or anything like that. It was clear when they were talking to me that they knew everything about me – who I had been staying with, who I had seen, everything.'

Lendl has recalled being chaperoned on his international trips, though as the years passed and he loosened the ties with his country of birth, and with the tennis federation, he was able to travel without Big Brother tagging along. Among other surveillance techniques – they also intercepted mail – there was the belief in the 1970s and 1980s that the StB would routinely listen in on international phone calls. So Lendl, being no fool, is understood to have been careful about what he said. As were his parents Olga and Jiří, so when Lendl and his mother and father spoke they would censor their news. That wasn't the only precaution that Lendl took; someone who spent time with Lendl in the 1980s said that the player was in the habit of scanning hotel lobbies and restaurants for possible Czech eavesdroppers. 'Yeah, they are very friendly guys,' Lendl once said of the StB, 'funny like a heart attack.'

Like everyone else in the Republic, people in tennis were jumpy about the StB. Midway through Navratilova's appointment at the Manhattan immigration offices during the 1975 US Open, an official asked to speak to her alone, and the tennis player's manager was terrified that an StB agent would bundle her into a cab, jab her with a hypodermic needle and hustle her on to an aeroplane bound for Czechoslovakia. 'I wasn't as fearful as he was, but it happened to other people,' Navratilova once recalled. 'They were sedated and jammed on a plane and you never heard from them again.' As she left the building, a voice in her head was telling her that StB agents would chloroform her, and take her to the docks, and on to a boat. To guard against the possibility of being kidnapped, she checked out of her hotel and into her equivalent of a safe house, a friend's apartment in Greenwich Village. She was also given FBI protection. Walking into the stadium to play her matches at that year's US Open, she would be looking for the men in trench coats, trying to establish, in this off-court game of surveillance and counter-surveillance, who was the FBI and who was the StB. When Navratilova returned to Prague for the first time since her defection to represent the United States, for a Fed Cup match against Czechoslovakia in 1986, she was aware of 'secret service guys still behind my back; they were monitoring where I was going, and what I was doing and who I was talking to'. For years, Navratilova would look at route maps to see whether flights passed over communist territory – if they did, she would make alternative arrangements, because she knew that the StB's reach was global. In addition to infiltrating Czechoslovak émigré communities, they were widely believed to have run an extensive worldwide network of agents and informants, and it was subsequently disclosed that some British MPs had been passing them information. One former spy has claimed that the security services had plotted to catch British Prime Minister Ted Heath in a honey-trap, which they had hoped would allow them to blackmail him.

Lendl certainly wasn't aware of this at the time – and if he had been, you have to imagine he wouldn't have spent another night in the place – but at one stage he owned an apartment in the same Manhattan block as an StB super-spy. Karl Koecher is regarded as the most successful Czechoslovak spy of the Cold War, having infiltrated both the CIA and New York's high-society; he was held in such high regard that when he returned to Prague, after the governments exchanged prisoners, he was rewarded with a new Volvo and a villa outside the city. Doubtless Koecher would have passed anything of interest about Lendl back to the security services. However, there is no evidence to suggest that there had been an StB plot to have Lendl and Koecher bumping into each other in the lobby or in the elevator, especially as Koecher had tried to blackball Lendl. Koecher had been serving on the building's board of directors when Lendl made it known he wanted to buy one of the apartments – as part of Koecher's efforts to maintain his cover story, the spy had sought to block the tennis player from living there on the grounds that he couldn't possibly live with 'a commie'.

Little about Czechoslovakia's Big Brother operations could ever be described as amusing or light-hearted. But the thought that an StB agent wearing headphones and a pained expression was obliged to take extensive notes of Olga Lendlova's phone calls, detailing every last comment of the tennis instruction she was giving her son, does raise a small smile.

Any StB agent who listened in to Ivan Lendl's calls with his parents would doubtless have been treated to an exhaustive analysis – even after her son had established himself at the top of the sport, his mother liked, whenever possible, to give him her critique. Or, if she hadn't seen the match on television, she wanted to hear his detailed account of what had happened. That was even the case after he had only been appearing in unsanctioned and meaningless exhibitions; so when he once played in one of those in Atlanta, and didn't call his parents to let them know how it had gone, Olga was very distressed. Lendl couldn't understand it, telling his mother: 'Mom, it was four o'clock in the morning for you when the match ended, and it was an exhibition.' To which she responded: 'I don't care. I need to know. I couldn't sleep.' Lendl's mother wanted to know everything about her son's professional career, and then she wanted to comment on it. Sometimes, when Lendl wasn't in the mood to listen to another of his mother's monologues he would hand the phone to his coach. Or he would place the receiver down on the side table in his hotel room, read for a couple of minutes, and then pick up the phone again and say, 'You know, I think you're right about that.' As it happens, if an agent had been listening in, zoning out from the Olga monologues wouldn't have been among the options available to him. All mothers have an impact on their sons' personalities, but few have been as influential as Olga Lendlova was with her only child – as we shall see, she informed Ivan's approach to tennis and to life, including his work ethic, and his distrust of showing emotion in public.

Tennis has seen a few Tiger mums down the years, but, with the possible exception of Gloria Connors, the mother of Lendl's rival Jimmy, has anyone in the sport ever shown her stripes and claws as Olga Lendlova did?

Lendl's story would later feature another strong woman – in his fifties, he would be employed by a player whose own mother, Judy Murray, would come under sustained attack for being too fierce for Middle England's sometimes delicate tastes. For a while, Judy's post-bag attracted hate-mail from the letter-writing middle classes, with the poison generally free of spelling and grammatical errors, and neatly handwritten; understandably, this erudite, toxic mail was profoundly shocking for her. 'It was incredibly hurtful to get letters from people I didn't know – and who didn't know me – telling me that I was harming my kids.' Her correspondents informed her what an awful mother she was, how she was too brash and strident, and how they loathed the way she behaved while watching Andy play, crying out and shaking her fist. Why, some of these letters would have implied, couldn't she be more like Jane Henman, quiet, inoffensive and conservative with a small 'c'? And if Judy Murray wasn't being abused privately, she was being abused publicly; there was the occasion during one Wimbledon when the broadsheet newspaper that published her column also ran a takedown piece by a feature writer which accused her of being a pushy mother whose tennis elbows had been sharpened to the point that they could take Andy's opponents' eyes out. Lendl's old rival, Boris Becker, once appeared to suggest that Judy's continued involvement in her son's career was stopping him from realising his potential; to which she responded that he didn't know anything about her family.

But only one of those three ladies – Olga Lendlova, Judy Murray, and Gloria Connors – had ever tethered her young son to a net post, so as to avoid interruptions to her own practice sessions, which often continued until the sun had gone down. And that mother was Olga, who had previously been in the habit of wheeling her son on to the court in a cart; the day that cart tipped over was the day she went looking for a length of rope. So Lendl had only just been exposed to the sport, and here he was on a leash, tied up like a goat in a field, his clothes smeared with red clay from the court, and that, as John McEnroe noted, 'couldn't have helped his personality'. An alternative, more generous reading of the use of that leash was that it was the sporting equivalent of an umbilical cord.

Speaking both literally and metaphorically, was there much sunshine in Lendl's formative years? Even by the standards of the Eastern Bloc, his home city of Ostrava, in the east of the country near the Polish border, was a hard and dark place, said to have been born under a black star. The *New York Times* has since said the city 'epitomized communist-era bleakness'; you could say that Lendl is Ostrava's greatest symbol, or you could suggest that it's the city's 1,000-foot slag heap. Some who believed every newspaper caricature of Lendl in the 1980s may be surprised to learn at this point that we're discussing his origins in Moravia rather than Transylvania. Ostrava doesn't feature on many people's bucket lists, and the few tourists that it does attract tend not to venture into the suburbs. One recent international visitor who did wander into suburbia reported that, although Ostrava has 'a relatively nice and historical centre – there's decent beer and Moravian restaurants where you can get a good piece of pork leg – the city's suburbs are awful, half-Dickens, half-Kafka. It was like we were still in 1974.'

If you do make the trip into Ostrava's suburbs, perhaps you'll find yourself on Bachmačská Street and standing before a four-storey apartment block that, a quarter of a century after the collapse of communism, still lives up to every Iron Curtain stereotype – it's a dirty, breeze-block grey and it looks cheap. There's nothing remarkable or memorable about the building – it's just another grey box in another grey neighbourhood that, during the communist era, housed thousands of small, failed and thwarted lives. It was there, in their third-floor apartment, that Lendl and his parents lived. From that street, Lendl only had to walk a few blocks to the NHKG Tennis Club, which was sponsored – nowhere was untouched by heavy industry – by a company that manufactured trucks, trams and railway carriages. Given his parents' immersion in the sport, and there being little else to occupy a young boy's time in Ostrava – Lendl has said that he couldn't recall there being a swimming pool – he was always going to play tennis. In Lendl's words, he started playing tennis 'uncommonly early' – after starting with a bat and a ball against the wall, he then graduated to a wooden racket and he played a lot of it, which he attributed not just to his tennis-obsessed parents, but also to being an only child. The club has since been given a makeover, rebranded as Ostrava Sport Centrum, with a clubhouse and a restaurant serving cuts of meat and vegetable soup. When Lendl returned there recently, he thought the food was good.

Nevertheless, three of the original courts are still there. On those courts, Lendl would play under a coating of filth from the factories. 'There was so much smoke that if a good wind was blowing, you weren't able to play,' Lendl has recalled. 'Or you were able to play, but you couldn't breathe. And it smelt so bad.'

But let's not overstate this and imagine that Lendl's childhood was one of great material deprivation. Of course, in this Republic there weren't officially any classes, but the Lendls – with a lawyer father who knew his way around a chessboard, and a mother with a decent job and tennis ambitions – were about as middle class a family as you would have found that side of Prague. Lendl has recalled feeling perfectly safe in Ostrava, so as a child he thought little of walking home from practice in the dark on his own, though the low crime rate might have had less to do with the uniformed policemen on the beat than the fear of the StB: Lendl's own recollection is that, 'if somebody committed a serious crime, within two months they were gone: either executed or locked up for ever'. So when *Sports Illustrated* magazine once suggested that 'one of the major things missing from the childhood of Ivan Lendl was a childhood', it wasn't commenting on poverty blighting his upbringing, but articulating an opinion on Olga and Jiří's parenting methods, many of which would horrify the parents' forums of today.

You don't have to have read Freud to be curious about Lendl's early years. There's a great temptation, and one that

McEnroe has succumbed to, to look back at Lendl's child-hood – at little Ivan being kept on a tether, and at other disconcerting stories from his early years – and to speculate what drove Olga to behave as she did, and also to wonder about the effect of her actions on her son. And Lendl himself has shown in the past he isn't above that temptation; he has all but psychoanalysed his own mother.

For all that Olga accomplished on a tennis court – she was a spirited, bloody-minded player who was ranked number two in Czechoslovakia – he has sometimes wondered whether she was frustrated that being a mother, carrying her only child and then raising him, had prevented her from realising her potential. This wasn't someone who feared hard work or hardship – there was the time when, unable to walk as she waited for an operation on a torn knee cartilage, she was said to have bitten back the pain and scrubbed the family apartment on her knees. In communist-era Ostrava, there was pent-up frustration and internalised disaffection all around you; and, privately, did Olga feel as though her own tennis ambitions had been thwarted not by the system, or by her own failings, but by the responsibilities of motherhood? Even as a mother, Olga had applied herself on the practice and match courts; after a morning's work she would often leave for the tennis club straight after lunch and then train for as long as daylight allowed her. And keeping Ivan on that lead meant she could concentrate on her technique. And yet, did she still wonder whether, if she had been childless, she would have superseded Vlasta Vopičková, the sister of men's Wimbledon champion Jan Kodeš, as the country's highest ranked female tennis player? And what could Olga then have gone on to achieve, given that Vopičková played at the grand slams? So what if Vopičková was generally considered to have been more talented than Olga; as Olga saw it, talent could only take you so far. This was about doing everything you could do to make yourself a better player. So, in Lendl's overactive, overimaginative mind, he sometimes wondered whether his mother must have been thinking to herself: 'I could have been great if not for this baby.' That's not a thought that ever entered Andy Murray's mind about his own mother. Like Olga Lendlova, Murray's mother hadn't fulfilled all her ambitions as a tennis player, but it wasn't motherhood that had ended Judy's competitive career, but the realisation that she didn't have what it took to make a living competing at international tennis tournaments. Although she was successful at a domestic level, that success wasn't replicated on the world stage, where she often found herself taking long-distance bus journeys between tournaments, as she hadn't won enough prize money to afford the airfares.

Tying up her toddler was about as close as Olga Lendlova was going to come to a tennis career unencumbered by motherhood. While Lendl's late father, Jiří, also played tennis to a decent level, and was ranked in the country's top twenty, Olga was the more influential of the two in almost every sphere of his life. As the StB noted: 'In Lendl's family, he was most influenced by his mother, and did not respect his father as much as her. Lendl has always respected his mother very much, and while he played at NHKG he always reflected her views in various discussions.'

It was Olga's, not Jiří's, attempts to force-feed Ivan discipline, order and cold vegetables, which bordered on the fanatical; there were times when it must have seemed as though Ivan's entire world centred on the plate in front of him, still piled with uneaten peas and carrots. Once, and this anecdote from *Sports Illustrated* magazine tends to support the idea that Olga felt her tennis ambitions had been held back by Ivan, she alleged he wasn't eating his vegetables because he wanted to upset her before she played at the national championships. Certainly, Ivan was often scared of his mother's furies. If Ivan didn't eat his vegetables, Olga would sometimes strike her son. On occasion, his mother would set a timer for ten minutes and leave the room; Ivan would know to clear his plate before the alarm brought her back in. There was enough force in one of the blows, according to a profile of her then adult son in an American magazine, to have destroyed her wristwatch; thereafter, she had to remember to hit Ivan with her right hand rather than her left lest she break another. Olga would tell little Ivan, 'If you don't eat, I'm going to call the zoo, and the elephant is coming to get you', knowing her son was scared of elephants. Lendl has recalled: 'I always tried to push her as far as I could, but then I would just swallow everything.' In the end, he always submitted to his mother. Lendl once made a telling remark in an interview with *Tennis* magazine, saying that, after becoming a father himself, his hope was that his children would have genuine respect for him, and 'not just obey their parents like a machine'.

While Lendl always knew that Olga was different from other kids' mums, he wouldn't want anyone to think that she was a monster, and he has questioned the truth of a comment he supposedly once made to a former friend, George Mendoza, who quoted him as saying: 'My mother was always snapping at me to eat my peas and greens. But the more she yelled, the more I resisted. Then she would start hitting me across the face. It hurt but I forced myself not to cry. If I had, she would have known that she had got to me – and I couldn't let that happen.' Lendl has since questioned whether he would have said that, even if it was a fair recollection of what happened. 'Whether it's true or not, I would never say that,' Lendl said in an interview with the *Sunday Times*. 'My mother did a fantastic job, working, playing tennis, taking care of me. I will not complain about my mother. She had a hard life and I am not going to say a word about that. Was she tough on me? Of course, she was. But maybe that's what helped me. One parent is always tougher than the other, one is a disciplinarian and the other is not. In our family, my mother was the disciplinarian, but making quotes like that … no.'

Being an only child had its disadvantages. If only, Lendl would find himself thinking, he had a brother or sister, because then his mother would have someone else to order about. There would have been someone else living under these house rules, such as his mother's insistence that, even if he was only in the apartment for an hour, he had to change from his 'street clothes' to his 'home clothes' before then changing again before going out. And Lendl wouldn't, as most boys would, fling the clothes on to the floor – he would carefully put his trousers and shirt back in the cupboard. There was no idle or dead time in Lendl's day. After he had finished lunch, he would help to wash and dry the dishes, and if the waste bin was full he was expected to empty it. Wouldn't it have been easier for Lendl if he had a brother and a sister with whom to share these duties? Still, when Lendl thought about it for a little longer, he did wonder whether, if his mother had indeed had another baby, he would have been jealous of his sibling.

If there was deprivation in Lendl's childhood, it was emotional, with Ivan secretly wishing that his mother would be softer towards him. 'I can never remember my mother cuddling me in her arms or saying, "I love you, Ivan." I wanted her to be softer to me, and I once saved up to buy her flowers and a box of sweets,' Lendl has been quoted as saying. 'But it made no difference.' On other occasions, he thought that cleaning the family apartment, or doing the dishes, would make his mother softer towards him, but that didn't always work either.

Even the secret police, after their background checks on this 'well-known tennis family in Ostrava', thought of Olga as a formidable woman, who 'controlled' her son. An StB intelligence report in 1981, which analysed information provided to them by friends of the Lendl family, as well as from informants at the local tennis club and at her workplace, observed that Olga's 'only vice was that she always wanted things done her way even if she was not right'. Olga was nothing if not hard-working and efficient. According to the files, Olga worked at the Technical University of Ostrava, as a part-time technician in the Department of Iron, Steel and Coal in the Metallurgical Faculty, and was 'well-evaluated, as she performs her tasks precisely and quickly, and is completely reliable'. It was said that her connections at the university were of 'general character', and that she 'kept closer relations with people who play tennis or who are in some way engaged in tennis'. Away from work, she was said to have had 'the positive qualities of thoughtfulness, thriftiness and diligence', as well as being a 'very meticulous' lady who kept a strict control of the household budget. One report noted that, 'due to her controlling nature, Olga has not been popular with some people'. However, another included the line that, 'everyone describes her as a selfless and helpful woman – she is the exact opposite of her husband'. The StB could seemingly overlook the fact she wasn't 'politically organised'.

By contrast, the StB's informants saw weakness in Lendl's father, Jiří, claiming he 'always let his wife influence him just so he would keep a happy marriage', with Olga always the head of the household. 'Through the background check it has been found out that Jiří Lendl had never been popular for his peculiar behaviour and manner – he was unattainable to most people,' the StB concluded. According to the secret police, Jiří, who had a doctorate degree in law, and who was employed as a company lawyer by a government agency, was 'a loner at work'. Even so, the StB believed in the 1980s that Lendl's father could influence his son's thinking: 'As a lawyer, Jiří used to be very cunning, and Ivan used to cling to him because he gave him advice that Ivan would accept completely. It is possible to say that his father was one of the many people who had great influence on Ivan.' The StB believed that 'from his mother, Ivan inherited his persistence and leadership tendencies, and from his father he perhaps inherited his intelligence'. As we shall see, it was Lendl's intellect that would persuade his future mentor on the tour, Poland's Wojtek Fibak, that the Czech had a strong future. But it would be one of the qualities passed down by Lendl's mother – his perseverance – that enabled him to be so successful: central to his story was striving to improve his mind and his body.

From the age of four or five – by which time he was presumably allowed off that leash every now and then – Lendl was spending 'every free minute at the club', and by the age of six he was ballboying at the national championships held in Ostrava. 'I was the youngest ballboy we ever had, and I did it for eight or nine years, every match at the Czech Nationals for the whole week. You had your own court and you were there all day. If you were good there were just two of you, and two of you running a court is a lot of work. I would come home and drop dead. I ballboyed until I was about fifteen, then I umpired until I was eighteen. I was on the court all day just watching matches and unless you are asleep you will start understanding why a guy did this or that, and that is how you will get a feel for strategy,' Lendl has said. 'If somebody starts teaching that when you're twenty-four, it's too late.' A couple of years after Lendl became Ostrava's youngest ever ball kid he started playing against some of the older boys at the club, which forced him to improve quickly as he didn't like the experience of being bashed around the court. Soon after that, Lendl started travelling to matches outside the city; part of the appeal was the degree of independence that those jaunts gave him. As his parents didn't always accompany him on those adventures, he had more choice over what he ate – they were breaks from the battles that raged over his plate of greens.

It was on one of those escapades out of Ostrava that Lendl saw the Russian tanks advance through Czechoslovakia in 1968. 'I remember my parents were in Prague for club matches and I was with my grandparents in another town. They came to pick me up and we went home on the train and at every station there were tanks aiming at the trains,' Lendl told the *Sunday Times*. 'That wasn't terrifying because you're only eight and you don't understand. My parents were very upset and I was warned not to use words like occupants or to laugh or spit or say anything like that. People went to jail for using words like that.' It wasn't the sort of day that you tend to forget. Martina Navratilova's world 'changed over' when 'those frigging tanks came out of nowhere', and once, after beating a Russian girl at a tournament, she said to her vanquished opponent at the net: 'You need a tank to beat me.' You can imagine that those memories would also have shaped Lendl's thinking. When Lendl first started playing in international tournaments – according to a book published in the 1980s, *Hard Courts* by John Feinstein – he couldn't look Russian players in the eye. His memories of 1968 were so vivid, according to this account, that he hated them all.

You wouldn't necessarily describe some of Lendl's childhood experiences on a tennis court as playful. Almost from the beginning, Olga was hard on him on the practice court. While Ivan didn't take long to learn how to play a forehand – the shot that would go on to make him tens of millions of dollars – hitting backhands didn't come so easily to him, and that was the source of many of his disputes with his mother, which often ended with her screaming at him, and then walking off the court, abandoning her pink-eyed, blotchy, dejected child. They each knew how to irritate the other – he by not applying himself, she by screaming at him, or turfing him off the court. When Lendl's father was coaching him, the sessions would usually pass without incident, as Jiří could explain shots and strategies in a calm manner. With his mother, it was quite different; she would become frustrated and often use force to remove her son from the court. So Olga would say to her son, who at the time tried to mask a weak backhand by attacking the net at all opportunities: 'We're going to practise backhand cross-courts, and you can't come to net.' But Jiří would try to introduce an element of competition, saying to his son: 'We're playing backhand cross-courts and you can come to net on the eleventh shot.'

Olga Lendlova simply didn't know how to make tennis fun. 'One of us always ended up in tears. She because I wouldn't listen, or me because I thought she was being too rough on me,' Lendl told the American journalist Peter Bodo for his entertaining book *The Courts of Babylon*. 'In the end it was the similarity between us rather than the difference that caused all the problems. One part of me told me that my mother really loved me. The other part didn't understand why she was doing certain things. Now I can understand why she was doing those things. Now I can understand it and accept it as I get older. It was all part of the way she was educating me for tennis.' Later in life, Lendl would show a desire for self-improvement that bordered on the fanatical, and that can be traced back to how his mother spoke to him. 'She was always critical because she wanted me to do better,' he told *New York* magazine in the 1980s. 'That's why I do as well as I do in tennis – because I will never be pleased. I'll always want to do it better. If I go to school and get an A, I shouldn't be complimented, because that's my job. If I get an F, I should be in trouble.'

To say that Lendl had no childhood whatsoever would be to dismiss the moments of joy he experienced as a boy. Such as waiting by the window for his father, who worked for the country's tennis federation, to return home from international tournaments with stories of one of Ivan's idols, Rod Laver, and other greats of the game such as Ken Rosewall and John Newcombe. Although, if Ivan ever stopped eating those vegetables, the stories would immediately pause mid-sentence. Not all Lendl's tennis idols were mythologised Australians – another was Jan Kodeš, for whom Lendl had ballboyed, and whose victory at Wimbledon in 1973 had come when Lendl was at the impressionable age of thirteen. There was also pleasure to be had as father and son war-gamed ice hockey and football matches on their kitchen table before enjoying the live broadcast. Some of Lendl's happiest childhood memories are of him ballboying for his mother, of making sure that he could return to her the same ball with which she just won the point, while his father would be watching courtside. And the next day, Lendl would watch his father play chess, 'and it was boring, sure', but what he enjoyed was the family being as one and supporting each other. Having the three of them all together – mother, father and only child – made Lendl happiest. What upset him was when his father, having promised to play a game of table hockey, or to tell him some stories from the tennis tour, informed him at the last moment that he would have to cancel because of pressure of work. He would remember this clearly when he became a father, and always tried to make himself available to his children.

Part of Olga's formidable approach to tennis was that, as her son recalled, she would 'fight like a dog' on court. She regarded herself as stronger mentally than her husband, saying once: 'Ivan's father was ready to bow when he was met by a stronger opponent, but I never did. My adversary had to exhaust me totally to win.' As Lendl has also recalled: 'My father was the one who used his mind better when he was playing, and he played a smart game, but he didn't have the will, so when the going got really tough and he started feeling tired, he would just let go. My mum was the one who would never give up. Ever. She was kind of a bully. She'd say, "I'm going to break you down", and she would.' So Ivan knew that, in her eyes, the worst thing he could ever do on a tennis court would be to accept defeat. Growing up with a mother like his, it's hardly surprising that Ivan would come to despise losing, at tennis or anything else, almost as much as he loathed communism.

For Lendl, part of the appeal of tennis was that he alone was responsible for whether he won or lost. He had tried team sports, and hadn't liked them, as he hadn't been amused when others didn't try: 'I played a couple of basketball matches at school, and I had trouble handling the kids who didn't give their best. It was pissing me off.' Playing tennis, Lendl wouldn't have to rely on others, and couldn't be brought down by others' sloth or ineptitude.

But it's not as if playing solo on a tennis court, just him against his opponent on the other side of the net, left him constantly fulfilled and satisfied. Being a competitive bastard – his words – a young Lendl would suddenly go into an atomic rage if he happened to lose a game of table football to his father, threatening to flip the table on its side. Worse was if he was being beaten by anyone on the tennis court. He was a moper. He was a moaner. He was also a shouter and a sobber – sometimes his eyes would be so full of tears he couldn't see the ball. He wasn't, however, a great trasher of rackets, though one good reason why he didn't destroy his 'bat' was that he only had one of them. Young Ivan wasn't exactly, to borrow Barbra Streisand's description of Andre Agassi, a Zen Master – in fact, Lendl himself has recalled how his behaviour was often terrible, and the moping and the shouting was sometimes so embarrassing that his mother would have to intervene during a match and effectively default her son by removing him from the court. So, Lendl would have had some understanding of Murray's rage on a tennis court, of how a young Murray had once been nicknamed Bamm-Bamm, after the character from

The Flintstones who was always smashing things up, and how as a professional player Murray had occasionally become so angry that he bloodied his knuckles by punching a clenched fist against his strings.

If there was one thing that Lendl's mother hated more than the thought of her son giving up, it was displaying emotion, as she made plain to him: 'If you're going to cry, go home.' Olga's view was that 'emotions don't help you – never show your opponent that you're upset'. And that message seems eventually to have got through to Ivan, as by his late teenage years – when he was seventeen or eighteen – he had just about learned to control his temper. Lendl's parents also didn't believe he should be looking over at them after every point, as it made him appear needy and insecure. So they did their best to discourage him. 'During a match, we taught Ivan not to look our way,' Jiří once said. 'If he did, we turned, showing no reaction whatsoever.' So Olga and Jiří were blank, expressionless spectators at tennis matches long before Ivan was – though it's not true to say there was no movement whatsoever, as sometimes Lendl made a mistake, couldn't resist looking over, and caught his mother rolling her eyes. Olga's cold, hard approach to being a tennis mum was picked up on by the StB's informants at the club, with one report noting: 'Even though Olga is enthusiastic about her son, she doesn't show it very much.' There's a clear contrast here with Murray's mother. There was the occasion when Lendl turned to Judy Murray after one of her son's matches and said: 'If you're going to sit behind me again, can you bring ear plugs for me?' And there were times during Murray's childhood when he was playing doubles with his mother, and after missing a shot, she cursed under her breath. Probably the only time that Judy had been reticent to show emotion was when she was receiving those poison-pen letters, and she retreated into herself for a while, but she soon went back to her old self.

What is clear, though, from the story of Lendl's childhood is that long before he became fixated on beating McEnroe, Connors or Becker, he was obsessed with beating his mother at her own game. Even if he never won Wimbledon, one of the greatest achievements of Lendl's tennis life – perhaps above some of his tournament victories on the tour – was the day that he beat his mother for the first time at the Ostrava club. After that, their relationship would never be the same again. Even getting to play a match against his mum was a prize in itself as he didn't get to do that very often – that was because she was still playing competitively, and so didn't always have the time for someone still learning the game. 'It cannot be said that Lendl's parents contributed to the growth of his tennis skills, as they rarely played with him,' the StB noted. Perhaps the Lendls weren't as ferocious towards each other as the Connors family – Gloria would urge little Jimmy to 'play like a crazed animal', and 'to knock the ball down my throat, and he learned to do this because he found out that if I had the chance I would knock it down his'. But, be in no doubt: Olga wouldn't have been at all charitable towards her son; there wouldn't have been any Fisher-Price, mid-court fore-hands coming from her strings, and she certainly wouldn't have let him win so as to offer him encouragement. Tennis was a hard and unforgiving game; he was going to have to learn that.

Years later, Lendl was able to recall many of the details of that great victory. He was fourteen, and about a year had passed since he had defeated his father for the first time. He had been obsessed with beating Dad, a more regular adversary at the local courts, but never as interested as he had been in conquering the Lendl tennis matriarch. They were playing at the weekend. It was just before lunch, and they were on Court Number Four at the tennis club. They were tied at four games apiece in this one-set match, but Olga wouldn't have been worried given that she was to serve next, and she had always found a way of beating her son. This time, though, Lendl just kept on smashing winners past his mother, and he broke her, and then held on his own serve to complete the victory. If Ivan was delighted – 'I couldn't wait to get home to tell my father, and I was grinning from ear to ear' – Olga couldn't take any pleasure from her son's progress. At first, Olga said nothing, hardly speaking after her son's triumph, and then, on breaking her silence, she is understood to have announced that she wouldn't be playing with him again. Plus, he would have to get his coaching elsewhere; she wasn't going to be passing on any more instruction after that. There's no similar story from the Murray family archives. Andy and Judy's matches were certainly competitive, but they didn't have the intensity or the significance of the Lendl family's encounters. Murray probably took more pleasure from playing against Judy than Lendl did from facing his mother, with those matches helping Murray to develop his tactical mind, as he had to play intelligent, astute tennis if he was going to give himself a chance.

This wasn't East Germany – the state didn't steal Lendl's childhood for the future glory of the Republic. While some might suggest that, if the state didn't steal his childhood, that's only because Lendl's parents had got there first and robbed him of his early years, they're quite wrong about that. Lendl's mother could hardly have been harder on him, and it didn't always look as though Ivan was having much fun on court, but he wouldn't have continued playing so much tennis if it wasn't something which gave him a purpose and, despite appearances, some pleasure. So he would hang around the tennis club until sundown, and play against anyone who turned up; if no one came, he would play against the wall, though that was never as satisfactory. An StB report commented on his will to win: 'Since his childhood, Lendl has been strong-willed, with his best friends turning into the worst enemies on the tennis court, and Lendl doing everything he can to win. Since he has started to grow – physically and tennis-wise – he would subordinate everything to tennis. He would be constantly luring people into playing tennis with him.' No wonder Lendl was upset when his mother suspended him from going to the tennis club as punishment for biting his nails – she would look at his hands, and for every nail he had chewed he would miss a day of tennis. And he hated missing tennis, considering that a waste of a day.

It was up to Lendl, and his parents, whether he would have ambitions in tennis. So when it became clear that Lendl's forehand was going to take him a long way – that it was a shot capable of blasting great holes in others players' ambitions – he became part of the system, the so-called Czech Tennis Factory, but he wasn't scooped up or swept away; he was a very willing participant in this. He wanted to play. As we shall see later, that wasn't just because of some pure love for the game, or because he enjoyed the visceral thrill of putting forehand winners into the backstop (one coach at the NHKG Tennis Club, Olvrich Lerch, told him that you should never push the ball when you can hammer it), but also because of a desire to better himself.

A year had passed since that great victory over his mother and so well regarded was the fifteen-year-old Lendl in Czechoslovak tennis circles that he was taken on chaperoned trips to play junior tournaments in the United States. Though Lendl's school gave him special dispensation to miss lessons in order to play tennis, his parents still expected him to excel in exams, and he lived up to that demand, achieving mostly A and B grades, showing particular aptitude for maths and logic. So there were strong early indications that he liked to take a systematic approach to life; certainly, from his mid-twenties onwards, and especially on the practice and match courts, he didn't do much that hadn't first been thought through. One subject he didn't enjoy was history: he regarded the curriculum as communist propaganda: 'I hated it, because if what they feed you isn't right, why bother with it?' Even after Lendl won junior grand slam titles at Roland Garros and Wimbledon, and held the junior world number one ranking, his father was concerned what might happen to his son if he failed as a professional tennis player, so he made him enrol at the Technical University of Ostrava. But soon enough – with Lendl winning matches and moving up in the tennis world – it became apparent that this young Czech wasn't going to need the back-up plan of a university degree. As befits a future president of the country's tennis federation, Jiří Lendl wasn't a rule-breaker or a revolutionary – according to *Sports Illustrated*, a teenage Ivan once hoped to play in a professional tournament in Austria but was blocked by the federation's board, which wanted him to play in an amateur competition in France; the deciding vote was cast by his father.

So Lendl was ambitious for himself, but there was often reason to ponder whether his parents took his tennis more seriously than he did. Sometimes he would look at their faces after one of his defeats and think, 'Oh, come on, guys.' Every time he lost, there were two agonies: the match itself and then the debriefing with his parents (you can't imagine that any-one in the Lendl family would have been in a sunny mood on the occasion of his first match at a proper tournament; he was eight and he lost 6-0, 6-1). And, while Olga had backed off after losing to her son for the first time, she still wanted to be involved in his tennis, believing she had much to offer.

Jiří didn't want to be a bystander either. Even after Lendl graduated from the junior circuit to the senior game, played at the senior grand slams and had paid coaches travelling with him, Olga and Jiří would make observations. That's why, when his parents flew from Prague to watch him play at the US Open, he would make sure they didn't sit in the courtside box; he didn't want to see his mother roll her eyes when-ever he made some crass error. But putting them somewhere else couldn't stop the post-match debriefs, couldn't stop his mother from criticising him or talking to him as if she was his coach. And when his parents weren't in the same city as their son, they would telephone. And who would pay more attention to what Olga said? Her son? Or the StB? This much we do know: when Lendl became Andy Murray's coach, he didn't copy his mother's approach of passing on opinion and instruction through the use of monologues; he would take a far more collaborative approach, having realised that this was the most effective way of improving the Briton's game.

Tennis was, according to many in the Politburo, for the idle rich. For the hardliners within the Czechoslovak Socialist Republic, wafting a racket at a felt-covered ball was a bourgeois leisure activity, one of the most decadent of sports, and as offensive to their ideals as a round of golf or an afternoon's yachting. But life is never as simple as it initially appears to be in any ideologue's mind; the Republic ended up having a conflicted, complicated relationship with the sport. 'So the government thought tennis was a bourgeois sport, but they were still using us for publicity,' Tomás Šmid told me. 'They realised that if they let us out of the country, to play tournaments and to compete in team competitions, we would be promoting the country. Of course, by letting us out of the country to play, they were also allowing us to make money.'

From time to time – and it was almost as if they could contain themselves no longer – the state-controlled media would rip into those who led a life of privilege on the international tennis tour, who spent more time in capitalist countries, earning dollars, than they did with comrades in the East. 'Tennis was perceived with scorn as a capitalist sport,' Ivan Lendl's father, Jiří, once noted. The communist thinking was this: unlike a team of ice hockey players who all played for the common good, a group of tennis players were an inherently selfish bunch who thought only of themselves. And they were right. On the tennis tour, you eat what you kill, and the sport's ethos has always been closer to Thatcherism than to Marxism. And yet, for all their disapproval, Prague could hardly ignore the propaganda value in glories on the world stage: how better to promote their ideology than to duff up the West at their own pastimes? And it was propaganda to be pushed out at a domestic audience, as much as for an international one, with tennis one way of distracting your Czechoslovakian everyman from his daily grizzling. And, a few times each year – and this was much more in line with Prague's thinking – tennis players did compete as a collective. While the state media would never publish details of the prize money available on the tours – because the party officials found the numbers to be offensive, and also because they didn't want to unsettle the proletariat – the press delighted in covering the collective and national triumphs in the Davis Cup or in the women's equivalent, the Fed Cup.

So the Republic was never happier with Lendl than when he was part of the team that won the Davis Cup in 1980 after beating Italy at Prague's Sportovní Hall; the weekend that Czechoslovakia became the first Eastern Bloc champions was the closest he came to resembling a poster boy for the regime. Nothing he ever did at the grand slams could top that. Lendl was doing his compulsory military service at the time – that didn't mean he was about to join a tank regiment, just that he would have to play tennis for a military club, for Rudá Hvézda Praha, or Red Star Prague, and that during the week of the final he wore an army uniform whenever he appeared at a press conference or was near a television camera. Those who saw Lendl at close quarters thought the uniform must have been for show – the jacket was several sizes too big for this tennis soldier, and the trousers hadn't been tailored.

It was almost as if someone in Moscow had written a memo about which sport each of the countries in the Eastern Bloc would specialise in, so as to spread the propaganda benefits around – while East Germany juiced up for track and field, Romania would be a country of gymnasts, and the Soviet Union went big on weightlifting, Czechoslovakia was to become the communist tennis powerhouse. Tennis had been around in this part of the world far longer than communism – historians have traced the first organised Czechoslovak tournament to 1879, which was just a couple of years after the first men's competition at the Wimbledon Championships. And Czechoslovakia had had fine players and defectors before Lendl came into the wider world, let alone the tennis world – defector Jaroslav Drobný won the men's Wimbledon title in 1954. 'At the time, the communists realised far better than Western democracies the tremendous propaganda of international sport,' Drobný once noted, and after 1968, when the hardliners regained strict control of society, they started to care more about producing good tennis players.

After football and ice hockey, tennis was the most popular sport. If the apparatchiks in Prague had never put a system in place to manufacture tennis players – such as they would to produce tractors – it's perfectly possible that you would never have come to hear of this Ivan Lendl. For those doubting the success of the system, just consider how an American tennis magazine advised its readers after the 1986 US Open to 'get used to pronouncing funny-sounding names'. All four of the singles finalists at the tournament – Lendl defeated Miloslav Mečiř for the men's title, and Martina Navratilova beat Helena Suková for the women's trophy – were from this small Eastern European country. Lendl may despise communism, but he was very much a product of the Czechoslovak Tennis Factory, as were Martina Navratilova, men's Wimbledon champion Jan Kodeš, women's Australian, French and US Open champion Hana Mandlíková, and former doubles world number one Šmid and others; as Lendl has acknowledged, the country produced a disproportionately high number of leading players.

Among the truths you often hear repeated in tennis is that systems don't produce champions; parents do. But that's not always the case. Of course, Lendl's parents were influential in his own career – with a couple of racket-heads for parents, it was hardly going to be any other way – but there is no disputing that Czechoslovakia's system of finding talented juniors was efficient, with bright young things given plenty of attention and direction. And there was no doubting that this was a subculture that encouraged drive and ambition. Naturally, the players didn't have the same reasons as the state for wanting success on the tennis court; they weren't playing to keep the communists supplied with little propaganda nuggets. For any thrusting young player, the endgame was the same: to use their skill at swinging a racket as a means of escape, to be airlifted over the Iron Curtain to a new life of travel, opportunity, excitement and wealth. While the standard of living in the Republic was tolerable, and higher than in other countries in the Eastern Bloc, it was still a place where personal ambition could die a slow death in the long queue at the bakery, or anywhere else that reminded you of communism's limitations. Where was the reward for hard work, ambition or enterprise?

It could have been worse in Czechoslovakia, but it also could have been so much better. Prague in the 1970s and 1980s, according to the text that accompanied a recent exhibition of the StB's surveillance photographs, was a place of scaffolding, peeling façades and Soviet-era, two-stroke-engine cars. So the population had been promised 'socialism with a human face'. What they got, as Navratilova has noted, was George Orwell's description of the future – a boot stamping on your face for ever. Any drop in the standard of living for the post-1968 generation was said to have resulted in an uplift in cynicism and alcoholism. This was the era of 'Dumpling Socialism' – that, according to the *Harvard Gazette*, is the term for ironic nostalgia that some Czechoslovakians have used about that period of history. Just consider, as Lendl once did, free medical care. That sounded good, but it wasn't equal for all: if your wife was having a baby, you shouldn't expect the doctor actually to call, unless you were a public figure or if you had passed him money on the side. Who dared or bothered to be ambitious living in what Václav Havel called the 'entropy' of life in the Republic, with every citizen subjected to 'a prolonged process of violation, enfeeblement and anesthesia'. Few banked a high salary – with doctors, lawyers and other professionals not earning a great deal. Since there was no private legal practice, Lendl's lawyer father was on a depressed salary; some calculations would suggest his annual income was lower than the price of a cheap car, while it would have cost him a couple of months' wages to buy a television.

There was money for the few, not for the masses; one way of securing a relatively high income was to shimmy up the pole of the communist party hierarchy; or you could, if you had some talent, try for success as a singer or actor. And, for those who couldn't sing, act or fake devotion to the Politburo, there was tennis. However small any one individual's chances were of growing rich playing the game, playing the sport could at least give you hope. 'At that time of totalitarian darkness,' Kodeš has reflected, 'tennis offered one of the few opportunities for travel to the West.' So it was perfectly clear why the juniors were so competitive with each other at their domestic tournaments: everyone knew that only those who showed great promise would be given permission to travel abroad to foreign events. As one put it: 'It's like a war – to get out of the country.' Šmid told me that tennis was the only way you were going to make money and be free: 'They were the two big motivations to play tennis. As a junior, maybe you went to a tournament outside Czechoslovakia, to somewhere in the West, and then you saw for the first time how other people lived, and so then you could make a comparison between your life and what others had.' And Lendl wasn't deaf to the siren calls of America's personal freedoms and greenbacks. A career as a tennis player certainly had more appeal than a lifetime of working in the Ostrava coal-mining or metalworks industries, which was what was facing many young men in the city.

'Ivan was very clear early on why he was playing tennis,' Boris Becker told me. 'True, Ivan loved the sport, and he wanted to become number one, and he wanted to win as many titles as he could, but he also wanted to make as much money as he could. I believe he always saw tennis as a business.' As Lendl has said himself, as a young man he was motivated by the prospect of leaving Czechoslovakia and making money. 'When I was growing up the thing that drove me in tennis was the idea that it could get me out of Czechoslovakia. That was my goal. Then, when I had got out for a while I didn't really have any motivation. I had done what I wanted to do. Money then became my [sole] motivation.' Some within Czechoslovakia used to believe that the political freedoms that followed 1989 would lead to a Czech tennis boom, but that never happened, perhaps because the young players didn't have the drive to use tennis to escape. Consider this: was Lendl a great player because of communism, not despite it?

CHAPTER TWO
IRON CURTAIN CAPITALISM

At one stage, the security services believed, Ivan Lendl only had one friend in the world. If that were true, it was hardly surprising that Lendl was heavily under the influence of this Wojtek Fibak, who was the personal tennis coach of Pope John Paul II. He was also Eastern Europe's first tennis capitalist, and a Pole who was said to have improved his English by reading the financial pages of the world's newspapers. Lendl, who was yet to become his own man, gladly followed Fibak's instructions. 'All the time,' Fibak told me, 'Ivan never said no.' Lendl had been in need of some guidance, and Fibak had found himself wanting to help, and he had been clear on the USA. 'America was the centre of tennis, they had the champions, and they had the tournaments – it was always everyone's dream to play tennis in America,' Fibak recalled. 'Ivan came to me and said, "I want to become number one". So I said to [him], "if you want to be number one, you're going to have to live in America – you can't stay in Ostrava".'

Fibak and Lendl had met in the late 1970s, while Lendl was still a teenager, and from the off it had been an unbalanced relationship; it was said that a teenage Lendl would trail around behind Fibak, watching almost all of his matches. And Fibak's first impression of Lendl had been of 'a sad-looking country boy'. Fibak's misreading of Lendl when the Czech was new to the international tennis scene may be forgiven: how was Fibak to know Lendl was from the Ostrava smoke-stacks and not from rural Moravia?

And this gloomy teenager looked back at the man from Poznań with nothing but awe and adoration. From those beginnings, Fibak would go on to become Lendl's coach, mentor, landlord, best friend, cultural guide, business adviser, image consultant and the man who introduced him to his future wife. To know about Lendl, you also have to know about Fibak, one of the most colourful members of the tennis cast in the 1970s and 1980s. Such was Fibak's closeness to the pontiff, it was said that during one of the Pope's hospital stays, the tennis player was admitted to the suite while the President of Italy waited in the lobby. Fibak would say that he would have withdrawn from any tournament in the world, even Wimbledon, to help improve the papal backhand.

No one has ever accused Fibak, once ranked among the world's top ten singles players, of for ever pulling sad faces, or of having a dull and uneventful life – after his retirement from tennis, he was so successful in business that one Polish newspaper once considered him to have been worth $50 million, making him the second wealthiest Pole in the world, behind only Barbara Piasecka-Johnson, widow of Jay Seward Johnson and heir to the Johnson and Johnson pharmaceutical fortune. Still, for all his success as an entrepreneur,

Fibak continues to pop up in tennis – he coached Marta Domachowska (who would pose topless for Polish *Playboy*) as well as assisting Novak Djokovic at the 2013 US Open.

When Lendl started shadowing Fibak, the Pole was at the peak of his powers on the tennis tour. Fibak was a grand slam doubles champion in 1978, when he won the Australian Open with Kim Warwick, and he peaked at number two in the world doubles rankings, while as a singles player his finest season at the slams was in 1980, when he reached the quarter-finals of the French Open, Wimbledon and the US Open. During his career, he won fifteen singles titles, fifty-two doubles titles, and the best part of $3 million in prize money. For Lendl, there weren't many other players from the Eastern Bloc who had had an impact on the international tour, so no wonder he idolised Fibak. But Fibak's accomplishments on the tennis court would only have been part of the reason why Lendl would have regarded the Pole with such reverence. Tennis may have been a bourgeois sport, but that didn't mean that the tour was populated by renaissance men. Fibak, who had studied law and who spoke several languages, rightly regarded himself as being among the sophisticates of the locker-room. Unashamedly ambitious, he saw himself as being more cultured, educated and urbane than your average tennis player; one visitor to his house noticed a Sotheby's auction catalogue, as well as a picture of a foxhunting scene above the fireplace, and a bookshelf filled with back issues of *Kultura*, an intellectual Polish magazine printed in Paris. Off the court, and out of his tennis togs, he wore expensive clothes. There was something of the outsider about Fibak and Lendl was drawn to him.

Fibak also saw something of himself in Lendl – he, too,

had once been an Iron Curtain innocent trying to make his way in the tennis frat house. And Fibak saw something else in Lendl: this boy had potential. As Fibak saw it, there were all sorts of problems with Lendl's game; he wasn't the most gifted player, and he wasn't the most robust and resilient, but he thought that this miserable youth, both sad and soft, had a fine mind, possessing 'an extraordinary brain quality, and powers of insight that would take him very far'. Fibak would help to transform Lendl's game, his mentality and his image.

Fibak was right to have spotted potential in Lendl – note the Czech's progression in the space of five years. In 1978, the year Lendl turned eighteen, and the season he made the switch from the juniors, he was ranked among the world's top one hundred players in the senior game. A couple of years later, he was a top-ten player, and in 1981, a few months after celebrating his twenty-first birthday, he made his first appearance in a grand slam final when he was the runner-up to Björn Borg at Roland Garros, and two years after that he first held the world number one ranking.

While Fibak wasn't universally popular in the locker-room, Lendl was, especially in the early stages of their relationship, almost blind to any faults the Pole might have had. Fibak hadn't expected Lendl to be quite so susceptible, so impressionable; he could have said pretty much anything and Lendl would have done it. If Fibak was courtside when Lendl was playing, Lendl was always looking over at him, sometimes after every point of the match. For long periods, Lendl would move around the tennis world without a coach or even a companion – he would book his own flights and hotel rooms, with only a pocket cassette player with earphones for company, and looking very lonesome. But, even at those moments, Lendl wouldn't have been on his own, as he would have had Fibak's advice and encouragement in his head. After a match, Lendl would phone Fibak to update him. Sometimes they would share a match court, playing doubles together, but Lendl was always Fibak's creature, someone who, according to his old teacher, 'listened blindly to everything I said'. Such was his interest in Lendl's life that Fibak turned up in Prague, arriving in his Porsche in the week of the 1980 Davis Cup final; he knew Lendl didn't always find it easy playing in front of an expectant public and he wanted to help him find the right mental state. Lendl wanted to flee the interference and control of his parents and the state, and now here he was giving himself over to Fibak.

'At the moment,' said one StB report in the early 1980s, 'Lendl perhaps trusts only Fibak and he takes him everywhere with him.' According to the information supplied to the secret police, Fibak's wife had filmed some of Lendl's matches with a video recorder, and 'Lendl and Fibak would then think of tactics to use when playing against his opponents'. The StB's intelligence was that Lendl wasn't friends with any of the male Czechoslovakians on the tour, or with players of any other nationality. 'Lendl does not have any other friends abroad, and he once confessed to himself that the hardest times are when he does not play and he has to be by himself,' according to the StB.

If Lendl is The Man Who Made Murray, Fibak will doubtless regard himself as The Man Who Made Lendl. Fibak was instrumental in Lendl pioneering an ultra-aggressive brand of tennis, which many came to know as 'a power-baseline game'. Others described it differently, with the late American novelist David Foster Wallace, in the course of his superb

New York Times essay 'Roger Federer as Religious Experience', calling Lendl's tennis 'a kind of brutal art'. That's one of the few times, incidentally, that anyone has been known to put Lendl's tennis and art in the same sentence, the general view being that his game could be an artless, grim spectacle. Whatever your own personal choice of words to describe the ungodly power of Lendl's racket arm, this much everyone should be able to agree on: the way that Lendl played in the 1980s, with that ferocious serve and with the might of his forehand, is how most of today's players go about their work. There are, of course, exceptions to that generalisation, such as the sophisticate Federer, and Lendl's very own Andy Murray. But, 'for the most part', as Pete Sampras observed at the 2014 Australian Open, 'it's just everyone staying back and throwing rocks'. This was among Lendl's gifts to the modern tennis world – the baseline firefight. While Jimmy Connors had been playing a similar game, he didn't have the power in his shots that Lendl did, and that, after all, was key. 'Lendl loved smashing Connors,' Pat Cash told me. 'They played the same sort of game, but Lendl had more power than Connors.'

And Lendl couldn't have developed a power-baseline game without Fibak. During their time together, especially during the early years of their association, Fibak had put a great deal of work and thought into breaking Lendl down and then putting him back together again. According to Fibak, at the beginning of their time together, Lendl had a weak and flappy backhand wing. Truth be told, Lendl didn't have a backhand that was fit for purpose on the men's tour – he wasn't going to have much of a future in the sport if he couldn't attack on that side. As Lendl has remembered it, he had a 'harmless chip backhand' and you don't get very far with harmless ground strokes; though he would rarely miss with the backhand, 'it could be attacked with impunity'.

To cover up that flaw, as a junior, Lendl had been a committed serve and volleyer, rushing the net at every chance and half-chance, trusting his volley more than his backhand. 'Ivan didn't have a backhand – he just had a slice backhand, and it was a very conservative slice backhand,' Fibak told me. 'The game he had when he was eighteen years old, he couldn't have achieved anything with. As a junior, he had always served and volleyed, and do you know why? Because he had to, because if he didn't, his opponent would come to net after returning his second serve, and Ivan didn't have a shot to pass him. So when I met Ivan, he didn't have a flat first serve, he only had a kick serve. I know this is hard to believe now, but his game then was a kick serve, and serve and volley, and no backhand.' Fibak didn't have to do much tinkering with Lendl's forehand, which he regarded as an 'amazing weapon' and 'one of the greatest forehands in the history of the game', but his recollection is that he completely remodelled Lendl's backhand – while Lendl was once only able to hit ineffective slices on that side, he was soon able to attack on that wing by applying topspin, pace and menace. Despite the obvious weakness, this was still a bold move by Lendl, who by then was in and around the world's top ten, to have essentially started again with one of his ground strokes, and at first he didn't find it easy always hitting his backhand with heavy topspin, but he learned quickly.

To appreciate the speed at which Lendl changed his backhand, just consider a couple of matches he played against Harold Shipman, an American opponent, in 1980. When they met on a hard court in Las Vegas, Shipman trounced Lendl 6-1, 6-1, and it was said that Lendl was in tears at the end, but just months later, also on a hard court, but this time at the US Open, Lendl annihilated Shipman 6-1, 6-0, 6-0. Still, even after relearning how to play a backhand, Lendl's game was built around the might of his forehand. Indeed, Lendl used that very modern approach – he was doing this a long time before it became a common sight on the tour – of running around his backhand to play inside-out forehands.

At first, Fibak had regarded Lendl as a real plodder. It wasn't just speed he was lacking; he also lacked the explosive power you needed as a tennis player. So skinny and gangly as a kid, Lendl had been known as 'Nit', or 'Thread', and then in his late teens, which was when he first came into Fibak's orbit, he was still a bony, angular figure, all arms and legs, and with cheekbones sharp enough to slice you open. 'When I met Ivan, he was slow,' Fibak recalled, 'so I made him fitter and faster.' One of Fibak's methods was to have Lendl playing against two opponents on the practice court, running and hitting, running and hitting, flooding his body with lactic acid. 'Ivan hated that,' said Fibak, who suggested that Lendl – despite the example he had been set by his workaholic mother – was as a teenager still learning that he needed to graft if he was to make the most of his abilities: 'Ivan wasn't a hard-working person by nature. He would become hard-working, but that wasn't his nature.' So Lendl's movement improved during his time with Fibak, and he bulked up, too; he became a better athlete with the Pole.

Still, Lendl's new physique and new backhand weren't the only factors behind this new power-baseline game; much of the credit for that has to go to the new technology, with Lendl among the early adopters of a composite or graphite racket, which allowed him to load up tennis balls with extreme amounts of topspin. Lendl couldn't have played the way he did if professional tennis had still been stuck in the age of wood. Only with a composite racket could the Czech have been the player he was. While Lendl wasn't alone in using these new rackets, with the others it was as if they were still playing wooden-era-style tennis with graphite frames. But Lendl, as Foster Wallace noted, 'was the first top pro whose strokes and tactics appeared to be designed around the special capabilities of the composite racket'. The ability to impart all that spin – to have the ball making all those rotations as it fizzed off his racket – allowed him to hit his shots with much greater power and pace. Without topspin, you couldn't be sure, if you were playing eyes-out tennis and really going for your shots, that you would keep the ball in the court, but a ball loaded up with topspin would be programmed to suddenly dip and then bounce inside the court. Lendl could stay on the baseline and throw rocks. He was also reinventing the geometry of a tennis court – somehow, now that Lendl had a composite racket, everything was different, everything was new. So Lendl didn't even have to be in the middle of the court to hit winners – the trajectories of these new ground strokes allowed him to hit winners when he was outside the tramlines. No longer was it just serve and volleyers who could hit angled winners, as you could do that from anywhere in the court, just as long as you put enough spin on the ball. This was a new kind of violence and brutality, but it was a controlled violence.

So why would Lendl's game end up being copied by so many? Why did he spawn the modern game? Because, and

Foster Wallace makes this point very well, you don't have to be a great talent to play like Lendl. 'It wasn't that Lendl was an immortally great tennis player. He was simply the first top pro to demonstrate what heavy topspin and raw power could achieve from the baseline. And, most important, the achievement was replicable, just like the composite racket. Past a certain threshold of physical training and talent, the main requirements were athleticism, aggression, and superior strength and conditioning.' It also should be noted that Lendl's serve was better than most imagined it to be. 'So he had a lot of power, and he was very much a modern player, with a big forehand, but he also had a very underrated serve,' Cash recalled. 'Most people didn't realise how good a serve he had.'

If the StB wanted to know what Lendl was thinking, they first had to learn what was inside Fibak's head. While Lendl could probably not have moved to the United States if Martina Navratilova hadn't already defected, he was none the less indebted to Fibak. Inevitably, many of the conversations that Lendl and Fibak had were about America, the promised land of the tennis world. Moving to the United States had transformed Fibak, and he strongly advised Lendl that if he wanted to make it as a professional tennis player he would have to live in America, not in some Eastern Bloc backwater. Lendl was easily persuaded to settle in America shortly after leaving his teens – after all, like every other young tennis player in Czechoslovakia, he hoped that the sport would enable him to see the world. It was also clear to him that trying to train in Czechoslovakia's hard winters, with the lack of decent indoor facilities, was all but impossible. How could you put in enough training hours in Ostrava during the winter months when there was only one indoor court, and you had to fight to get a sixty-minute slot each day?

Fibak had convinced Lendl that he had to be in America, so, in 1981, the year the Czech turned twenty-one, he moved to the States. Unlike Navratilova, Lendl didn't make that move by walking into an embassy or immigration office and seeking political asylum, so he wasn't defecting as such; what he was doing was taking advantage of some of the post-Navratilova freedoms and basing himself in the West. There was still an expectation that Lendl would regularly return to Czechoslovakia, as well as making himself available for Davis Cup ties. This was just the next phase of Lendl's transition from East to West.

Lendl didn't just cart his life over to America: he ended up becoming a Connecticut Yankee, living among the preppies, the captains of industry and the Wolves of Wall Street. You couldn't possibly have conceived of a more capitalist place to call home, or anywhere, with the possible exception of the Hollywood Hills, that a Prague hardliner would have found more repulsive. According to his mentor, Lendl lived with the Fibaks in New York for a while, before then moving with his surrogate family to their manor house in Greenwich, Connecticut. And then, not long after that, Lendl would have his own house there, just a few minutes from the Fibaks. Of course, there had been practical considerations when choosing Connecticut; from there he could reach more than a dozen tournaments in America by car inside four hours, and he was much more inclined to take mini road trips, when he could stop whenever he pleased to pick up a Coca-Cola at a gas station, than to be at the mercy of the domestic flight schedule. Plus, being so close to New

York, he was just a short journey and then a Concorde flight from London, Paris and the European tournaments. An additional part of Connecticut's appeal was the harshness of the winters: when it snowed it reminded him of Czechoslovakia. Still, above all those reasons, there was plainly something about the ethos of Connecticut that chimed with him. And which still chimes: more than thirty years later he still has a home in Connecticut, splitting his time between there and Vero Beach, Florida.

First, Lendl had to go through a fair amount of angst – more on that in the next chapter, which considers his fears and insecurities after landing in the West – but he would eventually reach a state of capitalist delirium, declaring from his country pad, 'life is like a dream'. No one had greater admiration for America, and love for capitalism, than Lendl; there were times in the 1980s when he would overhear natural-born Americans griping about their country, and he would interject, 'maybe you should go live in East Germany for half a year and come back and we'll talk about it then'. For Lendl, America was 'so good that it was almost beyond the point of understanding'. It was certainly far better than many spoilt Americans thought it to be. Soon enough he would regard himself as almost the embodiment of the American Dream – a self-made man from Eastern Europe, making millions of dollars a year, living in a big house and driving a fast car. Once fully formed, Lendl's politics couldn't have been more different from those held by Czech tennis's other celebrated émigré. While Navratilova was a liberal, he gravitated towards right-wing Reagan/Bush Republicanism. Towards the end of the 1980s, Lendl was at a Downing Street party when, according to her daughter, Carol, he astonished Margaret Thatcher by asking for the result of that night's Commons vote on the hanging bill, with *The Times* 'hazarding a guess that he shares Mrs Thatcher's views on the subject'. While Lendl gave law and order a big man hug, Navratilova was 'Martina the Complainer', for ever questioning authority. Lendl couldn't comprehend why anyone with Navratilova's experiences, who had lived behind the Iron Curtain, could ever have a world-view like hers. 'I can't understand how anyone who wants a free life can go the liberal line. I just cannot see her point of view,' he once said. 'Liberal is just a different name and a different stage for communism.' WHAT! LIBERAL COMMUNISTS!

Still, Lendl was all too aware during those early years that he had to be extremely careful about what he said and how he behaved, and that included what he said about his finances. Those freedoms could still be removed. In tennis's debating chamber, Lendl had to keep quiet about his own wealth. During the boom of the 1980s of yuppies and Gordon Gekkos, greed might have been good in the West but it wasn't on the other side of the Iron Curtain, so he couldn't let on how much he was earning – and in dollars, too – or go in for any conspicuous consumption, or lead what might have been considered a playboy lifestyle. Not wanting to antagonise the apparatchiks in Prague, Lendl knew to be discreet about how he was making the kind of money that your average worker in Czechoslovakia could not even have conceived of. You can understand why he and Fibak reportedly tried to stop stories appearing about his real estate in America. Travelling on a Czechoslovak passport, Lendl felt the terror of what an aggrieved Politburo could do to his tennis life if they thought he should be brought back under their control; it was still in the state's power to have damaged, or even shut down, his career by blocking his requests for visas.

As inconspicuous as Lendl might have tried to be about his wealth, the reality was that the StB's collaborators were regularly feeding them information on Lendl's earning power. 'Lendl's income is indeed huge,' the StB observed in a report in 1981. And they contended he wasn't afraid to push tournament promoters for extra compensation; for instance, their informants had told them that, at one tournament in Germany, Lendl didn't just receive an appearance fee of 60,000 Deutschmarks, and then prize money on top, but supposedly also asked for a Mercedes. According to the StB's account, the tournament agreed, and had the car shipped to America. An StB report in October 1982 estimated that Lendl's earnings in dollars could have reached eight figures: 'For the period between early 1982 and July 1982, Lendl's profit from tournaments [sanctioned events and exhibitions], has been calculated at $1.25 million. In tennis circles they say that this figure should be multiplied five times to find out Lendl's real income from commercial [deals]. This year it is assumed that Lendl's income will exceed $10 million.' That intelligence report also noted that tennis players in Ostrava were talking about an article published in a Polish newspaper in which Fibak was supposed to have said that 'the Czechoslovak authorities were being difficult with granting Lendl permission to invest his money abroad'.

The secret police were aware that Lendl was trying to be discreet. They observed, based on information that appeared to have come from sources in the tennis world: 'When discussing his income, he said he had been asked to do lucrative adverts for television and radio companies, but always declined, as he is able to earn money in an easier way without the whole world knowing about it. It is understood that Lendl is not only a great tennis player and a well-dressed man, but also a competent businessman.' During Cold War-era Czechoslovakia, being described by the StB as a 'competent businessman' wasn't a compliment.

In post-match news conferences, Lendl felt Western journalists were far more interested in politics than tennis – he has recalled how the first question was often, 'when are you going to defect?' – but, of course, he could never speak openly about his views on Czechoslovakia, America, and how he loathed communism. 'There was no freedom of speech in communist countries. I had to be careful about what I said, so I didn't upset the agreements or arrangements I had because if I was home they could have taken my passport and I would never have travelled again; would never have been heard of again,' Lendl told the *Sunday Times*. 'The first question at the press conference was always, "Would you like to live here? When are you going to defect?" Well, what could I say?' It's also true that, in the early days after moving to the States, Lendl was a little taken aback by how direct – aggressive, even – Americans were in conversation, talking openly about their ambitions and accomplishments. At first, he was as reticent and reserved as every other European. And even when he had got used to incessant questions, Lendl could never cooperate and give the media what he felt they wanted, which seemed to be for him to leap on to the table in the interview room and declare: 'I love America!' It was perfectly clear to most that Lendl didn't want to live in Czechoslovakia any more, but he was never going to say as much; he knew just how dangerous a few loose words could be.

It was widely assumed, one former Czech player told me, that intelligence officers stationed in Czech embassies around the world would have been taking note of what Lendl said during any newspaper, radio and television interviews. And that assumption was correct: the StB were interested in any media reports about Lendl's affairs; for instance, his file contained information gleaned from an article in the *Los Angeles Times* that detailed the cars in his garage.

As it was, Lendl proved that taking the Fifth Amendment was always the smart choice. Any candour could potentially have ended his career, especially on delicate subjects such as money or whether his feelings towards the Soviet Union had been affected by memories of their tanks rolling into Czechoslovakia. It was always better not to air any potentially controversial views in public. The new freedoms of this post-Navratilova world had hardly created a kind of utopia for tennis players. It's the informed opinion of Jan Kodeš that Lendl's problems started when he 'became a star', when it was no longer possible to hide how much money he was making, and when it became widely known that he was investing his wealth in America, including in real estate. Soon enough, people also learned that Lendl spent his leisure time driving around in sports cars listening to cassettes of The Beatles. There would be stories – how far he had come from that third-storey Ostrava apartment – of how he was looking to 'upgrade' from a 16,000-square-foot Georgian house to a house twice the size.

Some started to speak of Lendl as one of tennis's 'Iron Curtain Capitalists', a group of players for ever considering their loyalties and contemplating defecting to the West. As *Tennis* magazine noted in the 1980s, tennis players lived as

luxurious and as capitalist a life as anyone from a communist country could, 'but all this carries a price, for the East
Europeans live daily with a troubling uncertainty. Who are
they? Where do their loyalties lie? What are the limits of
the freedom? Should they stay with family and familiarity at
home? Or should they emulate Navratilova and others and
leave forever? Although they understandably say little about
it, the lure of defection tugs at every East European player. It
has haunted Lendl ever since he began living in the US.'

Navratilova wasn't Czechoslovakian tennis's only defector. There was also Hana Strachonova, who gained political
asylum in Switzerland, and she had known plenty of Czechs
who had wanted to defect but who had lacked the courage.
Some apparently even defected as juniors; there were reports
of three Czech boys, who were held in high regard by the federation, jumping off a train that was taking them home from
a tournament in Italy. After seeking asylum in Switzerland,
they were resettled in West Germany. And Hana Mandlíková,
who won four grand slam titles, would also defect to Australia.

There were, according to Kodeš, an increasing number of
officials in the communist party who regarded Lendl as 'a bad
ambassador' for Czechoslovakia, and as a 'bad example' for
the children of the Republic. The feeling among those hardliners was that Lendl was becoming too rich and powerful,
that he would have to be disciplined and brought back under
state control. 'Ivan gave up his education early, and put all his
focus on becoming a tennis player, and making money in the
West,' said Kodeš. 'So some in the party thought you would
have hundreds of young kids trying to do the same, and then
they wouldn't make it, and they would end up on drugs and
become homeless.'

There was something schizophrenic, most agreed, about Lendl's situation; this member of the Davis Cup-winning team of 1980 was a poster boy for both communism and capitalism. There was no doubt that Lendl was adopted by corporate America, and that he was a huge commercial success, even if that StB estimation of the tennis player earning $10 million in 1982 was on the steep side. Fibak claimed to me that, during his time with him, Lendl had the biggest endorsement contract in tennis, more lucrative than any deals signed by John McEnroe, Jimmy Connors or Boris Becker. Consider that Lendl has been estimated to have earned $100 million over the course of his career, with just over a fifth of that figure, some $21 million, coming from prize money, and the rest from endorsements and appearance fees. Or consider how McEnroe and Lendl reportedly reacted to a proposed new competition with a seven-figure prize-money pot. McEnroe was quoted as saying: 'If we take that kind of money, it makes us look like a bunch of money whores', while Lendl was reported as commenting: 'When someone offers you $2 million, you don't spit in their face.'

As McEnroe once asked: 'How much money does a guy need?' Well, by 1986, by which time he was a multiple grand slam champion, *Sport* magazine was calling Lendl 'The Six-Million Dollar Man', having reached that figure after talking to more than thirty people in the tennis industry and making informed estimates of the money he was making. Though, to answer McEnroe's question, perhaps even that sum was insufficient. That year, the same magazine had calculated, Lendl earned $50,000 for promoting Ray-Ban sunglasses, $300,000 for having a patch for Gleneagles Country Club on his right shoulder, $200,000 for having a patch for Avis on his left shoulder, $150,000 from Seiko watches, $2.5 million from Adidas for endorsing their rackets, shoes and clothes, $50,000 for Bow Brand strings, $2.5 million for exhibitions and appearances and $250,000 for smaller endorsements and bonuses.

Given how humiliating it would have been for Prague if Lendl had followed Navratilova by defecting to America, it was no wonder the authorities wanted to know what was in Lendl's head, and who his associates were. It was the StB's analysis in the early 1980s, based on intelligence passed to them by those close to Lendl, including sources on the tennis tour, that his allegiance to the regime could not be guaranteed. 'Lendl is currently surrounded by a high number of people who live off his fame and he is significantly influenced by them. He is very adaptable and easily succumbs to rumours and poor views,' one StB document concluded. 'Most of these people come from the Czechoslovak emigrant population … Lendl is currently under the strong influence of the current propaganda implemented in the West against socialist countries. At tournaments abroad he keeps very close connections with Czechoslovak emigrant Martina Navratilova. He speaks very nicely of Navratilova, and claims that our leaders should rethink their attitude towards this tennis player who has reportedly committed no offence other than criticising the disarray in tennis, and the existence of people who exploit the fame of leading tennis players …'

By now there was growing suspicion at Lendl's reluctance to spend any time in Czechoslovakia. One of the StB's secret collaborators at the tennis club in Ostrava reported suspicions that Lendl's mother, Olga, was holding back information about her son's intentions. 'It was discovered that Olga Lendlova got nervous when she was asked when

Lendl will next be coming to [Czechoslovakia]. She stated that Lendl is playing a tournament in Basel followed by a tournament in Vienna, after which he will fly out of Europe. He had initially intended to visit Ostrava for two days, but he changed his mind. During this conversation, Lendlova's behaviour suggested that she was withholding some information.' Another report from the tennis club claimed that Lendl had been invited to take part in an exhibition match on their courts, in exchange for some crystal, 'but since this match would be without any financial reward, Lendl did not even respond to the invitation which means he is not interested in a match of such nature'. Word reached the StB that even Lendl's mother had become exasperated at her son never visiting Czechoslovakia: 'On 30 September 1982, before a trip to Barcelona, Olga Lendlova said she was mad at her son. She does not know why he never comes to the CSSR.'

For all the 'secret collaborators' they had recruited on and off the tennis tour, the security services never came to know the full extent of Lendl's thinking. In the heads of the StB's intelligence officers, and so also in the minds of the politicians who were being briefed, there was for ever the suspicion that Lendl was about to defect. And yet, certainly in the first half of the 1980s, it would appear that Lendl didn't have any firm plans to relinquish his Czechoslovak citizenship for an American passport. Lendl didn't see himself as a political animal, and didn't care so much for politics; he wouldn't defect for ideological reasons, only if he felt that the Prague administration was stopping him from going about his business, whether that was winning matches or signing sponsorship contracts. So long as he could carry on representing Czechoslovakia, basing himself in the United States, and earning American sponsorship dollars, Lendl wasn't going to be making any bold moves.

By 1982, there were suggestions that the StB had instructed newspaper editors not to promote Lendl's achievements. 'In newspaper circles in Ostrava, it has recently been discussed that Lendl should not be advertised in our newspapers, and that the newspapers should only inform their readers about Lendl's scores at important tournaments,' a lieutenant colonel for the StB noted to his middle-ranking colleagues. 'These instructions reportedly came from our bosses, but no one knows whom in particular.' And the public opinion of Lendl also shifted, with Kodeš suggesting that your average Czechoslovak increasingly believed that Lendl was mainly motivated by money. Likewise, some of Lendl's fellow Eastern Europeans appeared to believe, according to an article published in an American magazine in the 1980s, that the Czech was 'out to get very rich, and he is rich not only because he wins a lot of tournaments but also because, living in the US, he has access to big-dollar endorsement contracts that cannot be secured in the East'.

Attitudes towards Lendl's parents were changing, too, according to the information that the StB was receiving, though it should be remembered that some of the informants may have been driven by jealousy, as Lendl's success had ensured a comfortable life for his mother and father. According to the StB's spies, there was considerable suspicion and ill feeling towards Lendl's father after Jiří 'rid himself of all the posts he had performed at the tennis club NHKG, merely remaining a formal member of the club committee'. It was said that 'his current outlook is a surprise to all ordinary members of the club and its officials', with some believing that he had only held those positions for as long as he did for opportunistic reasons, as he supposedly thought that would help his son's tennis career. 'Jiří Lendl has declared at the tennis championships of CSSR in Bratislava that he is not interested in the tennis developments in Ostrava. With this he has revealed his character and attitude towards the sports situation in Ostrava. It is most likely that he had previously engaged in all posts just so that his son could without any difficulties work his way up to being one of the top tennis players in Czechoslovakia, hence for opportunistic reasons.' The StB's collaborators also raised suspicions about Jiří's politics and his attitude towards the government: 'As far as politics go, he should have been expelled from the communist party in 1970. His relationship to the regime was good in the past. At present, he regards our administration as a necessity, and he manifests his superiority, regularly reminding people of his son Ivan's success.'

It was also noted that Olga handing in her notice at the Technical University – she apparently said that she couldn't continue working if she was going to be regularly travelling to watch her son compete abroad – was not greeted with universal approval among her colleagues in the department. 'This has met with disagreement from some university employees, perhaps out of jealousy in some cases.' One of the StB's documents stated how Lendl's parents were conscious that they were being talked about, and so withdrew from society for a while: 'Ivan's parents have been avoiding people. Lately, Ivan's parents have been very cautious about their behaviour as if they were trying to see what was being said about them.'

By the early 1980s, the StB thought that Lendl was no longer subject to parental influence, with one report noting: 'Since Lendl now lives in a rather high society, it is debatable to what extent he can still be influenced by his mother.' Indeed, their spies at one international tournament reported that 'Ivan paid very little attention to his parents'. One secret police report in 1982 recorded how Lendl had supposedly isolated himself, distancing himself even from his parents: 'Lendl has now become even more introverted. He isolates himself when he stays abroad. He manages his business and other matters over the phone from his hotel rooms. He only sees his manager. He has adopted this behaviour even towards his parents, whom he treats poorly, which is different to his previous relationship with them. People in tennis circles condemn his behaviour, and it's said that he must be tired out. This is supported by the fact that his behaviour at tournaments has been inappropriate. He fires tennis balls at the crowd and does not shake hands with his opponents, for which he must pay fines to the professional tennis association.' So Lendl's parents had lost much of their hold over their son, but Olga and Jiří were still regarded as good sources of information on their son. That's why the StB had infiltrated the local tennis club: 'To answer the question whether it is true that Ivan has been granted an emigrant passport, his mother said on 15 September 1982 at the tennis courts of NHKG that Ivan had never applied for such a passport, and that these assumptions are unjustified. Olga Lendlova said it must be a rumour started by some cop, but that isn't true.'

On learning that Lendl had bought a new house for his parents in Prague, the StB thought that such a purchase showed that his parents were not about to defect. 'Judging by its floor plans, the Lendls would have bought the house for at least one million crowns. It is a new build with two residential units,' the StB observed. The thinking was that Lendl had chosen to relocate his parents in Prague because, when returning to Czechoslovakia to visit them, he wouldn't have to waste time travelling between the international airport and Ostrava. 'Supported by the fact they have just bought a house in Prague,' the StB noted, 'there is no assumption that Lendl's parents will emigrate.'

Reading through Ivan Lendl's secret police file, it's plain there was one episode, above all others, that shaped his thinking, which had him turning further away from the Czechoslovak Socialist Republic, and towards the United States. This hugely regrettable affair would have reminded Lendl that, even when he was in America, or travelling the world, he wasn't untouchable; Prague still exerted control over him. 'It was all so stupid,' Jan Kodeš told me. 'Ivan gave so much power to his opponents – some serious problems started for him after this.' One of the most revealing documents in the StB file entitled 'Ivan' is one that was spawned by this episode, and was a pleading letter that Lendl wrote to the Minister of the Interior in the wake of the scandal.

Though Lendl had been warned against appearing at an exhibition tournament in Sun City in the Bophuthatswana homeland in apartheid-era South Africa, he had still gone ahead with it. The government was angered less by what they must have regarded as an obscene amount of money to hit a few tennis balls – some newspaper reports at the time put that figure as high as $400,000 – than by Lendl having broken the anti-apartheid sanctions. Prague didn't accept Lendl's protestations that the exhibition had taken place in an independent state, with a black president – he even produced photographs of the black leaders – and the United Nations didn't accept it either and blacklisted him. Part of Lendl's punishment – he was also given a six-figure fine and suspended from the Davis Cup – was to be given the Navratilova treatment, so he, too became a non-person in his own country. Lendl was, as Andy Murray would later describe it, disowned by his own government, with the media barred from reporting on him and his activities on and off the court. And the result, Kodeš has said, was that 'news about Czech tennis subsided altogether'; it wasn't just Lendl who was covered by the ban, as the media were also prohibited from anything relating to tennis. A planned biography of Lendl was also spiked. Lendl no longer existed. Tennis no longer existed. 'They blacked me out over there, so the kids didn't get to see me on television or play in person,' Lendl has recalled.

At first, Lendl didn't think he had done anything wrong, but he later admitted he shouldn't have travelled to Sun City. Opening himself up to the state, Lendl wrote a letter on 10 January 1984 to Minister of the Interior Vratislav Vajnar, much of which was an explanation for his involvement. As Lendl acknowledged in that letter, playing in Bophuthatswana 'caused uproar and shed bad light on myself and my views'. But he said that the reason he decided to play the exhibition after all was that the promoters had threatened to sue him if he withdrew. 'I had made the decision not to play in Bophuthatswana, but the organisers in the USA responded with a threat of a lawsuit followed by substantial financial sanctions, and I would not have stood a chance of winning. Despite my promise to [the Czechoslovak government], I therefore travelled to Bophuthatswana.' One option Lendl considered was faking an injury: 'I even considered injury reasons. However, given that I had just completed the Wimbledon semi-finals without any injury and that my contract stated that my health would be examined by doctors at the place of the match, I was forced to abandon this alternative.' Lendl also wanted to make it clear he wasn't racist: 'I took part in a meeting at a black school, and the whole time did nothing motivated by racial hatred, as that is very much against my beliefs.' Lendl expressed regret at his actions: 'I am not oblivious to, and I am sorry about, the fact although acting in goodwill, my behaviour caused trouble for Czechoslovakia and cast doubts on to the country's politics.'

Speculation intensified that Lendl, though already living in America, was about to defect to the United States, which would have meant giving up his Czechoslovak passport and starting the process of becoming an American citizen. The more successful Lendl became, the more matches and titles he won, the higher the stakes, for both Lendl and the Prague administration. Such was the concern in Prague that Lendl was about to join Martina Navratilova in the West, it was said that the President of the Republic, Gustáv Husák, was regularly briefed. Years later, Kodeš would reflect that Lendl had become a 'hot stone' that the politicians didn't know what to do with. It appeared as though Lendl was in a stronger position than Navratilova had been in just before she jumped; he was much more established on the international tennis circuit, so had a far greater profile, than she had when she sought political asylum.

But Lendl didn't want to defect; he sought something else. In that letter to Vajnar, Lendl explained in detail why he had not been a regular visitor to Czechoslovakia. He wrote that he wanted to 'eliminate confusion about myself that seems to exist both at home and abroad, including the assumption that I wish to leave the country illegally'. 'I have never contemplated the thought of leaving CSSR illegally, despite this idea being associated with myself in various contexts and on different occasions both in CSSR and abroad. I never behaved in a way to imply this. I am a citizen of the CSSR, represent CSSR and behave accordingly. I realise that because I do not return to CSSR people may conclude that I do not wish to come back at all,' Lendl wrote.

'The reason why I do not come back to CSSR is my worry that I may not be allowed to travel back abroad. This worry is not unjustified. In 1982, I was assaulted in anonymous letters and also in a report about my appearances abroad, which were addressed to top authorities of state and the Communist Party. It was always stressed that I wanted to fall out of contact with the CSSR. My name was associated with many fabrications that raised my well-founded worries. These were intensified by many facts that suggested that I would not be able to easily leave the country and thus fulfil my obligations towards organisers of international tournaments abroad. Another reason for my worries was the fact that, even though I am one of the world's top tennis players, the media barely report about me. This suggests their poor relationship towards me, and a poor understanding of what I do, and what playing internationally means these days, as well as what a player representing a socialist country must endure in countries that are hostile to socialist regimes, in order to retain his honour and pride and not give up. I think that I have made very few mistakes in this regard if at all. I have always presented myself as a citizen of CSSR who is well aware of what and whom he represents.' One of those mistakes, he conceded, was playing in that exhibition in Sun City.

Towards the end of 1983, Lendl had had a meeting with

the Czechoslovak ambassador to the United States of America to discuss his relationship with the regime in Prague. That was followed by a meeting in Luxembourg with officials from the Czechoslovak Tennis Federation, at which, according to Lendl's letter, the administrators 'laid out what duties I have and what guarantees there are for myself'.

In his communication with the Interior Minister, Lendl pleaded to be given legal permanent residency abroad. 'To reconcile relations at home and eliminate all misunderstandings that are associated with my name, both at home and abroad, and due to mutual interest, I thus ask for and wish to receive permission for a permanent residence abroad. I trust this arrangement is most appropriate.' Lendl listed the reasons why he thought it would be in his and the state's mutual interest for him to be granted a permanent residence abroad. 'It would not deprive me of my Czechoslovak citizenship. It would allow me to represent CSSR at international tournaments and competitions. Because it would resolve my financial situation given that our legal system is straightforward about the acquisition of foreign currency – in the event of a breach of the law, steps could be taken against me. Because it would rid me of the obligation to apply for entry visas to individual countries, which doesn't help my concentration and well-being during training. Because it would allow me to return to my homeland, to visit my parents and my friends and to stay in touch with the public.'

To placate the minister, Lendl offered to help broker sponsorship for a professional tournament in Czechoslovakia, writing: 'International tennis is afflicted by immense sponsorship from businessmen, and this has a negative effect on the possibility of holding tournaments in socialist countries.'

In the letter Lendl also claimed he hadn't started playing tennis because he wanted to be rich. 'My argument [for a permanent residency abroad] may contain certain loopholes. I am aware that some may question whether I am the right role model for our citizens and our youth given that I always stay abroad and my income exceeds the norm. I believe that this can be overlooked when taking into consideration that there have been many people who for whatever reason officially lived abroad, but made their homeland famous and kept returning home on a regular basis or even moved back after some time. I did not start playing tennis to become rich. It is the nature of international tennis that those who excel make profit just as in any other profession, with some being more profitable than others.'

Among the discoveries in Lendl's security services file was Lendl floating the idea of basing himself in Monaco, rather than in the United States. So there was a third way; this wasn't just a choice between Czechoslovakia and Connecticut. In that letter to the minister, Lendl wrote that, should his application be successful, he would consider relocating to the tax haven. So, in the course of the negotiations with his government, Lendl would sign a contract with the Central Committee of the Czechoslovak Union of Physical Education and Sport, and the country's tennis federation. As part of the deal, Prague would allow Lendl to have legal permanent residency abroad, and to travel to international tournaments. In addition, they guaranteed that Lendl would be able to return to Czechoslovakia – with no problems entering or leaving – and that his parents would be given exit permits to accompany their son occasionally to foreign competitions, in their role as 'escorts' (a concern for anyone who left the country was what would happen to the family members they left behind). In return, Lendl would be expected to 'behave and perform abroad in accordance with the interest of the Republic and the Czechoslovakian socialist idea of sports', a clause which covered making himself available to play in the Davis Cup, and being discreet about his wealth. In addition Lendl would still have to give a cut of his earnings to Prague.

However, despite Lendl signing the agreement, and sending a cheque to cover the fine, President Husák was against honouring the deal; Lendl was left feeling as though the administration, from the President down, had misled him. He was still being punished for that appearance in Sun City. 'My exhibition in South Africa was blown up into "case Lendl" – it's a pity that it ever happened,' he has said.

In public, relations between Lendl and the Republic weren't chummy either; as Lendl's StB file has shown, what was printed in the newspapers and broadcast on radio or television tended to be an accurate reflection of the state's feelings towards him at that moment, with government officials believed to issue editorial directives. You might have imagined that Lendl's first grand slam success, at the 1984 French Open, would have elevated his status and given him some protection from criticism, but that wasn't so. With his suspension lifted, Lendl returned to the Davis Cup, and yet he was roasted by the media after a defeat against Sweden, his critics claiming he could have done so much more. But there were also those on the Czechoslovak tennis scene who considered that Lendl had been unfairly treated, especially as, according to Kodeš, his 'psyche had been eroded by the unresolved negotiations about his passport and emigration status'. As much as Lendl blamed the cold winters for his not spending time in the country of his birth – he said he wanted to train in the heat – it was the political climate that would have stopped him from boarding flights to Prague. He didn't feel much affection emanating from Czechoslovakia.

Between early 1984, when Lendl sent that letter to the Minister of the Interior, and the 1986 US Open, a period of more than two and a half years, there was a shift in Lendl's attitude towards the Czechoslovak Socialist Republic. The Sun City affair wouldn't have encouraged Lendl to have felt any patriotism or loyalty towards Czechoslovakia; and nor would Lendl's belief that he had been burned in private, with the state not delivering on their promises, and burned in public, with the perception that the media were increasingly hostile. In those couple of years, there was also a change in Lendl's communications strategy: travel deeper into the 1980s and the world grew ever closer to the fall of the Berlin Wall, and Lendl became ever more assured of what he could say publicly. And that was whether he was discussing money, politics or his own situation. In 1985, Lendl made it known he no longer wished to represent Czechoslovakia in the Davis Cup, for what were described as philosophical reasons. By the time of the 1986 US Open, when he won the second of his three titles at Flushing Meadows, Lendl was openly saying that he considered America his home, and that he wished to play for the US Davis Cup team. That ambition would not have gone down well in Prague, with an administration which elevated the Davis Cup above anything he might ever achieve on his own. And this wasn't just bad news for the communists. 'For Czech tennis, Lendl never playing Davis Cup again was a disaster,' Kodeš said. 'We might have won the Davis Cup again, but all was broken.' In 1987, the StB were made aware that

Lendl had said in an interview with a Dutch newspaper: 'I cannot represent a country whose regime I deny. Both the Czechoslovak government and the tennis federation mistreated me.'

If Lendl's desire to become an American citizen, and all that longing, lobbying and politicking, had caused distaste in Czechoslovakia, it had also upset a few people across the United States. Blame the Olympics, and tennis being admitted into the programme – ending an absence that began in the 1920s – in time for the 1988 Games in Seoul. If tennis was going to be at the Games, Lendl wanted to be there, too, just as long as he could play for the Stars and Stripes. Lendl had only recently received his permanent resident status, or Green Card, and, if going through normal channels, you would have to wait for five years before becoming eligible to take a citizenship test – but he couldn't wait that long if he was going to be boarding that plane to South Korea in an American tracksuit. Playing in the US Davis Cup team was also a motivation, but it was the approaching Seoul Games that made this so urgent. In 1988, he would be near the peak of his powers, but, four years later, when the 1992 Olympics rolled into Barcelona, he wasn't going to be as well placed to win a medal.

This is where President George Bush Senior makes an appearance in the Lendl narrative. I was shown private correspondence between Lendl and President Bush that gives an insight into their friendship, as well as demonstrating why Lendl would have felt that he could have turned to the President for guidance and support in his attempts to fast-track his American citizenship. It was in the mid- to late 1980s, when Bush was the Vice-President, that Lendl is said to have recruited this Washington heavyweight to his cause. Though

President Bush 'couldn't recall any specifics from Ivan's efforts to retain citizenship', he did tell me, through his official spokesman, that he was 'very high on Mr Lendl'. This is believed to be the first time that these notes between friends, written during Bush's single-term presidency from 1989 to 1993, have been given a public airing. Archived in the George Bush Presidential Library, the correspondence showed that the pair bonded over a common political outlook and a shared love of tennis – in addition to playing an ultra-aggressive game, Bush admired others who were bold with their shots, which was why he was so taken by Lendl's baseline power. There was also the Connecticut link, as that had been home for President Bush, too. Once you get past the heading on these notes – those from Bush read 'The President' and 'Aboard Air Force One' – the most striking thing about their correspondence was their informal and breezy tone. Lendl may have been unloved by the American people, but he had an ally in the White House. One of the notes from Bush reads: 'Dear Ivan, did you know this about my family – now you understand why I have such a blinding serve and fan-jet forehand? Sincerely George Bush.' Attached was a copy of a newspaper clipping from 1935 that related the story of President Bush's father, Prescott Bush, the then president of the United States Golf Association, urging Prescott's uncle, Joseph Wear, to take the role captaining America's Davis Cup team.

There would also be an exchange of notes in late 1992, when Bush was in the middle of his unsuccessful re-election campaign for the White House, with Lendl sending his friend a handwritten message: 'Dear Mr President, Samantha [Lendl's wife] and I wanted to take a moment to wish you the best of luck during this year's Presidential Campaign. It's my first chance to vote and of course I'm voting for you and the Republican Party. Our thoughts are with you and your family and we look forward to enjoying your win in November. Best regards, Ivan.' To which President Bush responded, in a handwritten note from Air Force One on a flight between Washington and Boston: 'Dear Ivan, thank you for your great and encouraging note. The polls stink but I remain confident of victory. Give Samantha a hug. I still follow your tennis actions closely. Warm regards, George Bush.'

Bush wasn't Lendl's only ally on Capitol Hill – he reportedly also met with Senator Ted Kennedy, younger brother of President John F. Kennedy. And it was Lowell Weicker, a tennis groupie as well as a Republican Senator for Connecticut, who put a bill before the Senate Judiciary Sub-Committee on Immigration with a view to having Lendl playing tennis for America sooner than he would otherwise have hoped for. In Washington-speak, this was officially known as 'A Bill for the Relief of Ivan Lendl', which made the situation sound much more dramatic than it was.

There was disapproval on the American tennis scene – John McEnroe, for one, said he found the idea of being on the same team as Lendl difficult to accept – while others outside the tennis bubble simply found it objectionable that senior politicians in Washington were spending their time worrying whether a Czech could ever achieve his dream of standing on a podium, hand on chest, as a Korean band played its version of 'The Star-Spangled Banner'. One columnist for the *New York Times* – and the writer wasn't alone with this view – contended that this special citizenship bill threatened to be an embarrassment for the political process. 'To push through a citizenship bill just to get a gold medal for Lendl – and for

the United States – is an injustice to every Korean woman selling luscious fruit in Manhattan at 11 p.m., every Indian man
running a newsstand, every Russian immigrant driving a cab,
every hard-working Latin American who fled the poverty and
violence back home.' In the end, though, it appears that the
bill was blocked not by New York and Washington's commentariat, but by the administration in Prague not providing the
necessary waiver documents – the communists wanted Lendl
to win a medal for America about as much as McEnroe did.

For many Czech émigrés the period immediately following
the 1989 Velvet Revolution – the collapse of communism –
was potentially a troubling one. Under communism they had
known what they stood for – and against – and where they
wanted to live. Post-1989, those answers weren't always so easy
to come by. Just a year after the revolution, Lendl appeared
in front of the Czechoslovak tennis public for the first time
in years, playing in an exhibition match against Miloslav
Mečíř. Lendl made the most of that trip: he was also looking at German shepherds, as well as scouting young hockey
talent for the NHL Hartford Whalers, the team for which he
was a board director. Even so, he would later show reluctance
to broker Czech players to North America, regarding it as
exploitation or dealing in human meat.

Marc Howard, one of Lendl's former practice partners, told
me by email that he had once had a conversation with Lendl
suggesting that, in the early 1990s, the Czech-born player
was 'unwilling to embrace his former roots'. 'For me, it was a
striking conversation about Lendl's connection to the former
Czechoslovakia. During the summer of 1992, between my junior and senior years of college, I travelled a bit around Europe,
including several days in Prague and some other parts of what

was still Czechoslovakia (which split into the Czech Republic and Slovakia in 1993). And I was also a student of political science who was interested in that region and its transition to democracy (and much later I wrote an academic book about it). So when I saw Ivan that fall, I was eager to talk to him about my experience and my hopes for Czech democracy under the newly open leadership of Václav Havel. But before I could say much, Ivan quickly cut me off, dismissively telling me that, "everything over there is poisoned by communism", or something along those lines. He seemed to be filled with hostility for the country. Even though most of the leaders and institutions had changed by 1992, Ivan seemed unwilling to turn the page and to embrace his former roots.'

Three years after the collapse of communism in Czechoslovakia, Lendl went ahead with becoming an American citizen. There hadn't been a celebrity fast track, some gilded VIP channel to an American passport. Just like everyone else, Lendl had waited for five years after receiving his permanent residency status. It was in the summer of 1992 that he became an American citizen, with a small ceremony at the Immigration and Naturalization Service office in Hartford, attended by his wife, Samantha, and a few friends. It was reported that while these ceremonies are usually open to all, Lendl's was held in private. That ceremony came too late for the glory of the United States, or for Lendl's satisfaction of winning slams for his adopted homeland. The last of Lendl's grand slam titles came at the 1990 Australian Open. By the time Lendl became a fully fledged Yankee, his career was tailing off.

CHAPTER THREE

A SOFT HEART,
NOT A BLACK HEART

One afternoon in London's Berkeley Square, among the hedge funds and art galleries of Mayfair, Boris Becker sat down over espressos in his offices and disclosed to me what Ivan Lendl has been trying to keep secret all these years: 'Ivan has a soft heart.' It's comments such as these that can ruin a man's reputation.

'Like most people who come across as being quite harsh and difficult to deal with, it's because they are trying to protect themselves,' Boris said. Becker's take on Lendl – and the philosopher king of tennis has plainly put some thought into this – has long been that his old, supposedly hard-boiled adversary, a man he defeated in a Wimbledon final, lacked 'genuine self-confidence', and so 'put up a wall around himself so that his opponents couldn't get near his sensitive side'. 'Somewhere underneath that hard exterior, there is a soft heart, and a soft side. Ivan was, and is, just as sensitive as everyone else.' Coming just a few years after the disclosure that Andre Agassi's hair wasn't his own, here's another profoundly disturbing piece of information, of the sort to make you question your entire understanding of tennis history: you're being asked to believe that Lendl is a delicate sort, not a sociopath in shorts. But what if Lendl really was a much more complex and sensitive character than popular opinion, and John McEnroe and Jimmy Connors, might suggest? What if he successfully managed to suppress his personality throughout his career?

A conversation with Wojtek Fibak, who observed the Czech-born player when he was at his most needy and vulnerable in tennis, confirmed that this delicate Lendl really does exist outside of Becker's head. Fibak said to me – and here's a comment to skin a champion of his aura – that Lendl was never even close to being the hard man that the public and his opponents imagined him to be. It was Fibak who instructed Lendl that he needed to wear a mask to hide his fears. 'Ivan won a lot of tennis matches because people thought he was a tough guy like Clint Eastwood. But that wasn't so – Ivan wasn't a tough character like that, and he wasn't a fighter by nature and he wasn't a hard worker by nature, either. Ivan was never naturally tough like McEnroe and Connors were,' Fibak said. Pat Cash, who beat Lendl in the 1987 Wimbledon final, used to think of his rival as being like the Ivan Drago character from *Rocky*; he would have been shocked at the time if he had been informed Lendl was actually quite a gentle fellow. Naturally, the all-seeing, all-knowing Czechoslovak secret police were aware that Lendl was hiding himself away, with one StB intelligence report in the early 1980s observing: 'He plays with a calm face – he does not go off in stressful situations and does not let it show when he gets nervous.'

This is what is so compelling about Lendl's story. If there's a myth to be busted about Lendl and his image, it was that he was the great myth-maker, that he had helped to create this caricature of himself. This image of Lendl as a cold, passionless tennis machine was the one he chose to project to the world, and so that's how the world saw him; indeed, as recently as 2011 when his name was mooted as a possible coach for Andy Murray, Murray's mother Judy had a picture in her mind of that android from the 1980s. However, as with most people, on meeting him, she would quickly revise her opinion. As Murray himself has observed, Lendl 'worked a lot over the years to be able to disguise his emotions, and that's part of his nature – that's him, and you have to accept that'. Murray has also offered his opinion that there is 'a fear of emotion in tennis' and how 'it wouldn't make me feel good to bottle up my emotions, as saying nothing and standing there makes me feel flat'.

How could the public, the press and many of his peers have been so wrong about Lendl? How could such a sensitive man have invited so much abusive literature, such an unrivalled trophy cabinet of bile and insults? Say what you want about Lendl, as everyone else in the tennis galleries already has: Paranoid Android. Dr Doom. Dr Gloom. The Ostrava Ghost. Old Bone Face. Chicken-Shit Commie (that from Connors). A Chilly, Self-Centered, Condescending, Mean-Spirited, Arrogant Man With A Nice Forehand (*Time* magazine). The Choking Dog. The Choker-In-Chief. The Choke-Slovakian. The Blank Czech – An Android With A Cyber-Serve And The

Personality Of A Frozen Turkey (*New York Times*). Darth Vader In Shorts. A Cadaver In Shorts. The Champion That Nobody Cares About (*Sports Illustrated*). Count Dracula (*Spitting Image*). Ivan The Heartless. Ivan The Terrible. Czech Mean-Machine. The Tin Man. The Grim Reaper. The Man With An Iron Mask. Igor Lentil (one summer, the *Daily Mail* ran a cartoon strip of a tennis player, clearly based on Lendl, who rested in a coffin during the changeovers, with a ballboy knocking on the lid when the umpire called 'time'). And this was how one newspaper reported Lendl's arrival at Wimbledon one summer: 'An empty car arrived at the All England Club and Ivan Lendl stepped out.'

In the 1980s, everyone was a Lendl-basher. If you took even a passing interest in forehands, backhands and semi-Westerns (those were grips, not Americanised Eastern Europeans), you bashed Lendl. And there was absolutely no shame in it. One of tennis's longest-running champagne-bar debates still goes on: who, to borrow from the American tennis lexicon, is the GOAT, or Greatest Of All Time? No discussion is necessary, however, about who would be slow-handclapped all the way to the stage to receive the award for The Most Unloved Player In The History Of The Sport. So Lendl was as boring as hell, and he was sour, he was monosyllabic, he was stiff, awkward and robotic, he probably thought in binary – cut him open and you would find only ones, zeroes and circuit boards. He was totally lacking in refinement, sophistication or humanity. He was no fun at all. He was – perhaps the public just didn't see the contradiction here – someone who choked matches away because the tension got to him, as well as being a machine whose scientific approach to tennis had drummed all the art and joy out of the sport. An American tennis magazine once went to the trouble of counting all the criticisms levelled at Lendl. There were eight main ones:

1. He is cold, surly and impersonal.
2. He is unattractive.
3. He is boring.
4. He is a communist.
5. He is too private.
6. He is a choker and, worse, a quitter.
7. He has been successful only because Borg retired, Connors got old and McEnroe went on a sabbatical.
8. His game isn't entertaining.

Did Lendl deserve to be demonised like this, given that he shared an era with two of the great vulgarians of tennis history? The laughter count might be low, but, unlike Connors, Lendl never called an umpire 'an abortion' and neither did he ever, showing the comedic brilliance of a thirteen-year-old schoolboy, mime masturbation with his racket handle. Lendl's other great adversary, McEnroe, could be relied upon for his foaming furies; here, after all, was a man who once told an official at the Australian Open to 'just go fuck your mother', and you could fill dozens of therapist's notebooks with his rage against tradition, good manners and, with a poke at Wimbledon's Royal Box, 'bowing and curtsying to rich people who don't pay any taxes'. While Lendl would occasionally be boorish, crass and unpleasant on court – and he could gripe at officialdom and at other forces in tennis – he was, in contrast to the double-headed American beast that was Connors–McEnroe, generally a respectful man during matches. Never was he as self-indulgent as the natural-born Americans. Sadly for Lendl, the public no longer wanted tennis players who minded their Ps and Qs. This was a time for rage and rebellion on the tennis court, not the deathly application of science. What the public craved were players who moved them, who infuriated them, who made them feel alive and exhilarated, who left them sucker-punched with emotion, whether that emotion was love or revulsion. In short, they wanted to care. And yet, as Lendl would surely have come to appreciate in the first few months of coaching Murray, the twenty-first-century tennis crowds hadn't changed so much from the galleries in the 1980s; spectators still demanded to see a player's personality. And tennis crowds could still be cruel. 'The tear-inducing British exit from the grand slam tennis event exhausted itself as a breakfast-table subject long ago,' Paul Hayward once observed in the *Guardian,* 'so the middle classes make merry with character assassinations.'

If you wanted tantrums or comedy, Lendl once advised, don't come to watch one of his matches. Those who ignored such advice didn't feel much of a connection. How could they when he gave them almost nothing? Some players can't operate without a crowd, but the impression could easily have been formed that Lendl would rather have competed in empty stadiums, playing tennis in total isolation and without the hassle of human interaction. That was taking the argument too far. There was no doubt that Lendl never saw himself as a performer, as some funnyman with a racket. He was one of those tennis players who never appreciated he was part of the entertainment industry. So Lendl never revealed himself to the public, and Arthur Ashe wrote in a newspaper column that Lendl's 'relationship with the crowd is nil, and that's what they don't like about him – spectators always want sportsmen to make a gesture in their direction. Eventually, even Connors learned how to arouse sympathy. But Ivan is a blank.'

In another era, Lendl might not have looked like such a square. But in this one, when the tone was set by McEnroe and Connors, personality was deemed to have been almost as important as returning serve; never before had a group of players revealed their characters as this generation did. Consequently, the public could be quite indifferent to Lendl. Who, for instance, wasn't intrigued by Björn Borg? Who wasn't consumed by the tale of Becker, the kid from West Germany who hijacked men's tennis one English summer? And that larrikin Pat Cash, meanwhile, could hook you in with his disdain for the old niceties, never more so than when he ignored protocol after winning Wimbledon by treating Centre Court as a young child would a climbing frame. Tennis, some said, was exploding on the gunpowder of personality, and many considered that Lendl could never quite compete. A reminder of that truth came shortly after Lendl wondered aloud whether McEnroe ought to be considering early retirement, and *Tennis* magazine printed an open letter from a fan to Lendl. Should McEnroe depart the scene, the fan informed Lendl, the game 'would be about as interesting as the sawdust in your pocket'.

Some of this wasn't Lendl's fault. He couldn't help the way he looked. He couldn't help not having the same effect on female spectators as Borg did. Was Lendl really any less demonstrative than Borg? So why, if Borg wasn't known for being dull, was Lendl for ever being called boring? That had much to do with sex. About the only recorded example of a Western publication describing Lendl as 'sexy' came in a piece published in Britain's *Daily Express* on the eve of the 1984

Wimbledon Championships, under the headline 'The Sexiest Men on Court'. 'Lendl loves his mother. And he's interested in winning and thinking – he plays as if he has a microchip on his shoulder. He makes you long to bring a smile to that taciturn, well-shaped mouth. An obvious romantic, his tight jawline denotes a passionate, possessive but very permanent lover.' Mostly, though, Lendl was seen as a sexless figure. So fans watched Borg and wondered about his mind, but it was widely supposed that there wasn't much depth or mystery to Lendl. 'In some human beings, containment creates mystique, the unstated draw us in. In Lendl's case, neither happened,' *Sports Illustrated* noted. 'He confirmed our communist carica- ture of the grey, stiff automaton. In neither the movement of the muscles, nor the flicker of his eyes, could one sense any imagination, any playfulness, any reason to want to pry into him any further.'

It's a great pity, Lendl's coach Tony Roche once observed, that no one could feel anything towards the Czech. Either Lendl was the mighty ogre about to crush some hapless and hopeless journeyman, in which case the galleries sided with the underdog, or he found himself up against McEnroe and Connors, and most in the crowd, especially if the match was being played in America, would back either of the self-styled brats. The most convincing thesis is that Lendl wasn't so much hated as unloved. Indeed, there were probably far more spec- tators who loathed McEnroe and Connors than those who could be bothered to hate Lendl. Lendl's difficulty was that he couldn't even make a good public enemy; being a con- fected, cartoonish Cold War villain didn't count.

He wasn't a real villain, just a pantomime one. Brilliantly, there wasn't anything that needed changing; Lendl was already a Cold War villain almost to the point of parody. With the Transylvanian appearance and that unmodulated voice, he looked and sounded just as those in Middle England or America's Midwest might have imagined an Eastern European player should. As a bonus, during Lendl's early days on the tour he had worn all-black gear, a get-up that, according to one fashion critic on the tennis beat, 'made him look less like a tennis player than an exemplary worker in the Socialist People's Union of Dry Wall and Sheet Metal Fabricators'. You didn't want to get too close, either: when he was new to the tour and without regular access to laundry facilities, he sometimes resorted to washing his clothes in the shower. 'I think Ivan was in the wrong place at the wrong time,' said Mats Wilander, a former world number one, who used to live near Lendl, who appeared in eight consecutive finals and won three titles, at the US Open. 'Lendl was doing well at the US Open, which was supposed to be home for Connors and McEnroe, those two American crazies. So Lendl became this villain from the Eastern Bloc.'

On the tennis tour in the 1980s there was no ignoring the tanks churning up the Centre Court lawn; the Cold War was even being fought at the All England Club. This was a sport dominated by American money, populated by American names and with crowds who bought into President Reagan's 'evil empire' rhetoric. Many in the US Open's bleachers, seated around Wimbledon's Centre Court, and elsewhere in tennis, regarded Russia and Czechoslovakia as one and the commie same, with Lendl reflecting: 'I think the Cold War was a big part of it [his unpopularity]. Where I came from didn't do me any favours, even though I hated the communists more than anyone.' This wouldn't have concerned those living on the different side of the Berlin Wall to their friends and family, or those fretting that the world was always one small slight from Armageddon, but one consequence of the ideological warfare between capitalism and communism was that people thought less of a tennis player from Ostrava.

But, again, Lendl was never hated, just unloved. The problem for Lendl was that this Red Ivan was a useful fiction: at a time of such tension, of course there wasn't any genuine concern that communists taking over tennis would in any way unsettle the world order, but having him around on the tour was arguably a safe way for Westerners to confront their fear of Marxist doctrine. So Lendl was a spittoon for Cold War bile; cough up your angst and anger in the direction of this tennis player and you felt a little better. And this wasn't a state of affairs that was doing the American players any harm either; some thought that Connors encouraged the public to 'goof on' Lendl, as if he were every capitalist tennis fan's worst nightmare. 'You communist son of a bitch,' one American player, Eddie Dibbs, screamed in Lendl's face, not appreciating the Czech was that curious communist pin-up who was living in preppy Connecticut.

Some thought badly of Lendl because they considered he was the Politburo's tennis pet; conversely, some didn't warm to him as they considered him to have been too enamoured of capitalism, that he cared less about the sport's history and traditions than he did about where the next million dollars were coming from. As Becker told me: 'Ivan wanted to make a lot of money, and there was nothing wrong with that – everyone was in it for the same reasons – but as he got older he was just really open about talking about money, and that doesn't always go down well.' There were all sorts of myths and misconceptions about Lendl that made him so unloved. One former member of Lendl's circle, for example, has suggested that the tennis player was 'very threatening to American men because he was so much in control', and Lendl himself has suggested that the tennis public were frightened of perfection: 'When somebody is winning a lot, I think people are threatened by that.' If only the public had known then how much turmoil and emotional churning there was behind that impassive expression, how much effort had gone into making him look so disciplined and regimented.

Years on, the old Lendl images and caricatures persist. There's still, for instance, a media and public fixation about whether or not he smiles, as if that were the most interesting thing about him. Never mind the reality that a smile is not an exotic concept to him, and that he is, as he ever was, perfectly capable of smiling, and did so frequently when he was not sitting watching Andy Murray competing. Twenty years after retiring from his first tennis life as a player, Lendl's image is still that of a professional miserabilist or doom-monger. During grand slams, a half-smile from Murray's coach in the stadium would be treated as the most spectacular of aberrations, and almost categorised as a breaking story by the twenty-four-hour news channels. Alternatively, Lendl was teased for supposedly being so glum. 'Could someone please strangle a kitten?' someone once tweeted, 'as Lendl needs cheering up.' Still, Lendl can take the teasing, and has been more than willing to send himself up, once saying he doesn't want to grin for fear it would trash his image, and it's a moot point whether he was being serious when he said: 'Smiling is overrated.'

Has there even been, many seemed to be thinking, a grouchier player–coach combination than these two dark princes of tennis Lendl and Murray? It's nonsense, of course, to suggest that these two don't know how to laugh or smile. As we will see in a later chapter, their relationship was partly founded on bad jokes. But if a man acquires a reputation for being a grouch, no amount of smiling will shift that; he's going to be stuck with that label for ever. Murray is conscious of that. After winning the 2013 BBC Sports Personality of the Year Award, he allowed his clothing suppliers, Adidas, to release an image of him with the line, 'Not bad for a man with no personality'. Conventional wisdom is so often wrong. It's wrong about Murray, and it's wrong about Lendl. And it matters that it's wrong. Laugh along at jokes about Lendl, but the false perception of him is colouring and distorting the public's opinion of him, and his place in the tennis pantheon. You have to think that the tennis public would have a greater respect and admiration for Lendl's accomplishments if only he had been a bit more pleasant, smiley and presentable during his playing days. Or, conversely, a whole lot more awful and objectionable, as then he could have been added to the John McEnroe School of Tortured Geniuses. One of the two, pleasant or awful, just not something in between. To a degree, Lendl is still affected by the crowds in the 1980s having questionable taste in tennis players.

For Lendl, there was one unexpected, delayed benefit to the public being so harsh on him in the 1980s, and that was that, many years down the line, it would help to bring him together with Murray. And then, once they were in partnership, it would help to strengthen their bond. The more that Murray learned about Lendl's background, and what he had experienced during his playing days, the more he came to appreciate that his coach had also been misunderstood, and

he liked that about him. No one would quibble with the assertion that Murray had also suffered in the public relations
game, with many in the galleries basing their opinions on a
false picture of his character. There's no doubt Murray was
unfairly treated for daring to make a joke about the England
football team before the 2006 World Cup; for years, that was
the basis of many a ludicrous claim he hated the English.

Just as Judy Murray's problem was that she wasn't Jane
Henman, one of Andy Murray's greatest obstacles, at least in
the minds of some sections of the Centre Court set, was that
he wasn't Tim Henman. And then Murray made *that* joke;
dealing with the consequences of that one gag would become,
in the words of Henman, 'a pain in the arse'. Letters would
be addressed directly to Murray's locker at Wimbledon, telling him, 'I hope you lose every match for the rest of your life',
while he was once strolling through the grounds after a practice session and overheard a Home Counties woman saying
into her mobile telephone, 'there goes that Scottish wanker'.
When Murray started working with Lendl, his public approval
ratings were decent – it had taken a while for the Wimbledon
crowds to come to know, respect and even like him – but he
was still a long way from being popular. On occasion, Murray
was being trolled on Twitter and abused on the street, which
wasn't helping to shift his view of himself, after repeated failure in grand slam finals, that he was 'a loser'. Undoubtedly,
one of the key moments in Murray's relationship with the
British public came during his first Wimbledon with Lendl,
with that weepy occasion on Centre Court when he couldn't
hold back the sobs – this was the fourth time he had been a
runner-up at the majors – after losing the 2012 final to Roger
Federer. During his career, Lendl had never been a darling

of the crowds, far from it, but perhaps he could help Murray to achieve almost universal popularity; for that to happen, Murray was going to have to win Wimbledon.

Often you hear it said that no sport reveals an athlete's personality as tennis does – put someone in a tennis stadium, they say, and you'll see just who you're dealing with. But that's patently not the case with everyone who grips and swings a racket; you can fake it. And has anyone faked it as well as Ivan Lendl faked it? Born in a country whose government couldn't have been more image-conscious, Lendl was protecting himself. And what he didn't want you to know was that his head was full of doubts, insecurities, fears and concerns. Lendl would complain he was the most misunderstood tennis player in the sport's history – and he was undoubtedly right – but don't cry for Ivan, because he had hidden himself away. The Ivan Lendl you saw in the stadium, or on your television screens, was, to an extent, an act.

What was the greatest trick of Lendl's career? The supposed paranoid android convincing everyone he was made of flesh and blood? Quite the opposite; it was having his peers, the press and the public believe he had no feelings, that he didn't have a happy or a sad muscle in his face. Some of this goes back to his childhood, when his mother told him that 'emotions don't help you', they only betray your weakness to your opponent, and Ivan had learned to give up those fireball tantrums. But it was Fibak, guided by the motto 'win without playing well', and thinking that Lendl was 'very sad with a Slavic nature', who had urged the Czech to 'become a machine, hiding his feelings, wearing an unemotional mask on his face, and not reacting to anything'. Fibak looked back on his prime years on tour and considered he had been too soft, that he had cared too much about pleasing and placating others, and that wasn't the path he wanted for Lendl. As Fibak told me: 'When I was working with Ivan, I had to look at everything, not just the technical and tactical aspects of his game, but also the mental side, and I told him that he needed to put a mask on. As he didn't start life as a tough character, he needed a mask if he was going to be tough and serious.' So that was two influential figures in Lendl's life telling him that emotions weren't to be trusted.

And, as Fibak has recalled, Lendl would get the hang of leaving his emotions backstage, where the public would never go: 'Ivan [wouldn't] show his real face on the court because tennis was his profession. He wanted to be Ivan Lendl, superstar, number one. He wanted to be cool because that was his protection. If he had suddenly opened himself up, he could have been hurt.'

To this day, Lendl isn't a huge fan of psychoanalysis of sportsmen; he would far rather just deal in hard facts – the scores, and who did what when – than read a psychological profile. So if this probably isn't a discussion that Lendl will enjoy or appreciate, there's no avoiding the fact that the shutdown or suppression of his personality was key to his story.

Peter Fleming, McEnroe's old doubles partner, once remarked how his fellow American would sometimes win tournaments just by turning up, just by being John McEnroe. In truth, McEnroe didn't have any choice; he couldn't help but be his dark, funny and unpredictable self. (Incidentally, if anyone was faking emotions when McEnroe was on court it was the public; though they tut-tutted, it was generally only mock outrage, with most secretly exhilarated by this angry young man tearing into the Establishment.) At the same time,

Lendl was winning matches, tournaments, sponsorship contracts and reaching number one in the rankings and building a career and a life for himself by not being Ivan Lendl, at least not to those watching. 'Ivan helped to create this image of himself – it wasn't just the media and the public who turned him into something,' Wilander told me. 'For sure, there were a lot of fears and doubts underneath, and he didn't want people having a look at those.' And, for Lendl, moving to America meant there was plenty for him to be afraid of. Just going there for the first time, as a junior, must have been an unnerving experience.

The little that the teenage, gauche and culturally starved Ivan Lendl knew about the United States he had learned from watching old Chicago gangster movies. At the age of fifteen, the Czechoslovak Tennis Federation had paid for him to travel with a chaperone to compete in some junior tournaments in Florida; and in time, Lendl would realise that Americans didn't carry on like Al Capone.

That trip was memorable for Lendl competing for the first time at the Orange Bowl at Miami's Flamingo Park, the unofficial world championships for juniors (he would win the title on a future visit, in 1977) and for the culture shock: 'The language and the technology, nothing was the same.' The scale of everything – the size of the cars, the houses and the streets – was shocking for him. But that wasn't all; culturally, Lendl was floundering. Even when Lendl settled in New York City and Connecticut in the early 1980s, when he was in his early twenties, he was still pretty much a know-nothing when it came to popular culture – on seeing a headline about the fatal shooting of John Lennon, he found himself asking someone from his management company, 'And who's John Lennon?', while the first LP he bought was *Chipmunk Punk*, which was the Chipmunks' take on punk rock classics. While Lendl knew how to welly a forehand, almost everything else about his new life in the United States would be outside his knowledge and experience. 'I understand that adapting to a different culture was hard for Ivan,' Michael Chang told me. Lendl's solution was to become more American than the Americans themselves. When Lendl underwent this Yankee makeover, an important part of it, he felt, was immersing himself in the country's low-brow culture, so he bought himself a large television and sat in front of it for repeat viewings of *Police Academy* and *Beverly Hills Cop*. The local media would suggest that some of his other off-court activities, such as reading *USA Today*, playing golf and buying glass and chrome furniture, were also part of this cultural assimilation.

To Lendl's mind, moving from Czechoslovakia to Western Europe would have been a giant leap in itself, with all the opportunities and new experiences to be had on the other side of the Iron Curtain, and bounding on from there to the United States would have been another three jumps. And here he was making those four leaps all in one go. No wonder he was a little discombobulated; no wonder he became ever more reliant on Wojtek Fibak. Lendl had visited America as a junior, but only briefly, to play a tournament or two. This was different. Some would suggest it's irrelevant where a pro calls home, since a tennis player is essentially a citizen of the world's airport lounges, hotel lobbies and practice courts. But is that really so? You only had to look at what had happened to Martina Navratilova after her defection – she had binged on junk food, Big Mac-ing from coast to coast to transform herself into The Great Wide Hope – to appreciate that moving to the West wasn't easy. It wasn't just that America had Coca-Cola, sunshine and Cadillacs; this was an entirely new world, and one that was going to take some getting used to. We know what Navratilova had been eating. But what was eating Ivan? As Lendl once put it: 'I left a repressive, poor country and went to the most liberal, richest one on Earth. Those two or three years when I was getting the most criticism were the years when I suddenly had to decide where I was going to live, and who my friends were going to be. It probably looked smooth on the top, but on the bottom there were some pretty big storms.'

This shouldn't be underplayed. For the great majority of Lendl's old school friends in Ostrava, the biggest upheaval of their lives would come when they moved out of their family homes to a tower-block apartment of their own, and that often didn't happen until they had been married off – and sometimes, depending on circumstances, they didn't leave the nest then either. It wasn't that Lendl was suffering from homesickness. He knew that, if there was anything he wanted from Czechoslovakia, such as a particular food, or a piece of music, he could have it shipped to him. Rather, it was that this American assimilation wasn't straightforward. Any suspicions that Lendl had that he and his family were under StB surveillance would hardly have made him feel more secure and comfortable about his new life.

A fair number of leading male tennis players in the 1980s liked to think of themselves as outsiders; there was a certain vanity in that, as if they were somehow special or superior. John McEnroe saw himself as separate from the tennis pack, as did Jimmy Connors, whose 2013 memoir was even called

The Outsider. But no one at the centre of the tennis narrative was more of an outsider than the man from Ostrava's suburbia. He was, some considered, a career outsider, a career loner. 'Lendl is very, very much wrapped up in himself,' Becker observed at the time.

So Lendl wasn't entirely comfortable from the off, even if Fibak helped him out by first giving him a room in his New York apartment, and then in his house in Connecticut, where the lodger could store tennis balls, fur coats and his deep-rooted insecurities. Sometimes Lendl would travel into the city: not to search out the fleshpots, Fibak has said, but to look for a watch or a new telephone. He wasn't a gregarious young man; he couldn't be, not with his personality and his circumstances. According to Fibak, Lendl enjoyed being at home with his surrogate family. Even after Lendl moved out, into his own place in this capitalist playground, his house was nearby, so Fibak was there to assist. Fibak had talked him into coming to America, so it would have been understandable if he had felt greater responsibility for Lendl's happiness, or otherwise, in the States. Fibak appointed himself Lendl's cultural guide – there was a lot of work to be done with a man who as a twenty-something was once said by *People* magazine to have the sophistication of a fifteen-year-old American. Lendl needed to be taught everything from tax laws to table manners. Fibak introduced him to art, as well as to a doctor, a lawyer, someone to mow his lawn, and even to his future wife, Samantha Frankel. 'She was a friend of the family,' he said, 'and it was my idea that Ivan and her would become a couple.' Fibak, who said he didn't want to see Lendl repeating some of the mistakes he had made, also assisted his protégé with investments and managing his growing wealth. Lendl would suggest that, unlike Navratilova, he kept it together in the States; he didn't implode mentally or balloon physically. He was proud of that.

In some ways, not having grown up in the American tennis culture was no bad thing for Lendl   for one, he didn't mind that the US Open had been moved from Forest Hills to Flushing Meadows, having never known any different. Other players would say to him, 'This can't be the US Open', but he didn't care. As Stephen Tignor put it in his book *High Strung*, Lendl was 'the first top pro to make his debut inside the American tennis empire with no ties to its clubby past'.

But don't let's imagine that Lendl felt a great sense of freedom. Did he also suffer from the inferiority complex that dragged down other tennis players from Czechoslovakia? 'Part of being Czech,' Lendl once remarked to Jerry Solomon, his agent for much of his career, and who represents him now, 'was the feeling that you cannot excel.'

Both Navratilova and Hana Mandlíková had struggled for motivation after defecting. Was that in any way connected to Moscow crushing the Prague Spring? Navratilova has articulated the view that the Russian tanks had caused lasting damage to the Czechoslovak psyche: 'The Czechs and the Slovaks learned to swallow their feelings after the Russian invasion of 1968. We became a depressed society,' she has noted. 'You could see the difference: people just weren't optimistic about the future. It was all pretty gloomy.' Lendl's Iron Curtain background appeared to affect his attitude towards tennis and life; after realising his goal of using tennis to flee to a better life in America, where there was freedom and money, he was lacking a little motivation for a while, left wondering what he wanted to accomplish with his racket. In time, though, the pursuit of more cash and grand slam titles would give him a reason to get out of bed in the morning. So Lendl would say he wasn't like your average Slav, who was 'a little bit scared of success', and who had been 'brought up to be shy and laid-back'. He was more ambitious than that. He informed Solomon he didn't intend to be constrained by any Eastern Bloc inadequacies. Fibak's analysis was that Lendl was that rare creature, an Eastern European who thought he could be number one. Still, if that was to happen, Lendl's fears needed covering up; the impression is that he wasn't as assured of himself in the 1980s as he wanted you to believe.

Fibak's recollection is that Lendl didn't have problems picking up English, that he was soon speaking the language 'very eloquently and precisely, and with the correct grammar'. But others remember it slightly differently. During his early years in the States, Lendl certainly wasn't so confident about speaking the language in public – he was a long way off from the position he would reach later in his career, when he was as adept at making cocktail-party chit-chat as he was saying a few words at a sponsor's function. To improve his English, Lendl was said to have watched episodes of *Happy Days*, so The Fonz must take some credit for any improvements in his inflection and syntax. But what didn't change much was the heavy Czech accent – even today, after years of living in the States, his voice is more Eastern Bloc than East Coast America. So his English improved, but that still left him with another concern, his scattered, Iron Curtain teeth. For a couple of reasons, Lendl didn't always want to open his mouth.

It's not uncommon for young players new to the tour to experience loneliness – Murray felt isolated when he first started competing at the highest level. The theory that Lendl was a lonely figure on the tennis tour, unable always to communicate properly with those around him, was one advanced by his former chiropractor, Deborah Kleinman-Cindrich. 'Initially, he insulated himself so much from people because of the early disappointments that started, I think, with his inability to communicate. He didn't have good role models to teach him how to be sociable or even personable, so he learned to compensate for that by insulating himself and making himself believe that the loneliness didn't bother him,' she was quoted as saying in *Tennis* magazine, even claiming that he had to be persuaded to attend his own birthday parties: 'He shied away because he was afraid.'

A free press was another new beast for Lendl to contend with. At first, he was a little unsettled by the uncensored American press, and how someone with a deadline, a typewriter and a critical eye was able to 'write something bad about me'. And that initial unease never completely dissipated; years later, the American media would continue to have power over Lendl, as shown by how aggravated he was by a *Sports Illustrated* cover, marking his victory at the 1986 US Open, that called him 'The Champion That Nobody Cares About'.

The way it had worked back in Czechoslovakia, Lendl noted, was that 'when you're a big sports person, they have to write something nice about you because you are an idol for the kids, and unless you do something real bad, it never comes out'. One of the things Lendl had taken for granted, control of his image, had disappeared. It should be said that Lendl probably didn't become as exasperated with sections of the British media during the Wimbledon Championships as Chris Evert, John McEnroe, Navratilova, Boris Becker and others did some summers, but that was because his romantic life wasn't nearly interesting enough to be regularly splashed across a tabloid double-page spread.

Navratilova's droll observation on the media is worth repeating: in Czechoslovakia, there was no such thing as freedom *of* the press, and in the West there was no such thing as freedom *from* the press. In the early years, Lendl's dealings with the international media, and especially the American correspondents, weren't always cordial. Reading some of the stories back now, you form the impression that, when Lendl was new on the scene, the tennis player and the press weren't so fond of each other. It wasn't just that Lendl wouldn't speak openly about politics, and give them the answers they wanted about whether he would ever defect to the West; it was that he felt that he was for ever being quoted out of context, especially after making what he had intended to be jokes. 'I think the trouble with Ivan's image was because his English wasn't good, he felt quite insecure at first and many people misunderstood him,' his wife Samantha has said. Some contended that Lendl had been slightly intimidated by having to face the massed press, and so had tried to protect himself by being short and confrontational with his responses. Experiencing those awkward, staccato, sometimes fractious exchanges in the interview room, and then reading the resulting coverage in the next morning's newspapers, would have heightened Lendl's anxiety and self-doubt, as well as highlighting his struggle to assimilate. Perhaps Lendl was unaware of this reality until he moved to the States, but it wasn't the American media's job to make him feel welcome on that side of the ocean.

Part of the problem was that Lendl couldn't tolerate what he would regard as foolish questions. While he didn't appreciate

enquiries about whether he was about to defect – he reportedly cut a few interviews short, or at least threatened to do
so – he also didn't like being asked, 'What was the turning
point of the match?' or 'Were you disappointed after losing?'
Sometimes he vocalised his thoughts, saying in response to the
first question, 'Don't you know?', and to the second, 'No, I was
rather pleased.' Some reported that interviewing Lendl was
like conversing with a robot. But, as time passed and he grew
in confidence, he came to enjoy being so awkward, that there
was pleasure to be had in being combative and occasionally
uncooperative in his dealings with the media. One year at the
French Open, a British journalist sidled up to Lendl and asked,
''Scuse me, Eye-van, have you got a minute?' To which Lendl
responded: 'My name is Ivan, Ee-Varn. And the answer to your
question is no.'

Perhaps a line or two here is needed on how newspapers
shaped the public's opinion of Lendl, as it would appear that
their influence has been overstated. Lendl has said that newspapers created his image, as 'people read something and
whether it's true or not, that's the information being fed to
them'. But you have to imagine that the international armchair audience's view of Lendl would primarily have been
coloured by the images on their television screens. The public could work it out for themselves that Lendl could be a cold
fish; they didn't have to be told as much by some newspaper
columnist. To a large extent, the media were reflecting the
public's opinion of Lendl. When an American tennis magazine conducted a focus group about the public perception
of Lendl, the findings were that they couldn't relate to someone who didn't quite seem human. Or consider one reader's
letter to a tennis publication: 'I agree with the entire tennis

world that Ivan Lendl is, without doubt, the most dull, boring tennis player of all time.'

Even after Lendl appeared to have established himself in the United States – by which I mean he had worked through most of the insecurities about the culture, the language, and anything about his surroundings – he was never truly accepted by the American public. Would Lendl have been so annoyed by that *Sports Illustrated* cover, the one calling him 'The Champion That Nobody Cares About', if there had been no truth to it? For all the love Lendl had for the United States, and for Flushing Meadows (he once wrote a piece entitled 'Ten Reasons Why I Love the US Open') the American public didn't exactly hold him close. There he was, supposedly living the American Dream, so why wasn't the US public showing him a little more respect, love and understanding? As Becker observed, that would have been tough, commuting in from Connecticut to play at your local grand slam only to be treated roughly by thousands of New Yorkers.

There had been a Czechoslovak takeover of the 1986 US Open, with the men's final seeing Lendl beat Miloslav Mečiř, while the conclusion of the women's tournament had Martina Navratilova defeating Helena Suková. As Lendl kept on hearing, from newspaper commentators and television executives, American tennis was dying. If there was one small consolation for the American public, who had grown accustomed to their own players dominating the US Open, it was that the American-based Czechoslovaks finished as the champions. Lendl thought that *Sports Illustrated*'s cover – as well as the article itself saying that he had the star power to 'clear a stadium like a bomb threat' and he 'may someday empty entire cities' – had been 'uncalled for'. If you're looking for evidence of Lendl's soft side, of how vulnerable he was to unprovoked attacks by caustic columnists, then here it is: 'I just don't know what I did to deserve that. They don't want to like me, okay fine. But I thought that was over the line.'

Upset, Lendl refused to give the magazine future interviews. Tony Roche, Lendl's coach from 1985 onwards, told his employer to ignore media criticism: 'Don't worry about what they're saying. Once you retire you will become a better and more popular player.' It's worth remembering that John McEnroe wasn't immune from media attacks either, with the *New York Times* once contending he was the worst advertisement for America's system of values since Al Capone. The moment that issue of *Sports Illustrated* hit the newsstands was surely the closest that any leading tennis player has ever come to being stateless. Lendl had no intention of ever moving back to Czechoslovakia, where for a while he had been downgraded to a non-person, and at the same time he wasn't getting many bear hugs from Uncle Sam either. There was a time when Lendl would be asked whether he considered himself to be Czech or American, and some felt he tried to dodge the question; perhaps that wasn't because he was playing a diplomatic game, but because he didn't know the answer.

And that wasn't the only concern fizzing around Lendl's head. There were all sorts of other fears and vulnerabilities in there when he was new to the tour and new to the locker-room. As Wilander told me, 'you have to remember that Ivan wasn't a winner when he started out on the tour, and I can tell you one thing he was afraid of – he was fearful of fighting'. If Lendl was to make the most of himself as a tennis player, he couldn't keep alerting his peers to his vulnerabilities. That's why, for Lendl, tennis was always a masked ball; he could never just go uncovered. But there was another reason why he gave off all the warmth of a December night in Ostrava, and that was because he was concentrating so hard. Part of the effort required to win tennis matches, Lendl has said, 'involved total concentration that made him look impassive most of the time'. At the same time as hiding himself away in a full stadium, he could avoid distractions – on one occasion, he was so consumed by a match he didn't realise he was play- ing through a bomb scare. And, since he had been a young boy, he had appreciated the importance of concentration. The reason Lendl improved his behaviour, and learned to deal with all that angst and rage, was not because he 'wanted a gold star', or because 'the tantrums made me look like a jerk'. 'I shut up because all my own noise and turmoil affected my game. It was strictly a practical solution.'

Only a few people appreciated during Lendl's career that his nerves were sometimes fizzing like a bottle of dropped cola. One of those who understood this was Becker, who believed that it was pre-match anxiety that made Lendl so talkative in the locker-room. This is a subject that Lendl and Andy Murray have been over, the Scot commenting on how no one realised how nervous Lendl was, because of all the work he had put into hiding and disguising his emotions. 'Lendl's attitude on the court intimidated people. He never looked flustered. He always had the same expression, and no one really knew how he was feeling,' Murray has said. 'But I know from speaking to him that he got really, really nervous. Everyone gets nervous – but he got more nervous than most people, and he knew how to deal with it.' And as a coach, Lendl would still experience nervous tension at grand slams, especially when Murray was competing on the lawns of the All England Club. At the same time, Lendl would be urging Murray not to become consumed by anxiety on court, telling him he had to enjoy himself more and become a little freer.

Most players wouldn't have dared to be as cold as Lendl, fearing unpopularity. But that wasn't something that Lendl was too concerned about; he cared more for winning tournaments than he did for the love of strangers. That's not to say he didn't care about his image. As we have seen, he cared deeply about what people thought of him, but only when that potentially affected his ability to beat his next opponent. Was the real reason that Lendl came dressed as the Darth Vader of the courts because he imagined that wearing black clothes would make him appear to be more menacing? Arguably, he was his own greatest spin-doctor; he knew full well the benefits that he could derive from building an image, especially one that wasn't firmly rooted in reality. Take how he didn't go to great efforts to correct the myth about the Fuck You Forehand. And, as we shall see in a later chapter, Lendl worked extremely hard on his physical conditioning, more so than anyone up to that moment in tennis history had ever worked, but, as Wilander observed, he also dedicated himself to constructing an image of a strong man. 'Ivan wasn't the first guy to work out. But he was the first man to come into the locker-room and say, "Today, I rode fifty miles on the bike".' As one of Andy Murray's former coaches, Mark Petchey, observed: 'Ivan was a guy who wanted to let people know he was fitter than absolutely everyone else, and he felt that was a huge psychological advantage, and he used that to best effect.' It makes you wonder whether his decision to wear a legionnaire's cap at the Australian Open was part of the process of trying to intimidate; was he using his headgear to tell everyone else in the locker-room how he was ready to suffer?

Sometimes Lendl and his circle would go to extreme lengths to manufacture his image. As Tim Henman disclosed, Lendl wanted others to be impressed, even shocked, by his work ethic: 'Lendl told me a revealing story about a tournament he played in Estoril – it was his first clay-court event of the year – and he faced an out and out clay-courter. They played for three sets, and were out there for more than three hours, with Lendl winning 7-6 in the third set, and he came back into the locker-room and his coach said, "Right, put your running shoes on". So Lendl put his running shoes on, and they jogged out of the locker-room, and everyone was saying, "Oh, my God, he has played for three hours, and he's going for a run?" As they ran off, Lendl said to his coach, "I'm absolutely exhausted, there's no way I can run". And his coach said, "Yeah, yeah, that's fine", and they just ran into the nearby woods, and just sat there for forty-five minutes, and had a chat and a stretch, and then they ran back into the locker-room. And Lendl knew that everyone in the locker-room would be thinking, "Wow, he's like Superman". That was just part of the psychological warfare between Lendl and the other players.'

Dogs have always been an important part of the Ivan Lendl mythology. How strongly did Lendl object to the stories about his pack, including claims that one dog was trained to growl not only at trespassers but as it followed house guests around, while one had been taught to bite your leg and another to go for your throat? It's undoubtedly true that Lendl presented some of the dogs he bred to the local police department. After one particular experience that Lendl had had as a teenager – a Doberman bit him on the thigh, and the next day, during an exhibition match, the bandage on his leg became soaked through with blood – it would have been perfectly under-standable if he had had a phobia about dogs and preferred to avoid them thereafter. But keeping and breeding German shepherds suited Lendl. Anyone who calls their kennel and breeding programme 'Quantum Operations', because he wants his dogs to be quantums, or 'units of bursting energy', is not likely to be goofing around. Lendl let others in the locker-room have their delusions of rock'n'roll glory; he was chasing — through bloodlines and training – canine perfec-tion. Thinking that his German shepherds should be 'the best-looking dogs, the smartest dogs and the best-trained dogs', he used the time travelling to and from tournaments to study pedigrees, bloodlines and genetic-breeding charts. Whether breeding dogs, or later coaching a Scottish tennis player, Lendl didn't care for being a second-rater.

No doubt Lendl was comfortable with the image that went with being the master of the pack, of having these dogs under his control and protecting his home and family. What had he created for himself after setting up base among the Connecticut preppies? A home or a fortress? So Lendl had high stone walls, a grim look about him and the most sophisticated alarm system money could buy, one so sensi-tive that a small bird came down the chimney one night and tripped the lasers, waking the house and causing all sorts of confusion and concern. But surely nothing declared, 'world, keep out' as those dogs did. But why the need for all this canine muscle at all? According to an account in *Sports*

Illustrated, one of the reasons Lendl decided to keep dogs was because one evening he looked out of the window and saw an intruder on his property.

Who better to discuss fear, paranoia and Lendl's dogs than one of his former practice partners, Marc Howard, who was once set upon by one of the German shepherds, Cajun, his teeth going through Howard's jeans and into his upper thigh. Howard would notice too that the dog was 'visibly aroused'. All Howard had been trying to do, after arriving for a training session, was to pet the animal. At that moment, would Howard have bought into Lendl's assertion that, 'unless you're mice, my dogs won't kill you'? Howard, who at the time was on the Yale tennis team, didn't think it was a coincidence that Lendl had chosen German shepherds. There was no chance, he contended, of Lendl ever having a small, yappy dog like one of Andy Murray's Border Terriers. 'Ivan would never want a little pooch to sit on his lap, or a cute doggy that did silly tricks. Ivan selected a breed known for being strong, intelligent and obedient. He wanted dogs that could be trained to perfection. In short, his dogs were the canine versions of himself. I'm not sure if he literally wanted to scare people with his dogs, but I do think he was very proud of them.'

During one of his training sessions with Murray before the 2014 Australian Open, Lendl wore a Christmas present from his daughters, a T-shirt bearing the slogan: 'Leave me alone. I'm only speaking to my dog today'. Howard's theory was that, in the 1980s and early 1990s, the dogs helped stop Lendl from feeling lonely. 'After weeks on end of flights, hotel rooms and ruthless competition, it must have been comforting to return to the strong dogs that had complete loyalty and obedience to their master,' Howard said. 'It struck me that while Lendl had a wife and daughters, the unwavering pursuit of greatness must have left him lonely. His obsessive focus also seemed to be linked with deep feelings of insecurity – about his ability to compete, to perform, to win. And what could be a better antidote to loneliness than having a dog? Well, maybe having four dogs. Ostensibly, Lendl's dogs were meant to secure the perimeter of his property – as if the cameras and grounds-keepers weren't sufficient. I suspected that their real purpose, given their obedience and loyalty, was to secure the perimeter of their master.'

Howard's belief is confirmed by Lendl's disclosure that he did indeed buy his first dog because he was lonely. In time, Lendl came to enjoy the control and the discipline as much as the companionship. He seemed to get a kick out of having such control; he would show house guests how he could have his German shepherds sit waiting before bowls of food – only once he had given them the signal would they start eating. Lendl expected obedience and loyalty from his dogs at all times. If any of them didn't negotiate the obstacle course in his grounds as he expected – if they didn't follow instructions when walking the plank or climbing ladders – he would keep them outside until they did exactly as they were told. Lendl never shouted at his dogs, but he did feel that obedience was paramount. 'There must be no loopholes,' Lendl once said. 'He must know that when he receives a command from me, he has to do it.' The reward for all that training, Lendl contended, was that dogs could be better company than human beings: 'Many times you don't know if a person is loyal or just faking it. With dogs you always know that they mean what they're doing. And they have great sensitivity.' So if Lendl returned from the US Open in a sunny mood, the dogs would bound up to him joyfully; if he was feeling grouchy, they knew to leave him alone. Seeing that a pet food company were undertaking a 'Search for the Great American Dog', Lendl entered the competition, explaining in his entry form that his hound was his best friend: 'With my dog by my side, victories are more thrilling and defeats less painful. Win or lose, I can count on my dog to be there.'

Such was the giddy high of being invited to practise with Lendl that Howard wiped himself down and announced he was happy to play. He struck the ball quite decently that day, though the next day, when he awoke to bloodstained sheets, a doctor confirmed that the bite had been worse than he had initially thought. Some suggested that Howard should sue Lendl, but he wasn't inclined to. 'I'm not angry at all,' Howard told me. 'I don't think Ivan saw it coming, though perhaps he could or should have sensed that Cajun hadn't met me before and was acting aggressively. It all happened so quickly. Of course, I might feel differently, or be dead, if the "throat-dog" had got to me. Ivan was certainly very concerned about me, both at the time and over subsequent days. I have no idea if he was worried that I was going to sue him – as so many people suggested to me, though I never considered it for a second. I kept trying to play down the severity of the injury. Shortly after it happened, I insisted that I was fine to play, and we actually played two sets. And when he called me the next day, I told him that the doctors said Cajun's tooth had torn through my quadriceps muscle and I had to take two weeks off.'

Howard certainly isn't the only visitor to have departed from a visit to Lendl's home with torn trousers or a fear of dogs. Once, his chiropractor, Deborah Kleinman-Cindrich, came to the house to give Lendl some treatment and almost came under attack herself from a German shepherd, which jumped up, tore her trousers and threatened to go for her torso next. Lendl leapt off the massage table to call off the dog. A young Pete Sampras was also among those who visited Fortress Lendl and came away with barking in his ears and a little fear in his heart.

Howard didn't even mind that, as a result of the attack, he experienced 'scary flashbacks' when encountering police dogs during a year spent in Berlin. And nor is he aggrieved about the scar tissue; it's for ever a reminder of the occasion he trained with a man he regards as one of the most underappreciated players in the sport's history. 'Ivan was inaccurately portrayed by the media and misunderstood by the public. Most people, including myself until I met him, had the impression he was dour, boring and monotonous. But in reality, he was upbeat, lively and unpredictable. He had a wicked sense of humour, and he wasn't afraid to pepper his speech with profanity – both characteristics he shares with Murray, I hear.' In the weeks that followed the attack, Lendl called Howard a number of times – on one of those calls Lendl asked Howard, 'what size pants do you wear?', and promised that a replacement pair of jeans would be coming his way. 'But I never got those jeans,' Howard told me. 'I think Samantha actually did buy me a new pair, but Ivan forgot to give them to me. I would like to get a message to Ivan that my size – thirty-two by thirty-two – hasn't changed, and I am still looking forward to getting those jeans.' During one phone call, Lendl suggested that Howard photograph his wound and then send it to Cajun because, as Lendl sniggered down the line, 'he would probably lick it'.

Howard would never forget the messages that Lendl left on his answering machine. When he returned home from the Yale tennis team's tour of California, there were three or four messages from Lendl. The last one particularly struck Howard: 'Marc, this is Ivan. I haven't heard back from you. Maybe you're away. I hope you get this in time, because I have nobody to play with tomorrow.' Howard was astonished: 'Here was one of the greatest players in the history of tennis practically begging me to play. By the time I called back, the opportunity was gone – he was either travelling or injured. Lendl retired shortly thereafter. But that voice on that machine stays with me, evoking memories of his greatness and insecurity.'

CHAPTER FOUR

THE FUNNIEST MAN IN TENNIS

There's a locker-room *omertà* about Ivan Lendl's jokes, supposedly the filthiest in tennis, dirty enough to make a docker blush. Or at least it seems that way. Just you try to find someone who will dare repeat one of Lendl's bawdiest jokes on the record; it would be easier to uncover a Trotskyist on one of the All England Club's committees. One former player told me Lendl's humour was 'dark, sometimes a little warped, and some people get it, and some people don't'. But that former colleague wasn't going to be retelling any gags. Another former player said he couldn't think of any jokes that could be published: 'You can't repeat any of Lendl's worst jokes. They're unprintable. I don't think he does printable jokes. If Lendl did a joke book, there would be an introduction, and then the rest of the book would be blank.'

It was said in the 1980s that Lendl liked the work of the late Sam Kinison, a shouty American stand-up comedian known for the coarseness and viciousness of his work. But Lendl wrote his own material. Blacker than Ostrava coal, Lendl's own sense of humour could be savage, sharp, luridly unpleasant. A writer for *New York* magazine in the 1980s called Lendl 'an equal-opportunities offender, telling jokes about Jews, Poles, Italians and gays'. The implication was that there was almost no one he wouldn't dare mock. 'He's got a sense of humour that's very particular,' Pat Cash told me. 'He and his friends could laugh about it. But others didn't find it so funny. He told very inappropriate, politically incorrect jokes. There would be play- ers in the locker-room with different coloured skin and that wouldn't stop him from telling his jokes. Most guys would just sit there and look the other way, or walk the other way. Lendl was laughing or joking, and no one ever said anything. You just kept your mouth shut. If someone had said something, he probably would have backed down.' For instance, Cash wrote in his autobiography, 'there was an Australian guy who worked for the ATP. I'm not 100 per cent sure whether he was gay or not, but if he was, it certainly wasn't any of my business, or indeed Lendl's. Yet day in, day out, this poor bloke used to take a fearful hammering from Lendl's idea of humour. What could he say back? If he had told the world number one to piss off, then he would have lost his job.'

John McEnroe thought Ivan Lendl's jokes were worse than his father's; he observed that his rival had an 'odd, harsh demeanour and a mean sense of humour'. So not everyone laughed, or laughs, along with Ivan. 'I have a sick sense of humour – I can laugh at a lot of things other people don't find funny,' Lendl has said. Who else do you know who wakes from a nightmare and immediately explodes into laughter? But he does at least have a sense of humour, a fact that, until his re-emergence in the sport, had largely been kept from the tennis public. Of course, Lendl would say that he hasn't recently developed a sense of humour, it was just that others didn't get his jokes. Perhaps they didn't realise he was making any. Outside the locker-room, who knew about this? Certainly, the international media didn't always pick up on when Lendl was being sarcastic and when he wasn't, with the humour lost in translation, in the heavy accent, or – this was before the dentists had got to work – among those jumbled teeth. Anyone working in tennis knew all too well that Lendl has been making mischief for years, outside the locker-room as well as inside. And there were different types of Lendl jokes. Lendl could tell dirty, offensive jokes with the intention of making everyone laugh. And some of his gags weren't aimed at anyone – he would occasionally do something slapstick or absurd, such as roller-skating around a practice court – but there were also plenty of times when he would use humour as a weapon of assault. It was a rat-a-tat-tat of gags.

Inside the locker-room, Lendl was a long way from the media's portrayal of him as a man with a cold heart. This battery of sarcasm passing off as cocktail-hour banter, as someone once described it, appeared to have been designed in part to deflect attention from personal issues and concerns. These acid one-liners would have had his fellow players thinking about their own inadequacies, not his. Humour didn't just help Lendl to cope with any social awkwardness; it also allowed him to score points. Telling jokes, and humiliating and undermining others, was how he exerted a kind of totalitarian control over his contemporaries. The locker-room certainly wasn't bewildered by subtlety – there was little about Lendl's jokes and comments that was clever or sophisticated – but he could be relentless. Doubtless, some of the less robust members of the tour were weeping on the inside. And there was no remorse from Lendl; if any of his contemporaries were upset, they would just have to get over it. Lendl told jokes in pretty much the same way that he struck a forehand at some dumb player at the net; with gusto, and seemingly without even a moment's concern for any lasting damage he might cause. Think of Lendl as the master of the locker-room takedown. 'Lendl was always putting you down and giving you shit,' Cash told me. 'That was his way of saying, "I'm the king of this jungle". It was chest-thumping, gorilla stuff. For sure, he had insecurities under there. I'm sure a lot of his behaviour was just a way of trying to build confidence. We all go through times in our career when we're playing terribly, and we don't feel confident at all.'

This was the golden age of talking smack in tennis; never before or since in the sport's history have a group of players been so gifted at exchanging unpleasantries. When Lendl returned to tennis as Andy Murray's coach, he would have discovered that locker-room culture had changed quite considerably since his time. Now, whole seasons can pass without any proper feuding breaking out. And these modern-day manners haven't met with everyone's approval. When the Latvian player Ernests Gulbis, an uninhibited son of an oligarch, accused Murray and the rest of the big beasts – Rafa Nadal, Novak Djokovic and Roger Federer – of being so respectful they had tipped over into being boring, he wasn't alone. There are many others who believe that civility is slowly killing modern tennis. How some long for a return to those glorious days when tennis players were perfectly foul towards each other. Still, in the 1980s, at that time of verbal ping-pong, Lendl wasn't one of the great on-court sledgers. His domain was the locker-room. Lendl's decision to play his psychological games offstage, so out of public view, wasn't because of some desire to maintain his good image — the tennis crowds didn't hold him in high standing – but because he wanted to keep his focus and concentration during matches. While Lendl would gladly smash a forehand at his opponent's head, as that would help his chances of victory, there was a risk that flinging insults over the net would distract him from his forehands. Behind the scenes, Lendl's rivals saw a very different man from the controlled and serious one they read about in their newspapers, or saw in matches.

In the early days when Lendl was new on the international tennis scene, he had been more standoffish, and he had kept more to himself, giving the impression of being aloof and arrogant. But, as his results and his ranking improved, he became more vocal behind the scenes. 'You have to remember that there were some big egos in tennis then,' Cash told me. 'There were a lot of personalities and characters. Every day, you would see someone come into the locker-room, and just smash a bunch of rackets and just scream and yell. You don't see any of that stuff today. If you were upset about something, you would let it out. It wasn't unusual to hear one guy screaming across the locker-room at the guy he had just been on court with: "I'll beat the fuck out of you, the next time you do that, you arsehole". That was the way it was. But, even in that environment, Lendl was a loudmouth. I didn't like him. He was always aggressive towards people. You would walk into the locker-room, wearing a pair of jeans and trainers, and right at the back of the locker-room, there would be Lendl shouting: "Cash, you look like a complete idiot in those shoes – what are you wearing? You look like a dork, ha, ha, ha". So I would turn around and say, "Yeah, Lendl". I would be thinking, "Keep it up, mate, I'm going to kick your arse the next time we play". That would piss me off. A lot of players would go, "Oh no, do I look stupid?" Lendl would put people down, and be quite negative about you. He was a big talker. He was always mouthing off.'

Wojtek Fibak once observed that Lendl could be intolerant of others, including those who didn't dress well away from tennis, or who somehow demonstrated a lack of intelligence. That may have been so, but the most plausible analysis is that Lendl's comments weren't primarily fuelled by intolerance, but by a desire to destabilise and unsettle his rivals. Boris Becker also remembered the Lendl of the 1980s as someone with a loud voice. 'Lendl was always talking more than others, put it that way,' Becker told me, also claiming that Lendl's odd behaviour would sometimes extend to the on-court pre-match warm-up when he would repeatedly hit shots into the corner of the court, or with huge power, to prevent Becker from establishing any rhythm. 'Lendl and I were not the best of friends. Most top players in the 1980s weren't the best of friends, and there was no exception with Lendl. He did what he had to do to become the best player that he could be. And so did I. There was a battle going on, on and off the court, and we weren't exactly known for going out for dinner with each other.'

Lendl wasn't without locker-room allies, however. He had an international group of friends, a spirited and opinionated bunch that included South Africa's Christo van Rensburg, Argentina's José Luis Clerc and America's Bill Scanlon. To get an idea of what they must have been like when they were on the tour in the 1980s, consider what happened after their playing days when Lendl celebrated his fiftieth birthday with a party in Florida. Van Rensburg was among the guests who tried to 'roast' Lendl by standing up and telling embarrassing stories about him, or making irreverent comments about certain parts of his life or character. 'They tried to roast me, but since it was my party I got to talk last and after each guy I got to have a rebuttal,' Lendl has said. 'And after the third guy, when they realised that I had more stuff on them than they had on me, nobody volunteered any more.' It may surprise some to discover that one of Lendl's closest locker-room allies was Stefan Edberg, whose gentlemanly nature was such that the men's tour subsequently created a sportsmanship award in his name. 'Stefan had a sick sense of humour just like me,' Lendl has said of a Swede who in 2014 re-emerged on the tennis scene as Federer's new coach. 'You know what they say about quiet water making trouble? That's Stefan.'

Like Cash, Mats Wilander contended that Lendl went too far. The locker-room in the 1980s wasn't somewhere you went for tea and sympathy. But, even in that rough, abrasive subculture, Wilander felt that Lendl's treatment of other players, especially those much lower down the tennis rankings who Lendl knew wouldn't answer back, amounted to aggression. Certainly, there were things you could say as the world number one that you couldn't if you were ranked number eleven or twenty-one; that was the power of the office. To Wilander's mind, Lendl lacked tact and judgement, and didn't always pick the right targets. 'I think his sense of humour was so dry that sometimes it came off wrong, and sometimes it was directed at the wrong people. I wouldn't say that he was very tactful, and his judgement wasn't great. He would say things like, "It looks like you've put on a few pounds", or "You looked a bit slow in practice yesterday", or, "I kicked your ass out there". Or he would beat you and then say, "I thought you played pretty well today". It was weird, but he didn't do it to us – the top players – so much, but to the next level down. Connors didn't like him. McEnroe didn't like him. Back then, it was very easy not to like him.'

It's a sign of how Lendl's personality dominated the locker-room that he wasn't punched in the mouth for the comments he made. Brawls and bar fights have been started over far less. One occasion on which someone did react violently to Lendl's locker-room shenanigans, and in spectacular style, came one spring day at the Monte Carlo Country Club; that spot between the limestone cliffs and the Mediterranean is a place of beauty and serenity, but Pat Cash was red-lining as Lendl pulled the shoes from his feet and then started tearing them to pieces. 'I had just been given a pair of beautiful leather jogging shoes. They were the coolest shoes, and I wore them everywhere. I was sitting on a locker-room bench, talking to somebody, and he just came up and grabbed them, and ripped them, broke them. I wasn't going to take his shit. I just flew at him, I had to be pulled off him. I was ready to thump him. I just thought that wasn't right,' Cash said. Lendl's expression, according to Cash, was one of utter shock – he had imagined that, as a grand slam champion and a long-term world number one, he was free to behave as he wanted, without any backchat or come-back. Thereafter, Cash referred to Lendl as 'Mr Shoebreaker'. 'Funnily enough, Ivan came up to me just before the 2013 Australian Open, and said, "I've got a bone to pick with you – I've heard what you said about the shoes, and that wasn't me". He said it was my mate. Now, why the fuck would my friend, my best mate, do that to me? So Lendl's still denying it, but it was him, he did that to my shoes.'

Lendl has always loved a practical joke, so he would drive his car at high speed just to see his passenger's lip quiver, or to hear him beg to slow down. The one occasion when he did crash was when a squirrel ran on to the road, pursued by a golden retriever, and in trying to avoid them Lendl's Porsche skidded on wet leaves and he smacked into a tree. On impact, his head whacked the steering wheel, and he stepped out of the car with a great gash on his chin. There were also off-road japes, some of dubious taste: as he walked into a news conference on one occasion he snatched a beret from a journalist's head, pretended to wipe it on his backside and then flung it behind him. It has been said that he would invite someone over to his house and then casually inform him that his dogs were about to tear his liver out. When you were around Lendl's German shepherds you had to be careful not to put a tennis ball in your pocket; that would only encourage Lendl to give a covert fetch command, on which the dogs would launch themselves at your shorts. Or there was the time Lendl went cycling around Connecticut with a friend who was a professional golfer; when climbing one particularly steep hill, his companion dismounted and pushed his bike, while Lendl pedalled on. A few days later, Lendl had another friend call the golfer, pretending to be a writer for a golf magazine researching a story on fitness. They spent a few minutes chatting about diet and workouts before the bogus journalist said, 'Tell me, if you're cycling and you're going up a steep hill, do you ride your bike or do you push it?' There was a long silence on the line, and then the golfer responded: 'Tell Ivan to go fuck himself.'

Sometimes the joke was on Lendl. At times, he took it well. A groundsman at London's Queen's Club hid Lendl's bicycle to see what the reaction would be. 'You can't really imagine it now, the world number one cycling through London traffic. Can you imagine what would have happened if he had been knocked off his bike on the way to practice? I remember it was a white bike – it might have had a basket,' Graham Kimpton told me. 'Ivan would turn up and leave his bike by one of the pathways by the practice courts. We had some good laughs, some good banter, with him. Even then he had an image of being cold and grumpy, but once you knew him you realised how funny he was. He was always saying to us, "These grass courts are rubbish". One day he was on court, and I stole the bike and stuck it out the back somewhere. That day we had someone doing a demo with a new mower. So we were doing a demo on one of the other courts, when all of a sudden Lendl appeared, shouting: "Where is my fucking bike?" He looked as though he was getting very carried away. I think the guy showing us the mower was taken aback, with Lendl scream-ing and shouting at us. Lendl knew that I had done it, and he wasn't genuinely angry. It was tongue-in-cheek stuff.'

But on other occasions he didn't like it one bit, such as the time a friend arranged for an actor dressed as a traffic cop to knock on his door and arrest him for failing to pay a speeding ticket. According to an account published in *Sports Illustrated*, Lendl called out, 'Get me my lawyer', and then, a friend was quoted as saying, 'sweat was pouring off him, he was stutter-ing, and we had to tell him it was a joke. We were afraid he was going to break down.' Naturally, Lendl said he had always known it was a joke and, wanting to regain control of the situ-ation, he found one of his German shepherds, walked back into the room with the dog on the leash, and asked whether anyone was still interested in arresting him. On occasion, Lendl's jokes came back to sting him. On hearing that a certain player's wife had given birth to a girl, Lendl remarked to him: 'You're not man enough to have a boy. Better try again, girly-man.' Lendl would go on to have five daughters.

There was no need for any American wrestling-style fakery here, no need for McEnroe and Ivan Lendl to pretend that they loathed each other; they genuinely did. Among the insults McEnroe directed at Lendl was that it hurt the popularity of the game to have someone as robotic as him as the world number one. Another was that 'nobody gives a damn about Lendl and that's the bottom line – I could have no personality and be more popular than him'. One more was that Lendl was 'always going into strange sulks and weird head trips'.

You could see how they felt about each other from the way McEnroe foul-mouthed Lendl, even in exhibition matches, which were supposed to be amicable. Take the time they were appearing together at an event in Milan, and McEnroe, believing his opponent wasn't giving his best, and that the crowd weren't getting their money's worth, had a dig at Lendl: 'Listen, Ivan, you're acting like a pussy. Get out there and start playing, you wimp.' McEnroe, who has recalled how Lendl was bleating that no one should speak to him like that, later also called Lendl 'a quitter'. Lendl's memory of that match was that, after winning the opening set, he found himself trailing 1-5 in the second and he tried to throw McEnroe off his rhythm by taking much of the pace off his shots. It wasn't that he wasn't giving his all, just that he wasn't playing his usual game of slamming every ball with enough power to put a crack in a smokestack. 'So then we had that incident, and he started calling me names, and I almost hit him over the head with a racket,' Lendl has said. 'It was rather unfortunate, actually, because then every time we played, the press thought we were going to fight.'

Their loathing for each other was both real and intense. Even when Lendl and McEnroe weren't in the same room, they were often on each other's minds, the one seemingly a little obsessed about the other. When Pat Cash practised with McEnroe, the New Yorker would regularly bring Lendl up in conversation; and it was plain that 'McEnroe didn't like Lendl at all, not one little bit. They were both fiery, and both wanted to be the best they could be, and to win. I thought it made tennis entertaining,' Cash told me. 'They used to hate each other. Then throw Jimmy Connors into the works and, whoa there were some big egos going on there.' And if Bjorn Borg brought out the best in McEnroe, Lendl brought out the worst. As Michael Chang explained it to me, one of the reasons that Lendl and McEnroe didn't get along was that they had known each other for so many years, having first encountered one another in the 1970s at a junior tournament. By the time they made it on to the main tour, their feelings towards each other were well developed.

The suspicion remains that, even after all the New York vitriol that came his way, and despite the mutual loathing, Lendl still retained some awe and wonder for what McEnroe was capable of doing with a tennis ball. That would explain why Lendl seemed to care how McEnroe behaved towards him in the locker-room. What troubled him was that he never quite knew which McEnroe he would encounter. One day the American would be bordering on friendly, and the next he could be vile, 'and the day after that, he forgets what he called you on court'. Clearly, Lendl hadn't erased McEnroe's words from his mind. Sometimes, McEnroe would walk into the same room as Lendl and he wouldn't say a word; that silent treatment appeared to unsettle Lendl: 'Where I was brought up, when you come into a room, you say, "hello".' So here was Lendl, the supposed bully of the locker-room, whining that he wasn't getting a sunny 'good morning' before practice. McEnroe had made it plain that he wouldn't 'take any nonsense' from Lendl – in fact, he 'enjoyed getting on Lendl's case at every available opportunity'. The only other player who stood up to Lendl as McEnroe did was Connors, who once publicly accused him of being a 'chicken' for supposedly 'tanking' – not giving his best efforts – at the season-ending tournament one year. For a long time after that, whenever Connors saw Lendl he would squawk and flap imaginary wings.

For Lendl in the 1980s and early 1990s, it simply wasn't possible to 'really like your rivals, as you're trying to take the bread off each other's tables'. 'It's almost like in boxing, though nobody gets killed in tennis,' Lendl once said. 'It may be sad, but the lines are drawn. One fights against the other, one wins, one loses. Something else doesn't exist. And we always fight for more than just a few pennies.'

Sometimes Ivan Lendl just couldn't help himself and he revealed his soft side to others. Few saw more of that than Michael Chang, a Chinese-American who once humiliated the man from Ostrava on court. 'Most people have never had the chance to see the real Ivan, who is extremely talkative, very humorous, and likes to joke around, and he's very sociable.

I think that's too bad as people have a certain perception of him,' Chang told me. 'I hear what people say about Ivan and I think, "er, no, that's what Ivan is like as a coach when he's in the stadium, but that's not the Ivan that I know".' If ever there was a sign that Lendl liked Chang, it was that he didn't once try to assault him with a forehand. 'Ivan never tried to hit me, and I'm sure that was because I started on tour before my sixteenth birthday, and he didn't want to hit someone so young. He would have felt bad about that. Ivan was always very nice to me. Maybe the other reason he didn't go for me was because I was travelling with my mother, and he always got on well with my mom.'

From the first time that Chang encountered Lendl on a tennis court, at an exhibition match in Des Moines, Iowa, he saw that Lendl wasn't as nasty as people said he was. 'Ivan was supposed to be playing Boris Becker, and Boris pulled out at the last minute, and they were scrambling to find someone to fill in. I was sixteen at the time and Ivan beat me 6-2, 6-3. So we were riding back to the hotel, and he says to me, "Do you want to know why I beat you tonight?" And I said: "Sure, tell me". And he said: "Well, to be honest with you, you don't have a second serve, you don't have enough power in your game. You've got speed and footwork but, basically right now, you've got nothing to hurt me with. So if you really want to make it on the tour, you really have to work on those aspects of your game". I wasn't offended at all. I took it as, "Wow, here's the number one player in the world, and he's sharing with me the things that I need to work on". I took that as constructive criticism. He was absolutely right, and I worked on those parts of my game.'

Chang would end up beating Lendl in their most memorable meeting, a fourth-round match at the 1989 French Open in which the cramping seventeen-year-old American hit an underarm serve on the way to the most improbable of victories. Chang would go on to win the title. 'After we played in Paris, I didn't see Ivan again until we were at Wimbledon. We were at the practice courts and he was walking towards me. I was thinking to myself, "What's he going to say? What's he thinking?" You just never know whether someone is going to give you a sour look and say, "You seventeen-year-old punk". Ivan walked straight up to me, looked me in the eye, put his hand out, and said, "Michael, great job at the French Open, congratulations". That said a lot about who Ivan is.' Especially as, according to Andy Murray, that defeat still hurts Lendl.

Why, you might wonder, didn't Lendl ever press reboot on his on-court personality? Surely, this perfectionist would have wanted others to judge him based on accurate information? Surely that attack from *Sports Illustrated* should have told him that he should at least have considered showing the world his softer side? One thing that Lendl did do – and this must rank as one of the oddest letters ever sent to a newspaper – was to write to the *New York Times* to assure them, 'I am one of the happiest people in the world'. That wasn't Lendl's only musing on happiness. As Lendl saw it, you achieved greatness first and then you could chase happiness, and not the other way around. 'If you can become great, then you can become happy,' he once said, 'but if you're happy first, it's much more difficult to be great.'

That letter wasn't the only thing that helped to soften his image; Lendl didn't go through his entire career dressed all in black, with him and his clothing manufacturers embracing colour and geometric patterns. Still, even then he didn't look too friendly – who ever looked at Lendl in a shirt with a giant eagle across his chest and felt all warm and soft inside? Lendl also bought himself a new smile; perhaps he just wanted neater teeth, or maybe this was part of an attempt to help sell him to the American consumer, who rarely overlooked bad teeth. One member of the tennis writing pack, who had previously looked upon Lendl as 'a lockjawed night creature', would find himself thinking, as he stood there in the glare of about the best smile that tennis prize money could buy, that the 'new Lendl grin is so stunning that he looks perpetually as if he is working for a tip. Whereas he used to bare his teeth about as often as a full eclipse of the sun, now he wouldn't be out of place in the doorway of an airplane, grinning hello and goodbye to strangers.' That was a typical write-up – even when the media seemed to be hymning Lendl's virtues, they couldn't resist slipping in a few criticisms.

One year on the other side of the Atlantic, Lendl warmed up for Wimbledon by inviting the British tennis media to the Café Royal in Piccadilly, serving up dinner, drinks, and an evening of idle chit-chat. The cynics regarded this as a 'scrub-a-dub job' to reinvent Lendl as 'Ivan the Nice', but that was going too far. Relations between Lendl and Fleet Street did undoubtedly improve, with fewer insults directed at him. But that's not the same as saying that the columnists ever urged their readers to hold Ivan close to their hearts. Doubtless this was Lendl acting on the advice of his management company, who had long recognised that sponsors wanted someone with a touch of humanity. And, it has to be said, Lendl wasn't without international success; for someone who no one sup-posedly cared about, he certainly had a decent portfolio of corporate backers. There were clearly a fair number of com-pany executives who considered that Lendl's new smile was the best way of reaching Middle America and the rest of the global tennis market; for all the public's misgivings, Lendl was still the world number one for 270 weeks, and a winner of eight grand slam titles, and that counted for something in the endorsement market.

Still, the clothes and the smile were just small things. For all those modifications, what Lendl wasn't prepared to change was the fundamental way he went about his business on and off the court; if he was going to survive in this business, if he was going to prevent others seeing his vulnerabilities, he had to remain cold and hard, he had to keep that mask on. And perhaps he simply couldn't change; maybe he had spent so many years hiding his emotions away, and had become so good at it, that he no longer knew any other way to behave during tennis matches. Maybe he had simply come to believe his own myth. Maybe, after all those years of pretending to be tough and serious, he had eventually adopted that persona. And if and when that happened, you could reasonably say he had become himself on court, that it was no longer an act, that he was no longer faking it. Once the mask was on, there was no taking it off. Geopolitics changed faster than Lendl's approach to tennis; the Berlin Wall and the Iron Curtain came down, yet his guard was still up. He certainly wasn't going to be smiling, or showing any emotion, just because people told him to. 'I don't show my emotions because they are not everybody's business,' he told *Tennis* magazine in the 1980s. 'People say to me, "Do me a favour, smile on court". They don't know that I like to smile. I like to smile off the court; there I can smile as long and hard as I like. On the court, I have to be a certain way. I like it if people understand me, but I won't try to convince them.'

This pressure on public figures to emote – to dish up their desires and disappointments for the public's delectation – is supposedly a recent phenomenon. But look at Lendl. This was happening in the 1980s. Tennis then wasn't just a results game; as part of the entertainment industry, there was a demand on players to do more than hit the crap out of their forehand. Lendl never did understand the media and public's obsession with whether he smiled or not: 'Why is it necessary to explain all of this? Why does a man with tight lips need to justify himself, and a man who is grinning from ear to ear doesn't? Why is one better than the other? Why can't they just be different?' Still, he also recognised that people were only interested in seeing his teeth because he was winning grand slams; had he been ranked seventy-five in the world, they couldn't have cared less about his facial expressions.

'Sucking up', as Lendl called it, was out of the question. True, he wasn't above some fakery, but it seems he made a distinction between not sharing your feelings with the mob and your peers and acting out an emotional response to win over the crowds. Putting on that mask had won Lendl tennis matches; wearing a false smile, and gaining popularity, wasn't going to keep him at the top of the game. More than anything, Lendl couldn't fake a smile, not even with those new teeth. He had been called almost everything during his career, but one label he didn't want pinned to the front of his T-shirt was 'phony'. It wasn't Lendl's style to love-bomb the tennis public, to blow kisses in every direction, to land in whatever city he found himself in that week and to tell every cynical pro's beautiful lie, 'you're my favourite crowd to play in front of'. 'That's human nature to want to be loved,' Lendl once said, 'but I would rather be liked by a smaller percentage for what I am, not for who I am pretending to be.' Interestingly, Murray, too, felt the same way when asked to play the PR game; he hated the thought that anyone would ever consider him to be a fake.

And Lendl wasn't going to rebuild his game for artistic reasons. He knew that he could never possibly be as imaginative on a tennis court as McEnroe was. Lendl's game was all about clumping the ball, and he wasn't going to change that for anyone. When Lendl first came to prominence, he felt as though spectators had enjoyed watching him 'blow opponents away', but soon the novelty of his power tennis faded, and the public wanted players who could be more creative with felt, rubber, graphite and cow gut. You didn't have to remind Lendl that no style points were ever awarded on court; if Brad Gilbert, one of Murray's former coaches, was happy to win ugly, Lendl was perfectly content to do likewise, just so long as that was going to win him matches.

A final thought: what if being unpopular was the best thing that ever happened to Lendl, as it freed him to live his tennis life as he wanted? 'People didn't like Ivan, and I think in some ways he kind of liked that. I think he kind of found it funny,' Mats Wilander told me. 'He never did anything – and everyone in the locker-room kind of respected him for this – just to be liked. He was what he was, and he is what he is. With people not liking him, he didn't have to care about being nice, and he could just go about his business. He could be a little grumpy and fired-up if he needed to be. Coming from his background, he probably felt as though he wasn't just fighting against the players on court, but against the whole system.'

CHAPTER FIVE

A COUPLE OF LOSERS: A SHARED HISTORY OF FAILURE

Ride the Métro out into the south-west of Paris, step off at Porte d'Auteuil station and you'll walk out into one of the most boringly bourgeois parts of the city. So some say. Another take on the 16th arrondissement is that it's an elegant and agreeable place to watch old and new money sitting together at pavement tables sipping on overpriced *café au lait*. Others contend that this is a sleepy part of the city. It probably is unless you happen to be a professional tennis player passing through. For a fortnight every spring, this is about the most unforgiving and judgemental place any tennis player will visit over the course of the long season.

If you dare, you can discover your own worth at the closest thing to a tennis stock exchange. Any players who want to discover their true place in the world order, to know what their market value is in the sport, only have to pull a baseball cap down low and make that walk from the Métro station to the gates of Roland Garros – spend a few minutes listening to the touts who line that route and you'll soon discover who's on the rise and who's spiralling. There are touts everywhere in tennis, but none as excitable as these. How much will those without tickets pay to see you play? And then later, when a player makes their entrance, they will encounter the notoriously critical and vocal Paris tennis set. You're no one in tennis until you've been hissed at by a stadium full of Parisians. No opportunity to boo is passed up. They're the most expensively dressed mob anywhere on the tennis map, but there can be a viciousness, a cruelty, about Paris in the springtime. Funny, then, that it was there in La Seizième that tennis witnessed the most violent one-day swing in public opinion that tennis has ever known – in the space of a few hours on the orange-red clay of Roland Garros, The Choking Dog became The Man Who Wouldn't Give Up.

And this crude characterisation of Ivan Lendl as one of the great gladiatorial figures of modern tennis is the one that persists: in Paris and beyond, most still remember the Lendl of the 1980s as a relentless figure whose commitment never wobbled. Lendl, after losing in his first four appearances in grand slam finals, turned a two-set deficit against John McEnroe at the 1984 French Open into a fine, five-set victory that demonstrated his mental fortitude, his bloody-minded refusal to yield. Or did it?

What if the victory that appeared to have turned Lendl's grand slam career around, and stopped people calling him The Choke-Slovakian – as well as bringing him future employment in Andy Murray's entourage – didn't come about primarily because of his strength of character? What if he almost gave up that day at Roland Garros? What if a key part of Lendl's story – and so, by extension, part of Murray's – was all based on exceptionally good fortune, thanks to a voice which suddenly burrowed itself deep into McEnroe's brain? As Lendl once conceded: 'A lot of it was just plain dumb luck, but the good thing that came out of it was that the public came to think of me as a fighter.'

Speak to Wojtek Fibak, who was coaching Lendl at that time, and who says that Lendl 'wasn't a fighter by nature', and he will have you wondering whether this result requires an asterisk the size of an autograph hunter's giant tennis ball: The Man Who Wouldn't Give Up had been about to do just that – go tame in a slam final. On a number of occasions during the final – 'this didn't just happen once or twice' – Lendl's moaning to Fibak sounded as though he was considering abandoning his attempt to win his first grand slam title. According to Fibak, Lendl shouted: 'I don't want to play any more. What am I doing here?' So Fibak – or so he told me – urged Lendl to 'wait, wait, wait and fight'. And Lendl apparently responded: 'Wait for what?' To which Fibak said: 'Wait, wait, wait. How many times do I have to say wait?' So, once again, it would seem that some revisionism is required with the Lendl story. And that's not to say here that Lendl has made himself out to be someone he wasn't. As Lendl has acknowledged, it was the day he went from supposedly being a choker to being a warrior of the courts, and he has said that he didn't warrant either of those labels. This is the recurring theme of Lendl's life: he often wasn't the man others said he was.

On the *terre battue*, the beaten earth, of Roland Garros, such defeatist talk from Lendl was what some would have expected from him – after his four failures in slam finals,

they had come to think of him as someone who was too mentally soft ever to win a major. Everyone knew, McEnroe has
said, that Lendl choked away slams. When people spoke of
schadenfreude on the tennis tour in the 1980s, they weren't
talking about some unseeded German baseliner, but the
sight of Lendl's challenge dwindling away on a live transmis-
sion. The accusation was this – either Lendl would choke,
which was an involuntary shutdown of his ability to compete
and potentially to win, or he would tank, meaning he would
check out of a match and not give his all. You can only hope,
for her sake, and also for his, that Lendl's mother, Olga, one
of the most ferocious and competitive women ever to have
swung a racket in the East, and who expected her son to fight
as she once had, was protected from any such discussions.
Because of the way he was on court, suppressing his emotions and personality, people could get the wrong impression
of Lendl. Someone who is trying to hide his fears and vulnerabilities from prying eyes isn't always going to be growling,
shaking a fist, raging against himself, his opponent and the
world, or whatever else a player who finds himself in a scuffle
is supposed to be doing.

The morning of the match, the French sports newspaper
L'Equipe had published a cartoon of McEnroe pointing a gun
at a panicking, sweating Lendl; the artist was depicting the
common-held belief that when Lendl played slam finals it
always looked as if the umpire would have to step down from
his chair to perform the Heimlich Manoeuvre. Lendl has said
he didn't see the cartoon: reading the newspapers during
a grand slam was only asking for trouble but McEnroe had
come across the cartoon and, naturally, he had been thrilled
by such anti-Lendl imagery.

It would be hard to criticise Lendl for losing to Björn Borg in the 1981 French Open final; it was, after all, the first time he had experienced the pressures and the choreography that went with playing for a major. And Lendl even extended Borg, the greatest clay-courter outside Majorca in modern times, to five sets. But as Lendl racked up defeats in slam finals – he lost to Jimmy Connors at the 1982 and 1983 US Opens, and then to Mats Wilander at the 1983 Australian Open – the tennis commentariat started to consider whether he would ever be standing on the podium with a trophy and a gummy smile. Lendl had been telling himself not to worry, as 'if you get to seventy-five finals, you're going to win one of them, as you'll play well or the other guy will play badly, and the most important thing is to keep trying'. But did he truly believe that? Centre stage in La Seizième, it seemed as if Lendl had forgotten the pep talk he had been giving himself.

So, would Lendl choke? Or would it be a case of him not giving his all? Lendl's weakness, as Wilander told me, was that in the first half of the 1980s he was sometimes 'fearful of fighting'; the Swede recalled encounters at slams and other smaller tournaments when he felt as though Lendl 'didn't give his best efforts'. 'There was the time we played in the fourth round of the 1982 French Open, when I was seventeen years old, and the match went to five sets – I thought he threw in the towel in the fifth set. I played him not long after that, and I think he threw in the towel then, too. And then I beat him another time, and I thought to myself, "he's not being competitive".'

Suspicion and innuendo clung tighter to some of Lendl's performances than a pair of period-piece tennis shorts. It was at the 1981 Masters, the showpiece tournament at New York's Madison Square Garden, that Lendl's reputation for capitulation first properly took hold. He was said to have tanked during a round-robin match against Jimmy Connors; the reason for this was supposedly to give himself a softer semi-final, as the winner would play Borg in the knockout stages while the loser would go through to face what appeared to be an easier opponent in American Gene Mayer. Going on court, Lendl had hoped to win; at that stage in his career he still hadn't beaten Connors and wanted to experience that. And yet, after failing to close out his advantage in the first set, and feeling weary, he decided it 'wasn't worth trying', and that it would be a smarter move to save his energies for the next day. That didn't help Lendl's standing with Connors, who took to calling him a 'chickenshit commie' and teasing him about having a nervous pre-match bladder, and it didn't do much for Lendl's reputation with his peers and the public either. For all Lendl's initial denials that he had tanked, he would eventually concede that he could have done much more.

Tanking at the Masters was bad form, but not applying yourself in a grand slam final? That was among the biggest crimes a professional could commit. So the conclusion of the 1983 US Open final – when Connors ripped through the fourth set 6-0 to take the title, with his opponent offering little in response – led to Lendl being roasted by many who cared about tennis. According to the late Arthur Ashe, some former champions such as Rod Laver were saying that it looked as though Lendl – who had double-faulted when he had a point to lead by two sets to one – had given up, causing such embarrassment to the sport that he deserved to be fined or even suspended from future tournaments. Ashe's own view was that it had been 'inexcusable' for Lendl to have been so docile playing in front of more than 20,000 paying spectators

and an armchair audience of millions more. Ashe considered
that he had 'given the entire sport a bad name, as in the ethos
of competition, you always bust your ass'.

Still, Lendl felt any allegations that he hadn't applied himself were ridiculous – his view appears to be that he lost those
matches because he wasn't fit enough, and that he had never
given up. And his explanation for being bagelled – losing a
set 6-0 – against Connors at the 1983 US Open was that he
had been constrained by injury. Had this been the Ostrava
club championships, Lendl would have stopped trying, 'but
there would have to be something terribly wrong with your
brain to give up in the fourth set of the US Open final'. 'I
was treated very unfairly. What happened is that when I was
serving for the set in the third, set point up, I got a terrible
stomach cramp,' he has said. 'I just couldn't play afterwards.
Even when I was going home, I had to stop and lie on the hood
of the car. I had to bend over because I had a cramp the size
of a fist in the left side of my stomach. But nobody ever bothered to say, "he must have been hurting", or ask. Everybody
just said I didn't try. If you don't try in the US Open final, you
ought to have your head examined.' Unbeknownst to Lendl
at the time, Connors wasn't in the best shape physically and
beforehand he had checked with the tournament director
and umpire to clarify the rules about timeouts for sickness.

Perhaps, Fibak has previously considered, Lendl wasn't
'truly tanking', but, unable to handle the pressure, was suffering from a severe form of mental paralysis that went into his
stomach and legs and burned up energy.

Unfairly or not, Lendl wasn't someone renowned for liking
a dogfight on court, or for having the ability to compete when
the world was watching. That didn't really tally with Lendl's

view of himself as a 'competitive bastard', or with the stories about him for ever seeking competition, on or off the court. When the swimming pool froze at Lendl's Connecticut house, he would apparently challenge his caretaker to a game of ice hockey. In warmer weather he would invite other members of staff to try to beat him at basketball or racing miniature cars. To add spice to rounds of golf with friends, they would bet on the outcome, with money and sometimes press-ups riding on the result. Lendl once told his wife Samantha, an accomplished, experienced horsewoman, that if he ever took up riding he would be better than her within a month. And Samantha, who thought her husband had 'an incredible will to win', replied: 'Well, you're probably right.'

However talented McEnroe was, he couldn't strike the ball as hard as Lendl. No matter, thought McEnroe's friend and doubles partner Peter Fleming, who had been so sure that McEnroe would beat Lendl to win a first French Open title he had prematurely begun organising that evening's victory celebrations. In those first two sets, and during the third set, too, Lendl wasn't so much playing to win the title as playing for respectability, his ambitions limited to avoiding humilia-tion: 'We started and I was just basically getting blown away and just trying to make it respectable, that's all I was trying to do.' McEnroe was looking at his friends in the crowd and their faces were telling him they thought the final would be over in half an hour. Beforehand, the message that Fibak had imparted to Lendl was this: hang on for that moment when an error from McEnroe's strings might turn the whole match. 'I told Ivan that McEnroe would come to net on everything, but there would come a moment when McEnroe would miss, and after that one moment, the match would change,' Fibak recalled. 'And that was exactly what happened. McEnroe won the first two sets, and was leading in the third set, he missed a shot, Ivan broke McEnroe's serve, and then he went on to win in five sets.'

For all Fibak's years of instruction, it wasn't Lendl's spirit that changed the match and with it started his collection of grand slam titles. In the end Lendl put everything he had into becoming the first man since Björn Borg in 1974 to scuffle from two sets down in a Roland Garros final, working himself to the limit when he started to believe he might just have a chance of victory. One of his first acts as a grand slam champion, while waiting for the prize-giving ceremony, was to retch and vomit near McEnroe's feet; in addition, after lurching off the court, he 'splattered' the locker-room. Mentally and physically depleted, he was unable to recall either winning or, afterwards, talking to a friend backstage. When that same friend remarked to him a few weeks later that he looked really tired in that locker-room, and mentioned how white Lendl's face had turned, as well as the ice packs that had been stacked up on his head, the French Open champion looked confused and replied: 'What are you talking about? You weren't even in Paris.'

So Lendl didn't give up in Paris. But this story wouldn't have had a happy ending if all Lendl did was graft; he needed some luck amid the baseline dust-clouds of Roland Garros. McEnroe never needed much outside help in being irritable and emotionally volatile, but if noise hadn't been leaking from the headset of a courtside TV cameraman – which exasperated McEnroe so much that he grabbed it and screamed into the microphone: 'Shut the fuck up' – Lendl's run of defeats in slam finals would have stretched to five.

Whoever it was in the production team who was babbling down the line, he had inadvertently sent McEnroe into apoplexy and in doing so changed the course of tennis history. The Paris crowd booed, McEnroe's head was suddenly flooded with doubts – a telephone conversation with an old girlfriend the night before, in which they both admitted how much they missed each other, hadn't helped his mental equilibrium, and he would lose the third set and then the fourth – and Lendl would go on to win the fifth set 7-5. Still, as McEnroe has acknowledged, that member of the television production crew is probably still deaf to this day. Right in the middle of his finest year – in the middle of what was one of the greatest seasons ever put together by any player in the modern era – and just when it looked as though he was going to win the French Open for the first time, McEnroe was derailed by television. So the red-lining McEnroe would experience the most distressing defeat of his career; for a while, that result gave him sleepless nights, and there have been occasions on returning to Paris as a former player, to do television commentary, when memories of that match have brought on forty-eight hours of nausea. Losing a match in such circumstances was horrific enough; it was even more excruciating to have done so against Lendl, to have validated a man he didn't like, to have stopped him from being a failure. 'Lendl didn't beat me – I beat myself,' McEnroe would observe in his autobiography, *Serious*. 'Lendl got his first major, and I took his title, Choker-in-Chief, away from him.'

Backlit by flashbulbs and neon-signed agony, Andy Murray's life – with the private jets, the fat sponsorship and appearance fees, the hysteria of the Wimbledon picnickers – wasn't quite the gilded existence many imagined it to be. All those defeats in slam finals hadn't done much for Murray's self-esteem; a flight in a LearJet was hardly going to change how he felt about himself. Britain's most talented player since the 1930s was feeling like 'a loser, nothing more, nothing less'; he could barely bring himself to interact with his public, so on leaving the house to walk his dogs, or to buy groceries at the supermarket, he would sometimes lower his head to avoid the possibility of random conversation in one of the aisles. He was afraid of what strangers might say to him. We forget this now that he has won the Olympics, the US Open and Wimbledon, but there was a time when he was 'abused' on the street and trolled on Twitter, and he didn't just have barbs to deal with: he also had to contend with the warm words of encouragement, those cheery predictions such as 'Don't worry, it'll happen for your next time'. How was a 'loser', someone who felt as though he was letting everyone down, supposed to respond to that?

Such was Murray's mental state after three lopsided defeats in his first three appearances in slam finals that there was good cause to wonder whether it would have been easier on him to have departed all those tournaments in the first round, rather than getting anywhere near holding the trophy. It wasn't just that Murray had lost these matches – to Roger Federer at the 2008 US Open, to Federer again at the 2010 Australian Open and to Novak Djokovic at the 2011 Australian Open – for there was no shame in being beaten by opponents of that quality, but that on no occasion had he even come close to producing his best tennis. By his own admission, Murray hadn't shown much game, with his performances seriously lacking in poise and purpose. Those three grand slam finals hadn't even yielded a set for Murray. Can't win the big ones, people were saying of Murray, which was what they had once said of Lendl. So Murray had joined that exclusive yet unfortunate club of players to have lost their first three slam finals – the other members were Andre Agassi, who would go on to bag eight slams, including winning all of the four majors at least once each, and Goran Ivanišević, who was more than satisfied with his sole Wimbledon victory.

It wasn't as if many queried whether Murray had the talent to win a grand slam tournament, or thought that he wasn't a good enough athlete. It was understandable for Murray to have been a little overwhelmed in New York City's Arthur Ashe Stadium on the occasion of his first appearance in a grand slam final, especially when he was looking over the net at Federer, regarded by many as the greatest player in history, and who won his fifth consecutive US Open that evening. But it was Murray's subsequent performances, both of them at Melbourne Park's Rod Laver Arena, that were so exasperating to watch as he became far too conservative and passive. There were echoes here of Lendl's career; he, too, had once been accomplished at winning 'small' tournaments and at reaching the finals of majors, but then just couldn't win those title matches. There had been two Lendls in the early to mid-1980s, the one who could crunch opponents away from the slams, and then the one who played within himself at the majors. And now there were two Murrays; and there was no doubt that, had they ever met, Regular Touring Andy would have given Grand Slam Andy a horse-whipping (still, unlike Lendl, Murray was never accused of giving up in a grand slam final). Lendl had managed to turn his tennis life around, but could Murray?

It wouldn't have been any consolation to Murray, as he racked up defeats in slam finals, to have heard suggestions that he had the misfortune to have been part of a golden age of men's tennis (though he was a member of the Big Three and a Half, he would have to win a major for that to be expanded to a Big Four). While Ivan Lendl had shared an era with John McEnroe, Jimmy Connors, Boris Becker, Stefan Edberg and Mats Wilander, it is almost universally accepted that winning slams in Murray's era was harder than it was for Lendl in his time. Consider how Federer, Nadal and Djokovic had the sport in lockdown for seven years. From the 2005 French Open until the 2012 Wimbledon Championships, that trio won all the grand slams, with one exception – when Juan Martín del Potro was victorious at the 2009 US Open.

More background is necessary before we come to Lendl's intervention in Murray's life. Twice Murray lost in an Australian Open final and then went into a death spin of despair, moping from one tournament to another for weeks, even months, afterwards. It was the spring of 2011, and Murray had just experienced one of the darkest afternoons of his tennis life, playing a bloodless kind of match to lose on his opening appearance of the hard-court tournament on Key Biscayne to an opponent ranked outside the world's top one hundred. That followed defeats in his first matches in Rotterdam and at the Indian Wells Tennis Garden in the Californian desert; Murray was going through a horrible time on and off the court, still traumatised by losing that January's Australian Open final. And losing to opponents that the Wimbledon Queue would struggle to pick out of a line-up. Murray had been without a full-time coach since sacking Miles Maclagan after the 2010 Wimbledon Championships, but he hadn't lost his sense of humour; on April Fool's Day in 2011 he would kid some of the media that he had hired one of his closest friends, Ross Hutchins, as his new coach. There has been some criticism that at this time Murray had been surrounding himself with friends who dared not tell him hard truths, so part of the Hutchins joke was his declaration that he wanted 'another yes-man'. Despite the laughter, though, there was genuine concern about Murray's future. There was a growing body of people in tennis, including Murray himself, who wondered whether the Scot would finish his career slamless.

As early as October 2010, Lendl was offering the opinion that the decision Murray made about his next coaching appointment could go a long way to determining whether he became a grand slam champion or not. Talking to a small group of journalists, Lendl said he was glad that Murray wasn't rushing to replace Maclagan because 'if he makes the wrong decision, I don't want to say it would ruin his chances of winning a grand slam, but it would diminish them greatly. I think Andy would really benefit from somebody who will fit in well with him and his people and still be able to help him to go where he needs to go. It's probably a tough find, but it's a very, very difficult decision for him, and a very important one, too.'

In the spring of 2011, while Murray was in America, Lendl was competing at a seniors tournament in Zurich, and he let it be known in the global tennis village that he would potentially be interested in working with Murray. A few days after Murray was beaten in Miami, news of Lendl's interest in Murray was published in three British newspapers. This wasn't just played out in the media, but behind the scenes, too: Lendl and his representatives are understood to have contacted the American arm of Murray's management company. There was at least one key figure close to Murray who had some suspicions about Lendl's interest in the British tennis player, and who considered that Lendl had allowed his name and his interest in Murray to leak because he imagined the resulting exposure would help him to publicise his new tennis academy. Was Lendl trying to piggyback on Murray's slumped shoulders, to make money from Murray's despair? Lendl's interest in coaching Murray was genuine. This was no public relations stunt to promote his academy.

A shared history of failure had brought the pair together. Before most observers in tennis made the connection, Lendl had already seen strong parallels between his career and Murray's. Lendl didn't agree with Murray's analysis that he was a loser. Lendl saw great potential in Murray. He wouldn't have wanted to coach Murray if he hadn't thought that the Scot had the talent to go on to win grand slams, and if he didn't contend that he could possibly help him to accomplish that goal. Lendl liked Murray's technique and the way he moved around the court. With a few changes – to his mental approach, his body language and his tactics – Lendl thought Murray could achieve his ambitions. With that victory at the 1984 French Open, Lendl had seen for himself how an early run of defeats in major finals didn't mean that a player would for ever be precluded from becoming a grand slam champion; Lendl had made that breakthrough, and now Murray, with Lendl's help, would attempt to do the same.

Failure wasn't the only thing that Lendl and Murray had in common; both had been coached by their mothers, both had become known for their work ethic and relentless quest for self-improvement, both had felt unloved and unappreciated by the public and both would be defined by their success or failure on the lawns of the All England Club. But nothing drew them together like failure, the comparisons so strong that Lendl spoke of 'Groundhog Day'. 'Their paths are eerily similar, in the way their careers have panned out, and I think that's why Ivan was attracted so much to Andy,' said Darren Cahill, the Australian coach who would help to broker the deal.

But it's not entirely accurate to say that Murray and Lendl would bond over failure. What they would bond over was a response to failure. As we shall see, it wasn't until nine months after Lendl's initial expression of interest that it was agreed he would coach Murray (they needed a few lunches to establish whether they wanted to work together or not). But there's no doubt that it wouldn't have been long after Lendl's springtime intervention in 2011 that Murray would have developed a fascination for Lendl's story, with the Czech-born player creating his own boxed set of disappointments and setbacks, before going on to win so many slams. Murray didn't want a 'loser' to coach him; he wanted someone who had shed his 'loser' status. Lendl, after that early sequence of defeats, went on to become one of the most successful players in history, winning more majors than McEnroe and as many as Connors. No one now would ever call Lendl – who ended up with eight victories and eleven defeats from his nineteen grand slam finals – a 'loser', and Murray was intrigued to know how he had made that transformation.

Some observers, Wojtek Fibak included, would suggest that the similarities between Murray and Lendl have been overstated. Fibak's point is that, before Lendl won his first grand slam, he had been a much more successful and dominant

figure than Murray had been when he had still been looking to join the true elite of men's tennis. 'People forget,'
Fibak told me, 'that before Ivan had won his first grand slam,
he had already won the [Masters] a couple of times, and he
had held the world number one ranking, and, by winning so
many matches and so much prize money, he was dominating
the game apart from at the grand slams. He had clearly been
the best player in the world. Murray, when he started working with Ivan, was clearly the fourth best player in the world.'
While Fibak is undoubtedly right that Murray wasn't close to
dominating his era, and that Lendl had achieved a great deal
before winning a first major, when are you ever going to find
two players who have exactly the same narrative arcs? You
wouldn't find another great from the past whose back story
and experience was so similar to Murray's. 'I think it's amazing how similar Andy's career is to Lendl's,' Tim Henman
told me.

For most tennis players the hardest major to win tends to
be the first. There's the common belief that a breakthrough
major will validate your life choices. That's the hope anyway,
that, after winning that first slam, you will feel much freer on
and off the court. That was certainly the dream that Murray
was chasing (though life isn't always so simple after winning a
first major, as Lendl knew only too well).

Lendl has always agreed with the analysis that Paris in 1984
was devastating to McEnroe, his reputation and his career –
had McEnroe won that French Open, Lendl suggested, he
would have finished his career with between ten and twelve
grand slam titles, rather than seven, and now people would
be talking about him, along with Federer and Rod Laver, as
possibly the greatest of all time. Had McEnroe won at Roland

Garros, he would have been just an Australian Open away from the full set of slam titles. Lendl called it 'the most important match, in a negative way, of McEnroe's career'. But Lendl simply doesn't share most people's view that the result in Paris had been of enormous importance for his future and the rest of his tennis life. 'People always say it was the most important match of my career and I disagree – I think I would have won my share afterwards anyhow,' he has said. But consider how, after Paris, Lendl would go on to lose the next two slam finals he appeared in – at the 1984 US Open and the 1985 French Open – and you realise that he could very easily have been beaten in his first seven slam finals. What does a run of seven grand slam final defeats do to a man? The answer is nothing pretty. Who can be sure that Lendl would have fully recovered from a run of seven losses in slam finals, and would have gone on to win as many as eight majors? That unidentified voice in McEnroe's head didn't just help win Lendl a first grand slam title; it would also, years later, send the Eastern European into Andy Murray's orbit.

CHAPTER SIX

MONK-SOLDIER AND NEW-AGE WARRIOR

Little of what Andy Murray and the rest of today's bionic, neurotic tennis players do to prime themselves for competition should be regarded as being innovative. Essentially, they're only doing what Ivan Lendl did first when he employed a licensed funeral director whose background was in investment banking, a shrink with a love of ballet, plus the Prophet of Pasta, and an old-school Australian with a weakness for Filipino faith healers.

The modern tennis entourage was Lendl's invention. He also pioneered the idea of always looking for improvement, of putting your body and mind through a kind of endless Maoist revolution. It was Lendl, more than anyone else, who advanced the idea of having a posse of experts looking after your every need, and the approach of examining every aspect and detail of your game, body and lifestyle to maximise your ability to win grand slam titles. Officially, Year Zero for tennis's modern and professional era was 1968, when the sport went 'open' and left the shamateurism period behind, but the truth is that it was never truly modern or professional until Lendl resolved in the mid-1980s to chase perfection. Until Lendl's intervention, tennis players were generally still carrying on as if this was an amateur pursuit, recovering from a five-setter with a pint at the bar. Wojtek Fibak's sad-looking country boy would transform himself and, in the process, the entire tennis industry. In the words of Boris Becker, 'Ivan was the first true tennis professional – he ate tennis, he drank tennis, he slept tennis.

'Ivan was truly dedicated. He was the first player to travel with a proper entourage, the first to follow a proper diet, as well as the first to have his own racket stringer and his own conditioning trainer. He was very clear with his scheduling, looking carefully at when he should play and when he should train, and it was because of that that he stayed at world number one for so long. So all those who wanted to reach the top of the rankings looked at him and said, "That's how I need to train, that's how I need to live, if I want to become the best possible tennis player". The players today, the way they train, and the entourages they have, that's because of Lendl'. This is much more complimentary than some of the language Becker used about Lendl in the 1980s, when he was calling him 'grim' and a 'fanatic'.

There's only one player in modern tennis history who has demonstrated a greater desire for self-improvement than Lendl, and that is the man he would come to coach. Lendl was a disruptor. During the 1980s, he changed almost everything about himself – his mind, his diet, his body, the way he projected himself to the world and the country he lived

in – in the pursuit of greatness, all in order to better himself. This scientific approach to tennis was entirely in keeping
with someone with such a sharp and analytical brain, who as a
schoolboy had excelled at maths, physics and logic. And who,
as an adult, claimed to be able to solve Rubik's Cube in two
minutes, who buffed up before Scrabble matches by scanning
the dictionary, and who sat down in his library to read whole
chunks of the *Encyclopedia Britannica* as if it were a novel, still
marvelling at how he had bought this knowledge off a man
who had come knocking on his door.

There is an old Czech saying that Lendl sometimes quoted:
'More sweat on the practice field, less blood on the battlefield.'
But it had taken a while for Lendl to get around to embracing
science and hard graft. His triumph at Roland Garros in 1984,
the occasion that supposedly announced to the world that he
had finally broken through, turned out to be the victory that
led him to consider his own limitations. For a long time after
that win in Paris he felt so mentally and physically empty that
he was often unable to train for more than a quarter of an
hour. Lendl's body was flagging, useless, and he veered from
despondency, saying on the practice court, 'okay, flies, eat
me', to feeling terrified. After winning that elusive first slam
in his mid-twenties – at a stage in his career when he should
have been in his physical prime – was his career already over?
Would he be remembered for one fluky victory over John
McEnroe? He was worried he had glandular fever, or some
other illness that could have potentially ended his career. 'I
just couldn't recover from the effort. I was working hard and
getting tired and going nowhere,' Lendl once said. 'I really
thought my tennis days were numbered.' It was then that he
started to examine everything in his life, on and off the court.

This didn't look much like a power-baseline game. This was Lendl unplugged, and it was a pathetic sight. At that moment, he wasn't driven by megalomania, and the desire to push on from years of being ranked second or third and to establish himself as the world number one; he was motivated by wanting to dodge the horror of premature retirement.

What the victory in Paris, and its aftermath, had taught Lendl was that he was yet to reach his physical peak, or even come close to it, and that if he was going to make the best of himself he would have to embrace the new, the bold and the unknown. He had to experiment, to become an innovator and a risk taker. But perhaps the biggest risk would have been doing nothing new, sticking with the old routines and hoping for change, which was perhaps the approach that many others would have taken.

Like Lendl, Murray had also undergone a physical transformation – as a young player new on the scene, he was repeatedly accused of being weak and unfit, especially after he suffered from cramp during his first senior Wimbledon in 2005. By applying himself in the Bikram yoga studio, and on the track and in the gym, including at his punishing off-season Miami boot camps, he turned himself into one of the fittest athletes on the circuit. That great change happened long before Lendl came into Murray's life. So Murray wouldn't need Lendl to tell him to get in shape. But it would help their player–coach relationship that both of them had come to realise that you can't possibly play your best tennis without first being in prime physical condition. And, throughout his time with Lendl, Murray would continue to push himself.

You could argue that these changes to Lendl's body and mind were small modifications, mere tweaks, when set against the biggest transformation of all, when he had swapped his old life for a new one, making that giant and audacious leap from Czechoslovakia to Connecticut. As the months and years passed, and as Lendl's methods proved successful, many of Lendl's contemporaries, though they didn't like the guy, would end up respecting him for the way he had reinvented himself through a combination of new, fresh thinking and old-fashioned hard work.

Almost inevitably, McEnroe's take on Lendl's reinvention was more complicated than that. At once, it sounded as though he was both impressed and disturbed by the new version of Lendl who stood before him – still not smiling – on the other side of the net. If he hadn't appreciated it earlier, their meeting in the final of the 1985 US Open would confirm to McEnroe that he was no longer dealing with the old Lendl. McEnroe recognised that Lendl had shown himself to be the Stakhanovite of the locker-room, as it could have been tempting, as an elite player, to have felt satisfied, and to have relaxed and hung on to the old and the familiar. But that wasn't McEnroe's only thought on the matter.

Inevitably, McEnroe's view of Lendl was informed by the fact they had so little in common. As Pete Sampras put it: 'It was power against grace, and power won.' Of all the disparaging remarks that McEnroe made about his adversary (and there were many) the most revealing was his boast that he had more talent in his little finger than Lendl had in his entire body. Behind that remark was McEnroe's contention that tennis matches should essentially be decided on talent, and that Lendl, with all this sweat and science, was going against the spirit of sport. 'Where McEnroe believed in his God-given talent, which is not so different from an aristocratic belief in inheritance, Lendl the self-made American, put his faith in a Puritan's work ethic and self-improvement,' the American journalist Stephen Tignor observed in his book *High Strung*.

While McEnroe craved a regular life, saying that 'an urge for normalcy, together with getting married and having kids, helped save me from being a burned-out, completely bitter cynic by thirty', Lendl sought self-improvement, including with a radical new diet, and a radical new way of thinking on the court. He was getting off on hard work, on surviving the pain and punishment – whether inflicted on himself in training, or by others on the match court – and then enjoying the reward of greater physical capabilities and results. As McEnroe wrote in a column for the *Sun* during the 1988 Wimbledon Championships, he regarded Lendl, with all that self-denial and discipline, as an 'extremist': 'I realise I have to toughen up more in terms of physical conditioning, but I am not going to live the life of a monk like Lendl. He's an extremist. He sacrificed himself totally and in his case he has got results. But I don't think that needs to be the general rule. His way has made him stronger, and good luck to him, but my feeling is that somewhere down the road Lendl is going to pay for that as a person, because of what he has missed out on.' Lendl imagined that his way – constantly seeking perfection – could work for everyone. But, as others, including his agent Jerry Solomon, recognised, that wasn't the case – to transform totally your life as Lendl did, you had to have a certain type of obsessive personality. There weren't many players willing to go quite as far as Lendl, and to do everything in their lives to become the best possible players. Again, there are parallels here with Murray, someone who has been accused in the past of being a tennis obsessive.

McEnroe's reservations about his rival's approach – he once declared he detested everything that Lendl stood for – resonated with a public who generally preferred tennis matches to be decided by art rather than science. Was Lendl threatening to take all the joy out of tennis? Who wanted to watch tennis by algorithm? Without wanting to put an entire generation of tennis fans on the couch, were they scared of progress? Or perhaps it wasn't progress they had a problem with, but that it was Lendl, that old commie bogeyman, who was the one innovating?

Whatever the truth of that, one thing was plain; after the great Lendl revamp, which brought the Czech-born player a further seven grand slam titles, taking his collection to eight, McEnroe would never win another major, his last victory coming at the 1984 US Open when he beat Lendl in the final. How much was McEnroe's retreat from tennis, his sabbatical in the mid-1980s, connected to this new, fresh, energised and relentless Lendl? Victory, you must conclude, was Lendl's.

What could Lendl's detractors do but call him a tennis machine and hope that it would break down? Pitied as a 'monk-soldier of tennis, obsessed and sad' by Frenchman Yannick Noah, Lendl never did understand this notion that he was somehow committing a crime against tennis by dedicating himself to his game. Lendl recognised he wasn't as talented as McEnroe, just as Murray knew that he didn't have Federer's gifts. Though Lendl thought of himself as being more talented than 'the average person in the street', he didn't consider himself a natural. Lendl wasn't used to anything coming easily to him; he hadn't won his first grand slam easily, and he wasn't going to improve without putting some effort in. Just like his mother before him, Lendl was trusting that hard labour would allow him to bear down on the competition. That, and a level of dedication and organisation that meant even his naps were scheduled. As *New York* magazine put it in the 1980s: 'Lendl has turned his life into an ongoing scientific experiment, using himself as a guinea pig.' Think of Lendl, as McEnroe does now, as an early prototype for Murray's generation.

Exposed to cheeseburgers, sirloin steaks and Coca-Cola, Ivan Lendl was a fan of junk food during his early years in the States. After fleeing Czechoslovakia, with all the limitations and restrictions imposed by the state and by his parents, after all those years of cold vegetables, he had arrived in the Land of the Free and wanted to eat as he pleased. As a newly free man, Lendl would drink too many cans of Coke and eat too much red meat and too many puddings, while avoiding fruit and vegetables (though he certainly isn't alone in modern tennis history for having had a bad diet during the early years of his career – during one junior French Open, Andy Murray lived off baguettes and chocolate spread).

A typical day for Lendl would be five or six scrambled eggs for breakfast, a couple of McDonald's burgers for lunch and then steak in the evening. This disregard for what his mother and father had been telling him about the importance of eating your greens, had started to hurt Lendl's efforts on court: 'My parents were always telling me not to eat McDonald's, not to drink Coke and all that, and like any other youngster, I was saying, "What do you know? I know much more than you do". It turned out that basically they were right, and I learned the hard way. But I was lucky enough to learn the hard way without any damage.' In his teens and early twenties, Lendl had been guzzling and labouring away under the misguided belief that he was one of those lucky sorts who didn't have to watch what he ate. Lendl's exhaustion in the weeks after winning the 1984 French Open demonstrated how his diet had been clogging up his tennis. While with his metabolism there was no danger of developing a paunch that would then have to be lugged around the baseline as reminder of every bad choice he had ever made, and every bad meal he had ever eaten, he was lacking in speed, power and stamina.

Lendl's victory at Roland Garros precipitated the physical, psychological and existential crisis that followed the 1984 French Open, and Lendl had his agent contact the nutritionist Dr Robert Haas, who had been transforming Martina Navratilova's muscles and her moods, including finding a way to counter the effects of the parasitic disease toxoplasmosis from which she was suffering. Like Lendl, Navratilova was a Czech émigré who had binged on arrival in America. To get The Great Wide Hope back in shape, Haas had put Navratilova on his trademark low-fat, low-protein, high-carbohydrate diet – he didn't have much love for convention, for what was traditionally known as a balanced diet, or for red meat, eggs, salts and fats. It was said that, on the Haas diet, the only red meat Navratilova was eating was her opponents. What's more, Haas claimed, he was protecting her from premature ageing – do as he said, and you wouldn't only achieve tennis greatness, but also eternal youth. Haas was very interested in his clients' digestive processes; one journalist found himself in a hotel suite when Haas was serving Navratilova some chocolate brownies he had just baked, 'which led into a discussion of "transit time", the interval between eating and evacuating – it seemed to be an important element of Martina's training at the time'. Lendl was intrigued by how the Haas diet had changed Navratilova's body. 'I did learn from Martina,' Lendl once said. 'I saw what it did for her and I said: "Why shouldn't I try that?"'

With Lendl, Haas was perfectly clear. Lendl had already won a slam and he had held the world number one ranking, but his diet had been 'throwing up a brick wall in the way of performance'. Any weekend warrior in the 1980s could have broadly used the Haas methods to get into shape – all you had to do was pop into your local bookshop and buy a copy of his bestselling manual, *Eat to Win* – but Lendl's diet wasn't off the shelf. Before Haas did anything, he had to know what he was dealing with. Regular testing had always been key to his approach. Once a month, a computer would produce what became known as 'The Smartina Report' – after supposedly measuring Navratilova's blood in thirty-nine different ways, as well as examining her muscles and her reflexes, Haas would present her with a printout that gave her instructions on what to eat and drink for the next four weeks. Haas would prepare shakes and foil-wrapped vitamin packs. Haas and his computer did the same for Lendl, and the tests on Lendl's body would show – and this was quite shocking – that he was in the high-risk range for cholesterol levels for a normal male, and off the scale for an athlete in his twenties.

So Haas put together a customised diet for Lendl, based on what the computer was telling him, which would make him lighter, faster and stronger – he would have the muscle-to-fat ratio, and the cholesterol levels, that you would expect from someone with ambitions of tennis greatness. Essentially, there were three food groups for Lendl to think about now; primary foods were complex carbohydrates such as pasta and rice, while secondary foods, such as low-fat cottage cheese, met his need for protein, and the third group was all the rest on his plate, such as the steamed vegetables. And – there could be no clearer indication of how badly he wanted to win slams – he ate those vegetables without having to be scared into doing so, as his mother once had. Some of what Lendl needed for his body couldn't be pulled off supermarket shelves or ordered from restaurant menus; he would become very famil-iar with food concentrates and meal replacers, which were either blender drinks or powders to be mixed with water. And while Lendl could carry on putting dressing on his salad and eating chocolate fudge cake, they would have to be a special no-oil dressing and a cake made from Haas's own secret rec-ipe. Lendl didn't just have to change what he was eating; he also had to change *how* he was eating; he was under instruc-tions from Haas to 'chew every mouthful of food until it is liquefied into saliva'.

Lendl started a revolution at his breakfast table: he was the first leading player on the men's tour to rethink his approach to food. For all the recent interest in gluten-free Novak Djokovic's eating habits – such as how the Serb is partial to a cup of liquorice tea, and the first thing he does on waking is to eat two spoonfuls of manuka honey from New Zealand – they don't seem as outlandish as Lendl's appeared to be in the 1980s. For instance, Haas had Lendl drinking lots of water. Water, Haas told his clients, was the drink of champi-ons. Haas told Lendl that, like so many other tennis players, he wasn't drinking enough. Don't be a slave to the fashion for energy drinks, Haas was saying. Far better to drink what comes out of the tap, as dehydration, or what Haas called a 'water deficit', could cost you matches. And you had to be careful that you weren't derailed by a bottle of San Pellegrino.

During tournaments, Lendl would only drink still water, not going near the carbonated stuff, as Haas had told him that still water flushed through his system much more quickly.

Pure quackery, Haas's critics in the sport were saying. Okay, this Prophet of Pasta could help the likes of Cher maintain her place in the body beautiful, but that was show business and this was tennis. When John McEnroe was asked whether he, too, had been looking carefully at what he ate, he replied, 'No, but I am on the Haagen-Dazs diet', a wisecrack of which he was enormously proud. Others who had seen Haas at work could be dismissive, such as the member of Navratilova's entourage who referred to Haas as 'that nitwit nutritionist'. On the Haas diet, Lendl was soon shedding weight – he would eventually lose fifteen pounds or more – but some contended that he didn't look particularly healthy. He was gaunt and drawn, people said, forgetting that, even during Lendl's hamburger days, his face had never been podgy.

Even after all the help he had received from Wojtek Fibak and then Haas, Lendl was never going to be the greatest athlete or the smoothest mover on the tennis tour; he was never going to appear to glide. 'If you closed your eyes during a match between McEnroe and Lendl, it was easy to tell which man occupied either side of the court,' Peter Bodo observed in *The Courts of Babylon*. 'McEnroe's footfalls were as silent as those of a cat, while Lendl made an astonishing amount of noise – as if he were moving furniture complete with all the requisite thudding and scraping.' For all that, Lendl felt good on the Haas diet – he was now reaching balls he previously couldn't have imagined connecting with, and he was finding he had time to play the stroke he wanted to, rather than rushing, slashing and swiping at some ugly, improvised retrieval shot. No more lunging. This was great news: Lendl had figured out he needed to be quicker around the court if he was going to deal with McEnroe.

Maybe it didn't matter so much whether Haas had transformed Lendl's body or not, only that Lendl believed the Prophet had. 'Let's face it,' Haas once said, 'athletes are the most neurotic people on the planet. If they think something works, it works. Even if it doesn't work and it helps them psychologically, that's no less important.' There were limits, though, to what Lendl would believe – while he had borrowed Haas from Navratilova, he didn't follow her example of using a shamanic lady who said she could take you back to the womb through meditative massage.

Of course, you can't just carbo-load your way to success at the grand slams; a new diet wouldn't have counted for much if he didn't also grind and sweat. It was Haas, for instance, who had Lendl regularly cycling around Connecticut, packing muscle on his legs. Thanks to Haas, too, Lendl also had much more energy for life – while before he had been sleeping for up to fourteen hours a day, under the new regime he found that eight hours was sufficient. Previously, he had been waking up in the morning and telling himself, 'I'm going to sleep for another half an hour', but now he could attack the morning (though he was also – on Haas's advice – having twenty-minute power naps in the afternoon). For the first time in years, perhaps even for the first time since joining the tour, Lendl felt strong, and he felt alive.

No one was more closely associated with the Dark Ages of Ivan Lendl, with that time before he embraced sports science and psychology, than Wojtek Fibak. Lendl's reinvention would weaken his working relationship with Fibak. One day after practice in 1985, player and coach were talking about Lendl's desire to be a gym bunny, and, according to one account, Fibak turned to Lendl and said: 'I'm not a great believer in all this. I'm more of a natural person on the court and off, and it's probably better for me, too, if we split. I can move on to do things I want to do.' Ending their partnership was no small act. Most player–coach relationships wouldn't have disintegrated so quickly after a first grand slam title. But Lendl was in the process of looking at everything in his tennis life.

They had been working together since the late 1970s, in which time Lendl had gone from sad-looking country boy from Czechoslovakia to US-based grand slam champion, thanks to a power-baseline game that would radically change the sport. For a while, Lendl had referred to Fibak as his best friend; this ran deeper than forehands and backhands. Fibak told me it had been his idea to end his association with Lendl: 'I left him. It wasn't that he asked me to leave – I left him because I didn't want to travel any more.' And yet it would seem that there was a little more to this than any reluctance on Fibak's part to continue walking the tennis road; the indications are that he didn't share Lendl's enthusiasm for this new focus on diet and fitness. Gone were the times when Lendl would blindly say yes to everything Fibak said to him, and in that distressing period that followed the 1984 French Open – has a new grand slam champion ever had an unhappier breakthrough? – Lendl hadn't been sure he had liked what his mentor had been telling him. Fibak's solution for Lendl's fatigue was that he should train through the pain – that he would have to put in more hours on the practice court if he was to have some zest and zip about him.

And if Lendl felt tired, he could always walk off the court. Lendl thought differently – his view, and this would become accepted practice in men's tennis, was that he needed to put more time and effort into off-court conditioning work and less into bashing basket after basket of balls. There's a possibility that this wasn't just about steamed vegetables and aerobic fitness, and that what was really happening here was that the balance in the relationship had been altered significantly. At first, Lendl hadn't been far off being Fibak's tennis pet, a German shepherd in shorts who would react to commands. Fetch. Hit. Run. Jump. Sit. With time, it became less of a master–pet relationship and more of a partnership – Fibak's unofficial title would have been downgraded from mentor to coach – though Lendl, desperate to win a grand slam, still had enormous reverence for the man who had done so much to create him. Then he had his triumph at Roland Garros. To put this crudely, every match that Lendl won added to his power, and erased a little of Fibak's.

At first, Fibak has said, Lendl hadn't been a hard worker, and had to be taught how to apply himself. Now the Fibak–Lendl relationship had shifted – Lendl wasn't sure that Fibak could help him achieve greatness. Lendl once observed Fibak had missed out on greatness by not being in good enough shape, and he didn't want to have the same physical limitations. With different philosophical approaches to the sport, Lendl came to the conclusion he would be better off without Fibak. 'Fibak felt that I should work more on the court. I was twenty-four, and I thought I needed to work more off the court, running and bicycling and lifting weights. Fibak himself was a good player, but he could have been tremendous. He was just physically too weak. He just got tired. He just didn't have the force behind him, or in him, to go and work until it hurts,' Lendl told *New York* magazine in the 1980s. 'He couldn't help me to take the next step because he had a different philosophy than I did – and because he hadn't been there himself.'

When I spoke to him, Fibak had had the best part of thirty years to think about his split from Lendl, and he told me that he regretted his association with Lendl had ended when it did – it was, he said, 'a big mistake', by which the Pole appeared to mean it was a mistake for himself, as he wasn't involved with any of Lendl's future success. Those remarks were a big change from the glib, slightly unkind comments Fibak was quoted as making in the 1980s: 'It had to happen once he learned everything from me. In the end we didn't have that much in common. I'm a seeker. Ivan would be happy with his gates locked, his Adidas shirts and his dogs.' It's right that they could have achieved more together. Under Fibak's guidance, Lendl won one slam; he would go on to win a further seven, all with Tony Roche, an Australian who as a player had been celebrated for being one of the fittest players on the scene.

A gentleman of the courts from Wagga Wagga, a town in New South Wales, Roche was also someone who knew where to go for miracle cures in the Philippines. Still, this experience and knowledge of faith healers in downtown Baguio City, of knowing where to find men who could make openings in your skin just by passing their hands over your shoulder, wasn't why Lendl had been so attracted to working with 'Coach Roche'.

There were better reasons than that for wanting to partner up with Roche, not least that he was left-handed and at the time Lendl's greatest rival was the southpaw John McEnroe. Employ Roche, Lendl thought, and I'll learn to get inside the head of a lefty (McEnroe wasn't the only American lefty that Lendl had to contend with; there was Jimmy Connors, too, but it was McEnroe about whom Lendl was truly concerned). 'Hiring Tony meant I faced a lot of left-handed serves in practice. So he wasn't serving as hard as the guys I was playing, but he could always step two feet into the court, and the spin was there,' Lendl has recalled. 'I also got a lot of feedback from him about what left-handers liked to do and what they don't like being done to them. His brain was more valuable than anything else.'

Another factor was Roche's discreet and low-key nature; here was a modest individual, who had no desire to thrust himself centre stage. Lendl wasn't looking for another Fibak, a coach to micro-manage every aspect of his life. He was now too grown up, too worldly, to be in hock to another coach. From the off, Lendl would be running this arrangement and that suited Roche just fine – this became a friendship as well as a professional relationship so he wasn't just merely a member of staff, but it appeared as though this didn't have the intensity of the Fibak collaboration. In all their time together, Lendl and Roche never had a serious falling-out. All those who have worked with Roche during his post-Lendl coaching career – in Pat Rafter, Roger Federer and Lleyton Hewitt, he has had other clients who have held the world number one ranking – have spoken of his personable nature. This was someone who liked to do business on a handshake, who didn't think it was necessary to formalise arrangements with a lawyer and a contract.

It's also true that Lendl wanted Roche to improve his volleys for the Wimbledon grass and that he regarded the Australian as being tactically astute, but, above all, what Lendl liked about Roche was that he had himself competed at the highest level.

What Lendl bought when he hired Roche was the experience of a coach who knew what it took to win a grand slam singles title; while Fibak had been a decent player, he had never gone beyond the quarter-finals at any of the majors. And Murray was buying the same commodity when he employed Lendl: the experience of being a grand slam champion. For all the qualities of Murray's previous coaches, Miles Maclagan, Brad Gilbert, Mark Petchey and the rest didn't have a grand slam singles title between them. In the 1980s and early 1990s, Roche had the look of a wise man. In recent years, when the television cameras zoomed in on Roche during one of Hewitt's appearances, you couldn't help but consider that there was no other face in tennis that conveyed such wisdom – it wasn't just that his skin looked as though it had been toasted by the sun and the wind, but that his features had almost been cross-hatched with every match he has ever played or watched.

If not one of the tennis immortals, Roche won one singles grand slam title, at the 1966 French Open, and thirteen doubles majors. Roche was extremely fortunate to have won that sole singles slam in Paris; after injuring an ankle before the final, it had appeared as though his chances of victory were almost non-existent, but then his opponent, a very sporting Hungarian called István Gulyás, agreed to delay the match by twenty-four hours.

It was in 1985, while Lendl was still a one-slam wonder, that Roche and Lendl began a new tennis life together. This new Lendl wouldn't be manipulated by anyone. So Roche kept his base in Australia, instead of relocating to America's East Coast, and, rather than tagging along to every stop on the tennis calendar he tended to build his schedule around the slams. Roche sometimes worked Lendl so hard, having him

hit ball after ball without pause or reflection, that Lendl forgot what his name was. Sometimes, when they were doing
lob-and-volley drills, Lendl's legs would become so heavy that
he could only jump two inches off the court; just a few minutes
later, he wouldn't even get off the ground. Roche knew that
the way to get Lendl working until he dropped was to have
money, as well as pride, riding on any drills they did on the ·
practice court. Crucially, Roche supported Lendl's belief that
he should be working off the court to build up his fitness, but
that still left space in the schedule for these occasional oblivion
sessions. Some of this was just old-fashioned grunt work, done
in the knowledge that the fitter Lendl became, the more mon-
strous his power game would be. There were even indications
that Lendl could outrun machines: once, after completing a
seven-level fitness test on a treadmill, he was said to have sent
a message to the manufacturers saying they ought to rebuild
the machines with greater degrees of difficulty.

There was also Lendl's rhythm to consider – the hours
he spent on the practice court weren't simply about putting
the hard-, clay- and grass-court miles into his legs, but also
about ensuring that he didn't lose his timing and footwork.
While others could have long breaks without touching a
racket, Lendl was concerned that if he didn't keep practising
he would lose much of his muscle memory. He didn't want
to take the risk that his body would forget how to hit a topspin forehand; he didn't want his feet to forget how to move
around the court. Lendl's mother had been the same: 'If she
didn't play, she couldn't hit the ball properly. Neither can I,'
Lendl once told *New York* magazine. 'If I don't play for two
weeks, I can't hit a topspin. I just lose the timing, I can't move
on court; I lose everything.' So, to avoid the possibility of feet

and racket-arm amnesia, throughout his years on the tour he never once took a two-week holiday. 'I can't take a long break,' Lendl said while he was still on the circuit. 'I would love to, but I can't.' Surely, Roche thought to himself, there wasn't anyone in tennis who was working harder than Lendl? Or who cared more deeply about the number one ranking?

But their time together wasn't without a little mystery and voodoo. One of the most intriguing episodes of Lendl's time concerned Roche introducing his employer to the idea of using a Filipino faith or miracle healer. This is where Lendl's story really takes a lurch into the bizarre.

Not long after Lendl had lost to Mats Wilander in the final of the 1988 US Open he was disturbed to hear a specialist's opinion that his collarbone problem could keep him off the tour for up to twelve months. Anything that prevented Lendl having to miss a whole year of tennis was worth a try, and Roche suggested a faith healer he had known in the Philippines. The healer supposedly operated on Lendl without even picking up a scalpel. Instead, the faith healer's act of passing his hand over Lendl's shoulder opened up his skin, allowing him to reach in and clear up the debris. To close up the opening, the healer then passed his hand over the skin again, leaving only a red scar on the shoulder, and, rather than taking a fee, he suggested Lendl make a donation to the local church. When Lendl returned to the United States for a consultation, the American doctor didn't believe what he was hearing; the specialist was flummoxed, however, when an examination showed the shoulder had been 'cured'. Lendl further claimed that the healer's shoulder-dipping hand has been caught on film: 'Other people have made videos of this guy performing an operation – they can slow down the tape and actually see the guy's hand in there, up to the wrist. I can't explain it. But it worked. At least it did for me.' There's an irony here that the man who brought sports science to men's tennis didn't just use, say, an acupuncturist, but a faith healer who said he could put his hand inside your body. Still, given Lendl's sense of humour, it's not beyond the realms of possibility that the story is a joke.

This was a new Ivan Lendl and the greatest change was to his mental maturity. If Lendl's physical transformation possibly wasn't quite as great as he supposed it to be, there was no doubt in his mind that he had elevated himself above the rest. It appeared as though he came to need that feeling of having done everything in his power to prepare himself. And, it would seem, he also needed others to know how well prepared he was. It wasn't enough just to impress himself with his new, souped-up physical abilities; others had to marvel, too.

Occasionally, others players were invited into Lendl's world to train with him. Those guests, who tended to be younger than him, and those he didn't regard as immediate threats, among them Pete Sampras and Mark Philippoussis, would often come away totally spent, with burning legs and lungs. Sometimes Sampras came to hate Lendl for making him work to the point of exhaustion, but he felt as though it was an education: 'You know what the name Lendl means to me? Dedication, hard work, overcoming everybody, although he maybe didn't have the tennis talent of a lot of guys. I admire him immensely.' Others, though, would be discouraged by Lendl's endless regime of runs, bike rides through the Connecticut snow and practice sessions. 'If that's what it takes to become the world number one,' those players would think

left: Lendl learned to play tennis at his local club in Ostrava. © *ullsteinbild / TopFoto*

above: Even as a boy and as a teenager, Lendl was known for the ferocity of his forehand. © *Tennis Europe*

below: Lendl was a Wimbledon champion, but only as a junior – he won the boys' singles title in 1978. © *Michael Cole*

above: Lendl was part of the Czechoslovakian team which won the Davis Cup in 1980 – they were the first Eastern Bloc country to be champions. © *CTK/Alamy*

below: For years, Lendl has kept and trained German Shepherds at his Connecticut home. © *Getty Images*

right: After a long courtship, Lendl married Samantha Frankel in 1989. © *AP/TopFoto*

below: Lendl's parents, Olga and Jiri, always liked to give their son a critique after his matches.
© *CTK/Alamy*

above: To win his first grand slam title, Lendl came from two sets down to beat John McEnroe in the final of the 1984 French Open.

© *Sipa Press / REX*

right: Lendl had been beaten in his first four grand slam finals, making his first success, at Roland Garros, all the sweeter.

© *Getty Images*

above: A rare moment of levity during a Lendl-Jimmy Connors match at Wimbledon.
© *Leo Mason sports photos/Alamy*

below: Lendl's first Wimbledon final, in the summer of 1986, brought defeat by Boris Becker.
© *Colorsport/REX*

On his fourth appearance in
a US Open final – he had finished
as the runner-up the past three
summers – he won his first title
at Flushing Meadows, beating
John McEnroe in 1985.

© NY Daily News via Getty Images

Sports Illustrated

SEPTEMBER 15, 1986 $2.25

THE CHAMPION THAT NOBODY CARES ABOUT

Ivan Lendl Wins The Open

Never a darling of the American tennis public, Lendl took great offence at the *Sports Illustrated* cover story which followed his victory at the 1986 US Open. © *Sports Illustrated/Getty Images*

For the second and last occasion, Lendl reached a Wimbledon final – this time, in 1987, he was the runner-up to Pat Cash.

© *Leo Mason sports photos/Alamy*

left: Lendl did have some success at a grass-court tournament in London – he lifted the trophy at Queen's Club in 1988 and 1989.
© *Michael Cole*

left: The most hostile opponent of Lendl's career was John McEnroe.
© *NY Daily News via Getty Images*

To combat the heat, and
perhaps to show he was
willing to suffer in extreme
conditions, Lendl would wear
a Legionnaire's cap when
playing the Australian Open.
© Bongarts/Getty Images

Andy Murray's mother, Judy, with Lendl.
© David Lobel/Icon SMI/Corbis

above: Now they are playing senior tennis, Lendl and McEnroe can be a little friendlier towards each other. © *Alamy Celebrity / Alamy*

below: At the 2012 US Open, Andy Murray became the first British man to win a grand slam singles title for 76 years. © *epa european pressphoto agency b.v. / Alamy*

Andy Murray was delighted after hitting his coach with a forehand during a charity exhibition doubles match at Queen's Club just before the 2013 Wimbledon Championships. © *Getty Images*

above: For the first time, Lendl put on a tuxedo and went to Wimbledon's Champions' Dinner.
© *Getty Images*

below: Andy Murray was the first British man to win Wimbledon since Fred Perry in 1936.
© *Getty Images*

The first person Andy Murray embraced after winning Wimbledon was his coach. © *REX*

to themselves, 'then I don't think I would want to be number one.' That would have fed Lendl's belief that he could
cope with the suffering, with the pain that came during training and playing five-setters at the slams, better than others.
Sometimes, just a one-off practice session with Lendl could
traumatise others on the tour. He wouldn't have minded that.
'They usually don't play too well for weeks after practising
with me,' he once said. 'In fact, I've destroyed a few careers
that way.' Years later, while touring as a coach, Lendl wouldn't
have been urging Andy Murray to terrorise others, knowing
that the Scot didn't have the same hostile relationship with
his rivals that he had once had with his contemporaries. But
he would have expected Murray to display a certain tough-
ness and resilience, while he would have been delighted if
Murray ever fired a forehand at an opponent's head.

No longer did anyone consider Lendl to be a flake. The
locker-room recognised that he had changed mentally as well
as physically. 'Ivan was a choker – the players felt that as much
as the press did – and I think we were all surprised when he
overcame the tendency to get tight in big matches,' Wilander
told me. 'It had to be the physical training producing a psychological effect, because Ivan did things differently from the
rest of us.'

But Lendl was aware he wasn't a super-hero; knowing his
physical limits was an important part of his new approach.
Others, such as McEnroe, felt as though Lendl was destined
for tennis burnout, with the New Yorker concluding: 'Lendl's
crazy.' Lendl had been too busy stuffing his face with experience, ranking points and money to consider organising his
life any differently. With time, he came to realise that if he was
going to have sustained success at the highest level – which

meant at the slams – he would have to calm down and play a lighter schedule of tournaments away from the majors.

Lendl's increased power and energy hadn't just improved his mental outlook; it had also put a few doubts into the minds of his rivals. No longer would opponents expect Lendl to gag or fade away in a tight match. Now, if a match went long, it was much more likely that Lendl would grind his opponents into the cement or the packed clay (pressing their noses into the Centre Court turf below Wimbledon's Royal Box proved to be beyond him). 'I've spoken to some of the other guys about this, and they said they would hate to play against Lendl as they knew that by the end of the match, they would be much more tired than he was,' Michael Chang told me. 'That's not a great feeling for a tennis player to have, knowing that your opponent is fitter than you. Lendl prided himself on that, and he won a lot of matches because he was very well pre-pared physically, just very fit.'

Though Lendl wasn't the most popular man in the locker-room, the majority, but not all, of his contemporaries came to admire him. 'Connors didn't like him, and McEnroe didn't like him. It was easy not to like him. But at the same time, we also admired him, as he was working so hard,' Wilander told me. 'He earned the right to be the best player in the world. I'm sure that was the way he felt. After a while we thought, "Wow, he really has worked hard, he really is the best player in the world".'

Dr Haas, the Prophet of Pasta, wasn't the only person in Lendl's circle who had improved Lendl's mental fitness for tennis by working on his body. There was also the Florida-based psychologist, with a passion for ballet and a background in child and adolescent counselling, who, when watching

Lendl play for the first time, thought he was moving as if he had a broomstick nail-gunned to his chest. Alexis Castorri's was a bold approach – she contacted him through mutual friends, met up over bowls of beef barley soup, and made a thousand-dollar bet. And from that one memorable introduction, Castorri would go on to help two tennis players with their mental approach; in 2012, Lendl would ask the author of *Exercise Your Mind* to work with Murray.

This was early 1985, and Castorri believed that the reason Lendl had lost three successive US Open finals – twice he had lost to Jimmy Connors, in 1982 and 1983, and then in 1984 he was the runner-up to McEnroe – was because there was fear in his movements. Lendl's other problem, Castorri had concluded, was that he wasn't nearly flexible enough in his approach and his thinking so he couldn't possibly adapt to the fast-changing circumstances during matches. Castorri asked Lendl to work closely with her and to do everything she asked of him; if he did so, and he didn't win that year's US Open, she would owe him a thousand dollars.

Castorri's theory was that if she was to help Lendl's mind to become more flexible she was going to have to speak to him through his body; after all, she contended, wasn't Lendl, like all other athletes, a physical person who had spent his life listening to the needs and demands of his body? So ballet-based exercises it was for Lendl. At Castorri's suggestion, he started attending 7 a.m. aerobics classes with the women of Connecticut, sometimes finding himself 'bunched up with twenty-five ladies'. And, as Castorri told me, she has long been of the opinion that yoga can help tennis players: 'Back in the early days with my tennis clients, no one was doing any form of stretching outside of a few quick movements with their rackets. For me, it just made sense that relaxing the body and removing any tension was important for both mental and emotional preparation, so I recommended yoga, which no one was doing at the time.'

Lendl was trying something different, and behaving like a free-thinker. Was this really the behaviour of a tennis machine? While Castorri had been exposed to tennis before, having played a bit as a child, there was a risk here; unlike Dr Robert Haas, who had already been road-tested in elite tennis before he started working with Lendl, Castorri was an unknown. You can just imagine what McEnroe and Connors would have had to say if they had been privy to all the details of this arrangement, of how Lendl was entrusting his tennis life to a ballet enthusiast with some fanciful ideas about how tennis players, who thought they were putting all their energies into improving power and stroke production, and were neglecting their flexibility.

More than anything, Lendl craved greater mind control, and the ability to stay calm and collected at the moments of greatest tension and anxiety. What he needed to do, Castorri said, was to stay in the moment – to stop his mind from worrying, fretting, panicking, fast-forwarding, doing everything at double-, triple- and then quadruple-speed. Castorri shared with me the 'essential truth' that you wouldn't perform well if you were focused on outcomes: 'You need to focus on the specific task at hand. When your mind starts tracking and wanting to know how the match is going to turn out, you have stopped playing the match. You have stopped competing, and you have stopped doing everything you can to perform at your best.'

One of the steps that Lendl was instructed to take if he was to become a serial grand slam champion was to concentrate on a hairbrush. One of the mental-focus exercises that Castorri had Lendl doing required him to describe an object out loud for five minutes – it could have been one of Samantha's hairbrushes, or it could have been a cigarette lighter or a dime. It didn't matter, so long as Lendl's attention was focused solely on that object, and that, in Castorri's words, 'you're training the mind to see things that have always been there – you lose the ability to observe, because you're always thinking of three things at once'. Lendl's forehand didn't impress Castorri so much; what thrilled her was how he responded so well to this mental training. Castorri once called Lendl 'coachable to the highest degree', saying she had never worked with anyone with a greater ability to absorb information so quickly, and to then make changes in his life.

Another of Castorri's exercises for Lendl was called 'witnessing'. This involved Lendl talking about himself in the third person, and describing exactly what he was doing, down to the smallest of details. The idea, as Lendl has explained it, was to combat angst and all negative emotion by 'getting outside of my mind', by observing what he was doing. So in training he would 'witness' every act. Before competing, if Lendl felt as if he had a rainforest of butterflies in his stomach, he would talk to himself about that pre-match anxiety: 'You say, "Shit, Ivan is nervous today – but he's going to snap out of it". You describe what you are feeling, and then you let go of it. And it's over.'

Before going on court, Castorri told me, a player should fill his or her mind with the right thoughts. 'A player should have a strong focus on what they want to accomplish out there, some sense of the game plan, a feeling of commitment to keep the mind on one thing at a time in the most positive way possible, and making sure they use the time between points to motivate and inspire themselves.' So Lendl would sometimes stand in the loo before a match, closing his eyes and telling himself what his goals for the day were – for instance, he might have spoken about how he wanted to be strong, fast and self-assured on the court.

Bathrooms feature strongly in Lendl's tennis life, as, many years later at the US Open, Andy Murray would give himself the pep talk of his life behind a locked lavatory door. Before the fifth set of the 2012 US Open final against Novak Djokovic, Murray retreated to a loo by the players' entrance to the Arthur Ashe Stadium. This was the smallest of cubicles – there was barely enough room for a loo, a basin and a mirror – and in that enclosed space, he was thinking to himself: 'Why do I keep losing these finals? Do I lack something? How on earth did I squander a two-set lead?' Not wanting to return to the match in that sort of mood, Murray stood staring at himself in the mirror, imploring himself – his voice grew louder and louder – to leave everything out there on the cement: 'You are not losing this match. You are not going to let this one slip. This is your time.' No coach could have given as rousing a speech in that cubicle as Murray did. But when Murray later disclosed details of that speech, it was impossible not to hear Lendl in those words. If Murray hadn't been coached by Lendl at the time, you have to wonder whether he would have discovered that he was capable of delivering such rhetoric in a New York bathroom.

To maintain order and control in the stadium, to help him suppress his emotions, Lendl had his routines. Long before anyone was teasing Rafa Nadal for his habits and idiosyncrasies

– for picking at his underwear, for towelling himself down several times during a game and for his borderline obsessive compulsive disorder about the positioning of his water bottles, including the direction in which the labels point – Lendl had routines that both drove some of his opponents wild with frustration and resulted in little build-ups of sawdust at the back of the court. Preparing to serve wasn't just a simple matter of taking a couple of balls and stepping up to the baseline. The main purpose of taking a fistful of sawdust wasn't because it would soak up the sweat, but because it would absorb some of the tension and anxiety. It was *Tennis* magazine that listed the steps of what it called The Lendl Minuet: 'Step near the baseline, wipe the brow, rock the shoulders, tug at the sleeve, stare at and fiddle with the racket strings, dig sawdust from the pocket, sprinkle sawdust on the racket grip, place the left foot at the baseline, bounce the ball four times, adjust the grip and then, finally, toss the ball to serve it.'

But it wasn't true that Lendl would always bounce the ball four times – he only tended to do so that many times while preparing to hit a first serve; before his second he would restrict himself to three. And, when playing on grass, he tweaked his routines; seemingly concerned that too many bounces of the ball could result in the felt taking on too much moisture, and therefore flying just that little bit more slowly through the air, he would often bounce the ball just once before a first serve, and just a couple before a second.

And if Lendl wasn't sprinkling sawdust at the back of the court – some tournaments had their groundstaff clear up after him when the players sat down during the change of ends – he would sometimes fiddle with his eyelashes. Brad Gilbert has recalled how Lendl was for ever plucking at his lashes like a prom queen. 'He gradually edges up to the line to serve. I get ready, but he's not quite set to go into his first motion yet. He has some business to take care of first. He begins with his eyelash routine. You've seen that on the television. He plucks an eyelash and looks at it. Then he plucks another one and looks at it. Then another one. How he can have any eyelashes left at this point in his career, I don't know. He's been plucking and looking at them for fifteen years.'

Lendl was remarkably consistent; there wasn't much oscillation in the quality of his tennis; he would rarely spray a court with unforced errors. 'He was a difficult opponent to play against because he was almost like a machine,' Boris Becker told me. 'He never gave up, and there were never any weak moments on the court. He wouldn't lose a match. You had to beat him.'

Bounce, bounce, bounce, bounce. While Lendl was bouncing the ball, dropping sawdust and plucking eyelashes, he didn't have an empty mind; he was plotting his moves for the next point, and not just where he would serve, but also what he would do with his second shot. Why play on instinct when you can plan everything in advance? Lendl knew, after hitting any one of the serves in his repertoire, where his opponent was likely to direct his return. So Lendl had already thought through what he would do with his second shot. This wasn't tennis on a whim. This was about having greater control over his mind, the ability to restrain his urges to play spectacular but unnecessarily risky shots – for instance, in one possible scenario, he would know that an attempted pass down the line would work just once in every three tries, while if he went cross-court he would pull off the shot two-thirds of the time. From a young age, Murray has been interested in formulating strategies for beating opponents, and so as an adult there has generally been some structure to how he plays, but that's not to say that he is anything like as rigid in his thinking as Lendl was. While Murray always puts some thought into where to serve, and how his opponent is likely to respond, he doesn't plan rallies to the extent Lendl did. And Murray has certainly never recorded his thoughts on opponents and strategies – whether in his head or on paper – as his coach once did in the 1980s.

Lendl's dislike of surprises was such that he kept a video library of matches in his Connecticut home; he was the undisputed VCR King of Tennis, using the films for digging out information as well as for positive reinforcement. And that's why, in 1984, he created what we might call 'The Lendl Files', a large loose-leaf binder filled with his observations after matches against opponents he rated; before facing them again, he would look them up, process the notes and remind himself of the patterns of play. This was inspired by McEnroe – for most of the 1984 season, the New Yorker had been brilliant and dangerously unpredictable, with Lendl never quite sure what to expect from him: 'McEnroe was playing so well that there was no simple strategy that worked against him because he had so many answers to whatever I tried. I went on the court ready to do one thing and if he started counter-attacking, I had to change. I had to be readjusting all the time.' Lendl didn't want to be surprised again. So, as soon as he came off court, whether he had been playing McEnroe or anyone else who commanded respect, he made some notes.

And they were definitely notes, not unstructured thoughts doodled on a page. At the top of every sheet, he would state his opponent's name and then record six fast facts: where they played, the date, the surface, the result, the opponent's ranking at the time and the stage of the tournament. Below, he would restrict himself to a few sentences on any small adjustments he had made, and how his opponent had countered his move, if at all. On court, if Lendl didn't feel as though his game was working, he could make those adjustments, for ever looking for the small change that could have a big effect on the outcome of the match. It would have been suicidal for Lendl to have completely transformed his game, even against a particularly tricky opponent such as McEnroe. So he modified and made tweaks to his whole style of play, rather than totally revamping it. 'If one adjustment catches a little hole in someone's game, I try to penetrate through that hole.' And all those tweaks would later be detailed for future use, building up his bank of intelligence, and it shouldn't have taken more than four or five matches against one adversary for him to arrive at the best possible strategy. So Lendl was for ever looking for patterns, trends, anything that might tell him what the percentages might be if and when they played again. For instance, after one match against fellow Czechoslovak Miloslav Mečiř, an opponent whose varied, multi-speed game wasn't that dissimilar to Murray's, he observed: 'He plays in a very strange way. He plays angles that aren't there.'

Some information he omitted, believing it to be either irrelevant or a possible distraction from what he needed to be thinking about. So he wasn't just keeping his emotions hidden from the world; he was also hiding them from himself, as if he had recorded his feelings he could have increased the chances of falling into a pattern. Also missing was anything to do with his opponents' own excitements and agitations. He also tended not to record injuries, whether his own or those sustained by his opponents. This was cold, hard, weapons-grade information. 'I don't write about things that I cannot change or predict – wind, rain delays, bad bounces, my opponent's behaviour,' Lendl told *Tennis* magazine. 'I must accept conditions that I cannot control and work with them. Stay calm and cope. Don't get upset. Don't ever let the other guy initiate any problems inside you.'

This new Lendl, who believed in himself as never before, was ruthless and relentless. There was never any let-up. How better to illustrate Lendl's cold-eyed approach than the occasion he annihilated Wilander 6-0, 6-0 at an exhibition match in Barcelona? This wasn't how these big-money exhibitions were supposed to work – there was a general assumption among the elite players that these were meaningless, instantly forgettable occasions. The pair of you had been hired to entertain a crowd, and the understanding was that, even if one player was striking the ball far better than the other, you would at least conspire to make it halfway competitive. It wasn't unheard of for players to allow their opponents to win the second set of a three-set match, just so the exhibition would go to a decider, and the crowd and the promoters would get their money's worth (and you would potentially be hired again).

But that wasn't always how the new Lendl saw it. 'I was talking to Ivan about this not long ago, at a party for former number ones which the ATP put on in New York before the 2013 US Open,' Wilander told me. 'There was a group of us standing around talking at that party, and Björn Borg says, "Hey, Ivan, wasn't there a match when you beat Mats 6-0, 6-0 for no reason at all, as he didn't have his own rackets or anything with him?" So Ivan says, "Mats, let's hear your story first". I told them how I had flown in from New York without any rackets, clothes or shoes. And how I had to go and get rackets from a sports shop, and obviously they weren't customised or anything, just rackets off the shelf. And Ivan knew that. He says to me, "Do you want to warm up?" And I replied, "Why would I want to warm up with this racket I just bought from a shop?" So we started playing and he beat me 6-0, 6-0, and I just thought, "Why?" So we shook hands, he didn't say sorry or anything, and then early the next morning the phone rings in my hotel room, and it's his girlfriend Samantha and she says, "Good morning, Ivan would like to speak to you". I thought, "Wow, he's calling to apologise, he must be". So I say hello and he says, "This is Ivan, would you like to practise today?" And I said, "Ivan, I don't have any fucking rackets. No, I don't want to practise".'

Lendl viewed the exhibition quite differently, as he told the group of former players that night in New York. 'Ivan's story was that he had just won a tournament, he was playing well, and he didn't want his confidence to drop by letting me win a game or two, because he didn't have to do that,' Wilander said. 'Ivan wanted to keep on a roll. I didn't know that at the time, but it makes a bit of sense now I know that. He just wanted to bully his way through matches, even if they were just exhibitions.' Why put his form and his confidence at risk for something as trivial as entertaining a crowd? Lendl was many things during his career, but one thing he wasn't – and this despite all the times he was hired for exhibitions – was a crowd-pleaser. He wasn't about to drop a few games, or even a set, for the pleasure of the mob.

They were neighbours in Connecticut, and a couple of times Wilander practised on the court at Lendl's house. 'But Ivan never played at my court because I never invited him, and that was because he kicked my arse so badly. He was a monster in matches and situations that didn't mean anything,' Wilander told me. 'Most other guys, you're playing well, you're winning matches, and when you go to practice, you're going through the motions. I think he saw every one of our practice sessions as an opportunity to beat me really badly. He was good to hit balls with, but playing games was rough. Sometimes he would beat me heavily in practice, and I would think to myself, "This is bad, I can't do this, this isn't good for my confidence".'

One read of the reinvented Lendl of the mid-1980s and beyond was that he had started to use fear to his advantage. Once he would have been pulled down by fear; now it was spurring him on. So even if he was marmalising someone, he could keep on pushing himself, concerned that his opponent might still come back into the match: 'The most basic strategy is this: if you have your opponent on his back, step into his face and twist your foot. Don't give him the idea that he can come back.'

One of the most important conversations of Lendl's career took place in his head. It was during the 1985 US Open; Lendl was in the final again, for the fourth year in succession, and he was trailing McEnroe 2-5 in the opening set. Was Lendl on his way to yet another disappointment in New York, against the same opponent who had beaten him the year before? Defeat this time would cost Lendl's psychologist Alexis Castorri a thousand dollars, after the bet they had struck earlier in the year.

After winning that first grand slam title at the 1984 French Open, Lendl had another two runner-up finishes in a slam, losing to McEnroe at the 1984 US Open, and then a defeat to Wilander at the 1985 French Open. On that New York concrete, the early exchanges seemed to suggest that Lendl was in danger of not just losing another US Open final, but of his career record in slam finals moving to just one victory from his first eight appearances. Maybe the old Lendl would have folded, but 1985 was the year that 'it all came together in my mind', and there was no panic or despondency. 'I'm losing,' Lendl said to himself as he sat on his chair, 'but I'm doing the right things, it's okay.' So this time it was different. Lendl didn't retreat into himself; he kept going for his shots, and the result was that he beat McEnroe in straight sets. As Castorri described it, Lendl had had a moment of truth on the court. Lendl's reward was that, from that tournament on, he had the number one ranking in lockdown – for three unbroken years, the computer regarded him, as did almost everyone else in and around the sport, as the king of tennis. And being the world number one suited Lendl. Others, such as Wilander, discover on reaching the summit that they don't like the status and the pressures; Lendl, on establishing himself at the top of the rankings, found it to be even better than he had imagined.

One of the first calls Lendl made as the US Open champion – he was punching numbers within the hour – was to Castorri. He wanted to thank her. He would keep a framed photograph of the match on the white baby grand piano at home; that image was a reminder not just of the time he won a second grand slam title, but of the occasion he demonstrated to himself, as well as to others, that he could play well on the big occasion.

What was becoming clearer to Ivan Lendl, as he chased grand slams, was that he needed to feel that he was in complete control of his environment. Only then could he begin to contend with the doubts and fears in his mind. So he could never be a hard drinker, as even getting mildly tipsy was a loss of control. Alcohol didn't agree with him – once, after winning one of his Australian Open titles, his coach Tony Roche talked Lendl into having a beer and he became a little tipsy. One of the other rare occasions when he imbibed was when he drank a single glass of Scotch after boarding a flight back from South America to Europe and afterwards couldn't recall a single detail about the trip, which lasted almost twenty-four hours and required two stops, one of which also included a change of planes. An aversion to alcohol was something else Lendl had in common with Andy Murray, who hated the burn on his throat, and who was described by former coach Brad Gilbert as 'the only Scottish guy who doesn't drink'. However, Murray did indulge during his time with Lendl, drinking some champagne on a flight home from New York after winning the US Open – he ended up brushing his teeth with his girlfriend's face cream.

The more Lendl came to appreciate that the small details mattered, the more he wanted to be in control. Of course, as soon as the umpire announced 'play', he wouldn't have that mastery of his environment; it was only while preparing for matches, and then doing his recovery work afterwards, or during leisure time, that he could feel he was completely in control. So Lendl was a slave to his schedule; there wasn't much that would cause him to deviate from that, not even, a friend suggested, a papal visit: 'If the Pope was in Ivan's living room at bedtime, he'd say, "It was nice meeting you", and give that blank smile of his and disappear into his bedroom.'

Orbiting the tennis universe, Lendl wanted ritual and control, and everything his way – so he would have a driver wait outside a stadium while he was playing a final and then, still in his tennis kit, he could hop into the back and be taken straight to the airport in time to catch Concorde. According to one story that appeared in *Sports Illustrated*, Lendl also thought his control stretched to avoiding the paparazzi's flashing cameras – he wasn't pleased when he arrived at LAX once to a waiting pack of photographers strafing him with flashbulbs. The driver, seeing his passenger's annoyance, looked back over his shoulder and said: 'I guess that's the price of fame, Mr Lendl.' To which Lendl responded: 'No, that's the price of someone making a mistake. Someone will pay for this. Jerry [Solomon, his agent] will pay for this.' The driver replied: 'But the photographers didn't know anything about you coming. Diana Ross was on your plane, and you just happened to be there.' Travelling by road was better. Some tournaments in the States could be reached by sports car, and, the story goes, he paid someone to prep his vehicle before he set off on these journeys, filling it with petrol and highway tokens.

Before Jerry Maguire, there was Jerry Solomon. For Lendl, this wasn't so much about hollering 'Show me the money' down the line – though cash clearly mattered to him – but about commanding, in an unmodulated and heavily accented voice, 'Show me the love, the care and the attention to detail.' To a degree, all tennis agents, whether in the 1980s or today, have also to think of themselves as personal concierges, bag-carriers, counsellors and occasional dogsbodies. But no one in the history of tennis has ever demanded as much from his management company as Lendl did of Solomon and his colleagues at ProServ, including the occasion Lendl telephoned Solomon, telling him to drop everything and speed over to his house. Solomon did as instructed, intrigued and possibly even alarmed about what could be so urgent; when Solomon arrived, Lendl bounded over and announced: 'Jerry, I've learned how to dive.' Solomon couldn't find it within himself to be angry. No agent came close to giving his client this much attention; it has been said that when Lendl sweated, Solomon changed his shirt, and when Lendl was tired, Solomon took a nap. There are similarities in the guidance that Lendl and Murray would have given their respective management companies – neither cared so much for fame, with Murray making it plain during his first meeting with manager Simon Fuller, who also looked after David Beckham's interests, that he wasn't interested in empty celebrity. There are also differences in their respective dealings, among them that Murray has never been as demanding. Lendl and Solomon's time together as ProServ agent and client ended with legal ping-pong and then an out-of-court settlement. For a while, the pair hadn't been getting along as well as they once had, with Lendl perhaps not as willing to listen to Solomon as he had been in the past. Still, years later, Lendl would go back to Solomon; the firm bond they had built up over the years had even survived that very public, multi-million-dollar falling-out.

Some weeks on the tennis trail, Lendl didn't want anyone intruding in his world – on being shown his room, he would hang the 'Do Not Disturb' sign on the door and leave it there until he had either won the tournament or been beaten, although there were some who suggested that this sign was hardly necessary, given Lendl's reputation. Those weeks that he chose to withdraw from life, only emerging to train, play matches and indulge in some verbal cage-fighting with journalists, he would often ask for a VCR player to be brought to his room so he could watch tennis videos and Hollywood movies. When he was in that sort of mood, Lendl could also choose to eat all his meals in his room, as well as leave the curtains closed for a week and drop his clothes on the floor, where they would be left until it was time to check out.

However, the freedom to litter the floor of his hotel room wasn't as dear to him as the assurance that his rackets had been prepared to the highest possible standards. No one on the circuit came to care as much about grommets, graphite, grips and natural gut as Lendl did. Bouncing from city to city as they followed the sun and the tennis calendar around the world, most players had come to accept the unsatisfactory reality that their rackets would be restrung by a different technician and on a different machine each week. That was no way to achieve consistency of approach and service, so many of Lendl's rivals could never be sure they would end up with the tension and string set-up they had asked for when they checked their rackets in. For Lendl, it was different; he had Warren Bosworth. Wherever he happened to be on the tennis map, and wherever Bosworth happened to be, he knew he could always make a call – whether that was a scheduled conversation or an emergency – to his racket technician. And Bosworth would always pick up the telephone and, thinking that this would somehow put Lendl at ease, assume a heavy Slavic growl: 'Hello, Eevon, vere are you?' In a previous life, Bosworth had been a funeral director, and before that an investment banker. It was even said that his grandfather had invented the plastic tips that you find on the end of shoelaces. The stringing godfather, Bosworth was that rare creature, someone more in thrall to the detail than Lendl was. Anyone in the 1980s and early 1990s would be able to evaluate Lendl's worth as a tennis player by totting up the number of grand slams he had won – perhaps this was a touch crude, but it was really the only way of doing it – but he wouldn't have been the same player if, behind the scenes, Bosworth hadn't for ever been reaching for the calipers and micrometers. This was a life measured in thousandths of an inch. As Murray's would be, too; here is a player whose preparation for matches has often included having an osmolarity check to ensure he is properly hydrated, with the right percentages of water and minerals in his urine. And Lendl would bring a high level of detail to his coaching relationship with Murray, looking at everything in the Scot's environment; Lendl's interest in the minutiae was such that he advised his employer to move to a hotel in a quieter part of New York when competing at the US Open, as staying somewhere too exciting could have drained him of some of the energy he needed for the Arthur Ashe Stadium.

While the money was good, Bosworth wasn't doing this for the fame – as he himself acknowledged, no one in the stadium, or watching at home on television, would have known his name. But, backstage in tennis, people knew exactly who he was. In fact, he was so integral to Lendl's operations that the man from Ostrava took to calling the American his 'chief of staff'; 'racket technician' didn't quite cut it for someone who could potentially determine whether Lendl won a grand slam or not.

Such apparent regard didn't, however, mean that Lendl was polite to Bosworth. Theirs was a relationship built on profanity and light-hearted mockery; the first time they met was in the locker-room after Lendl had just lost to one of Bosworth's other clients, the American player Brian Gottfried, with Bosworth offering what he thought were words of encouragement to the beaten Czech: 'Oh, don't worry about it, you're going to be okay – you're going to be a top player someday.'

To which Lendl – unable to think of anything else to say at the time – responded: 'Fuck off.' As Lendl once said of Bosworth, who died in 2010: 'If I was nice to Warren, then he wouldn't feel good. I don't know what it is – Warren just invites abuse.' A great deal of this affectionate abuse was directed at Bosworth when they were on the golf course – Lendl was for ever telling people that Bosworth was the worst golfer he had ever seen. Sometimes he would stand on the first tee, look over at Bosworth and whoever else had joined them and say: 'Are you ready, girls?' Bosworth did try to get back at Lendl, but not always with success. On one occasion he tried to throw a cup of water over his client. Unfortunately he missed and, because he hadn't taken his foot off the accelerator, the golf cart he was driving collided with a tree – for some time afterwards, the sight of Bosworth's cuts had Lendl collapsing with laughter.

What gave Bosworth such satisfaction was that, once the match had started, he knew Lendl didn't have to worry, as other players did, whether or not his strings had been correctly strung. At any moment Lendl could select a new racket from the batch he had brought on court; this is commonplace today but at the time Lendl's habit of selecting a fresh racket at every ball change was revolutionary. Bosworth recalled watching one of Lendl's televised matches; when one of his strings frayed (something Bosworth couldn't have been faulted for), he fetched a new racket from his bag and resumed playing without first checking the tension. One of the commentators expressed surprise that Lendl hadn't first felt the strings, almost as if he thought he was being blasé about the racket he used. Before Lendl started working with Bosworth in the early 1980s, he would burn through huge amounts of time and money searching for the right tension – on occasion, he would need his rackets to be restrung three or four times before they felt quite right. And even then he wouldn't stop worrying that, if he were to break a string during a match, the replacement wouldn't be quite the same. By employing Bosworth, Lendl could silence some of those voices in his head.

What the commentator clearly didn't know was that Lendl was working with Bosworth, and that Bosworth and Lendl chased the same objective: perfection. Or, as Bosworth called it: 'A harmonious union between the player and his racket.' The saying goes that God is in the details. In men's tennis in the 1980s, Bosworth was in there, too. He had other alpha clients during his career, such as Jimmy Connors and Vitas Gerulaitis, but there was only one player with whom he shared a real kinship, and that was the one who, as a young child, had had to take particular care of his racket because it was the only one he had.

After establishing himself in the tennis elite, Murray would become a 'gold service' client of a company called Priority One, which provides a personal stringing service. But Bosworth was the one who created that industry. 'Warren is a wizard,' Lendl used to say. The wizardry began when Bosworth received the latest batch of frames from Lendl's racket suppliers. Bosworth and Lendl weren't going to simply accept what the sponsor had sent them – not when the company operated within margins of manufacturing errors, and imprecision could be so ruinous. Half an hour with the calipers and the micrometers would have confirmed that no two rackets in that production-line batch would have been the same, when what Lendl and Bosworth wanted was uniformity, every frame identical down to the last grommet, and to the shape and dimensions of the handle. What was fine for a weekend warrior wasn't fine for someone who aspired to win multiple slams.

All Lendl's requirements were kept on file – Lendl demanded each racket weighed 371.5 grams, with the balance point 321 millimetres from the butt. If Bosworth wanted to add some weight to the racket, he reached for the lead tape; if he needed to make the frame a little lighter, he drilled small holes. Naturally, Lendl cared deeply about the handle of his racket; this would have been measured with dial calipers and then either sanded down or bulked up until it was the required size. The shape also mattered a great deal; Lendl insisted that it should be perfectly octagonal.

No detail was too small for Bosworth – he scrutinised, measured and, where necessary, modified every part of the racket, including the string holes and grommet systems, where he would look for sharp edges or small defects that might cut or in any way weaken the strings; and if those flaws couldn't be corrected, the racket would be discarded. This process would take more than an hour. It has been said that Lendl didn't like playing with new rackets, finding them too stiff, so one of Bosworth's assistants would break them in for him. Once the frame was ready, Bosworth got to work with the super-thin natural gut, stringing the rackets to the desired tension of seventy-two and a half pounds of pressure per square inch – not half a pound out of whack either way.

Bosworth worked to a twenty-four-hour rule – he said that, no matter where Lendl was, he could deliver a new batch of rackets to his client inside a day. That was some claim, but Bosworth made sure he stuck to it. It wasn't unusual for Lendl, several time zones away from his chief of staff, to call Bosworth's Connecticut home at some ungodly hour; Bosworth would dutifully climb out of bed, walk down the stairs and pick up the receiver in his den. If tennis in the 1980s was a technological arms race, with players trying to get the most out of their rackets, no one was better placed than Lendl. Not only did Lendl have Bosworth, but Bosworth had voodoo methods – who, apart from Bosworth, knew how a sound-frequency analyser machine worked? So Lendl would be fretting down the line that his string tension didn't seem quite right, and Bosworth would ask Lendl to lift his racket up to the phone and to pluck at the strings, or to strike them with a small, hard object. This sounded, Bosworth thought, like the clanging of a San Francisco trolley car. Having recorded a clip of Lendl's racket strumming, he would then take the audio to his studio and link it up with his frequency analyser. That information would tell Bosworth whether Lendl's rackets had been strung correctly.

To prepare rackets for international travel, Bosworth would put a sandwich bag over the grips and then place each frame in cushioned plastic bags and insulated shipping cartons; next he would ensure that the package was on the flight leaving America, and that, at the other end, there would be a member of tournament staff waiting to collect them off the plane. From there they would be delivered by hand into Lendl's own sawdust-coated palm. Having a fellow perfectionist at the other end of the phone fed into Lendl's obsession with detail; it was said that he could tell, without looking at his racket, but just by the feel of the felt on the natural gut, whether his sponsor's logo had been stencilled on to the strings in red or black ink. Apparently the two colours played differently.

There is no better illustration of Lendl's obsessive nature

than the annual instructions he would give to the company that laid the practice court at his home in Connecticut. Lendl wanted the very same surface that had been laid across Flushing Meadows, so, after the company had completed their yearly resurfacing of the courts at the US Open, he would have them come to his home the very next day. Lendl couldn't wait even a week, as by then the crew might have forgotten about, say, the exact amount of sand in the mix, and then his court would have played ever so slightly differently from the Arthur Ashe Stadium. The level of detail extended to his choice of practice partners – before a key tournament, he would invite players whose games were as similar as possible to the rivals he expected the most trouble from. Only then would Lendl have what he needed: the illusion of control.

A couple of years after Ivan Lendl started the process of rein-vention, he was at the peak of his powers. That was 1986, the year he turned twenty-six, and the season he won two grand slams, the French and US Opens, and appeared in the final of a third, Wimbledon. The following year, Lendl was just as successful at the majors, with victories in Paris and New York, and a runner-up finish in London. It was plain that Lendl's physical and psychological transformation was having results. Still, for the public, there was one great shame about Lendl's time in his tennis prime and that was that he didn't play John McEnroe while both were at their best. For all the matches they played against each other – their head-to-head record shows that they butted skulls some thirty-six times at a senior level, with Lendl winning twenty-one of those and McEnroe fifteen – they didn't peak at the same time. McEnroe was never better than in 1984, when Lendl was still working out his physical and psychological issues, while Lendl's golden year came the season McEnroe disengaged from tennis. And even when McEnroe did re-engage with tennis, he couldn't reach another final of a slam, let alone win one of them.

Some would suggest that Lendl was extremely fortunate as, by the mid- to late 1980s, many of the big names of tennis were off the scene, thus making his life much easier. McEnroe wasn't the only one who had checked out. Jimmy Connors was no longer at his peak either, his last grand slam title coming in 1983, when he beat Lendl in the final of that year's US Open. There was plenty of fire and fury in this rivalry. Well, there was from Connors' side, with the American for ever wagging his finger and shaking his fist at Lendl. That didn't make Lendl particularly special, mind – Connors was like that with almost everyone. There was enough animosity to make their matches entertaining. But, ultimately, there was something a little empty and unsatisfactory about some of their encounters. They were just too far apart in age – Connors eight years older – for this to have become a proper rivalry. Lendl would win twenty-two of their thirty-five meetings, but this was an unbalanced rivalry; Connors won thirteen of their first eighteen meetings, and then Lendl was victorious on the last seventeen occasions they met.

It was true that Lendl didn't have to concern himself with Björn Borg, who had retired early, but it is worth noting that Lendl had given a good account of himself on the only occasion he played the Swede in a grand slam final, especially as that match, at the 1981 French Open, was the first time he had gone so deep at a major. Lendl extended Borg to five sets that day, and it was a shame for the tennis galleries that their rivalry ended before it had really begun. It would be preposterous to suggest that good fortune played a large role in Lendl collecting so many grand slams. Of course, there were other factors behind McEnroe's decision to take a sabbatical from tennis (not least parenthood), but it would be wrong to think that Lendl hadn't become something of an obsession with the American. And it's not as if there weren't other serious talents around in the mid- to late 1980s. The summer of 1985 saw the world premiere of Boris Becker, with the German winning Wimbledon at the age of seventeen. By the time he was finished, Becker would win six grand slam titles, the same number that Stefan Edberg, another name and face of the 1980s, would put in his racket bag. Then there was Mats Wilander, who was winning majors up until the 1989 season, in a career that brought him seven slams. And let's not forget Pat Cash or Michael Chang. Don't think that, just because McEnroe had slunk off, Connors was getting old and Borg was long gone, Lendl somehow had the stage all to himself.

Where better for this so-called tennis machine, this most modern and manufactured of players, than American concrete? Lendl never did play the US Open when it was staged on the grass of Forest Hills; for him, the tournament always meant the cement at Flushing Meadows. While the two European slams, Roland Garros and the Wimbledon Championships, made much of their heritage, and presented themselves in a more elegant and understated way, the US Open at Flushing Meadows has never been so afraid of modernity. This was a tournament in which you could speak openly about money, in which every last square inch of real estate in the stadium was up for sale to sponsors and in which the players competed on a surface not dissimilar to the parking lot or the subway platform. While Lendl was never the darling of the New York tennis public, this tournament, more than any other, was Lendl's territory. Nowhere was Lendl's power-base-line game more effective than on the New York concrete; in a remarkable run between 1982 and 1989, he appeared in eight successive finals. He lost the first three finals, to Connors in 1982 and 1983, and to McEnroe in 1984. His victories came in successive years from 1985 to 1987, against McEnroe, Miloslav Mečiř and then Wilander, and he then lost his last two New York finals, against Wilander and then Becker.

Let's make no apology for this fixation on how Lendl, who won a total of ninety-four singles titles during his career, fared at the slams. He had a great deal of success at the Masters at New York City's Madison Square Garden, where he played in nine consecutive finals, yielding five titles, but it is at the grand slams that you ultimately judge a player. We saw that with Andy Murray – when he was still slamless, it had reached the point when winning the biggest titles on the regular tour, the most important events after the majors, was almost making life a little less tolerable for him. If Murray could bag one of those, people wondered, then why couldn't he do the same at the majors? It took a while for Lendl to appreciate that the slams were what truly mattered – that he wasn't going to be remembered for the number of times he had won some mega-money tournament where, to borrow a Martin Amis line, the prize was something obscene like a gold helicopter. This was one of the messages that Lendl used to impart when he invited the bright young things of tennis to train with him in Connecticut – as well as telling them to work hard, he also implored them to build their careers around the majors.

Lendl played in fewer finals at Roland Garros than he did at Flushing Meadows – five times in Paris, eight in New York – but he ended up with the same number of victories, matching his trio of titles at the US Open with three wins at the French Open. Lendl's first appearance in a Paris final came in 1981, with defeat to Borg. Lendl's other four Paris finals were all in succession – after beating McEnroe in 1984, he lost to Wilander the following year, before beating Mikael Pernfors in 1986 and then overcoming Wilander in 1987.

The key moment for Lendl in Melbourne was not the time, as important as it undoubtedly was, when he spotted and then bought his first legionnaire's cap in a surf shop – it was the occasion when the Australian Open's executives decided to change from grass to hard courts. Lendl had reached a final when the Australian Open had still been played on grass – he had been a runner-up to Wilander in 1983 – but it was only after the tournament went synthetic that he prospered. For Lendl's sake, it was just as well that Melbourne's Rip Up The Grass Society (or whatever that pressure group or think-tank called themselves) got their way, for two majors played on grass, by far his least productive surface, would have been problematic. The Australian Open made the switch to hard courts in 1988, and in 1989 Lendl won the title for the first time by beating Mečiŕ and then retained it in 1990 when Edberg retired during the final. Suddenly, Lendl seemed to be in his element in Australia – not only was the tournament now being played on his beloved hard courts, he appeared to be getting masochistic kicks from competing in the heat. There were days in Melbourne when the sun would start to melt the tramlines – the real ones in the city, not those painted on the tennis courts – and that was when

Lendl could demonstrate he was a superior being; he had his legionnaire's hat as well as the appetite for suffering in the heat.

The following year, Lendl made a third successive final in Melbourne, but on that occasion he couldn't handle Becker's power. That match at the 1991 Australian Open was his nineteenth grand slam final and it would also prove to be his last. Every year since 1981, when he had been runner-up at Roland Garros, Lendl had played in at least one slam final – and his eight victories from those nineteen matches would leave him high up the all-time list of serial grand slam champions. In the 1980s and early 1990s, no one accomplished more at the slams than Lendl: he was level with Connors, one ahead of McEnroe and Wilander, and two above Becker and Edberg. Also, Lendl spent 270 weeks as the world number one – longer than anyone else apart from Pete Sampras and Roger Federer – and he held that top position for 156 consecutive weeks. Europeans, Britons especially, may find this a little vulgar, but perhaps we should be measuring his success in prize money: he amassed more than twenty-one million dollars in tournament winnings alone, a sum that, at the time of his retirement, put him at the top of the sport's earners.

Given everything else Lendl brought to the sport – the innovative way he prepared for matches, his pioneering power-baseline game, as well as those head-seeking Fuck You Forehands – it can also be argued that he was the most influential player of the modern era. Before Federer and Sampras, did anyone dominate tennis as Lendl did? But that's a subjective question. As Lendl's local newspaper, the *Hartford Courant*, once noted: 'In the perfect world of Ivan Lendl there is no subjectivity. There are no politicians, no newspaper columnists, no gray areas. There are facts, box scores, black and white.' So what Lendl would love would be for a tennis fan with a background in mathematics or computer modelling to create a formula that would allow for a totally objective comparison between players – so that winning a major, or a smaller tournament, or the weeks spent as world number one, would be worth a certain number of points. 'They would have to play with it a little bit, so it comes out with something decent,' Lendl has said, 'but it would be interesting to see what it comes out at.' So McEnroe had a greater hold on popular culture – watching the New Yorker frothing at the mouth on YouTube is always a fun, nostalgic trip – but it was Lendl who played a greater role in shaping the modern tennis world.

CHAPTER SEVEN
THE BIG RISK

Theirs wasn't a partnership with a Michelin-starred beginning; one of their first encounters was in a strip mall just off Interstate 95 in Florida, in a no-star, 'rubbish' Italian restaurant next to a hairdresser's. 'It wasn't some flash meeting, and that says a lot about him,' Andy Murray has recalled of the occasion in late 2011, during the short off-season, when he had lunch with Ivan Lendl beside a highway. The mediocre food appealed to Murray. Tennis's odd couple, as someone would later call this Dunblane–Ostrava collaboration with a twenty-seven-year age difference, weren't there for the linguini; Murray was there to confirm that he wanted this winner of eight grand slam titles, one of the all-time greats, and the cheapest of dates, to be his coach.

Nicknamed Killer, because of his polite and personable nature, Darren Cahill is one of the sport's most respected coaches; the Australian has worked with Andre Agassi and Lleyton Hewitt, he once declined the chance to travel with

Roger Federer and in recent years he has become a friend and confidant of Murray. While Lendl's interest in Murray had been common knowledge in tennis from the spring of 2011, with information leaking to three British newspapers, it would appear that Cahill's endorsement of Lendl was critical in ultimately bringing the pair together.

If Killer hadn't sold Lendl to Murray and his circle, which included his mother, Judy, the Scot could have ended up leading a very different tennis life. 'When Darren suggested Ivan's name to us, my only knowledge of Ivan was what I had seen of him during his playing days, and what I remembered of him as a player was that he had been a tough, driven, gaunt-looking individual who seemed to have no sense of humour whatsoever,' Judy Murray told me over a peanut-butter-bagel breakfast at the Lawn Tennis Association's headquarters in south-west London. 'The whole journey with Andy's tennis has been about listening to others and learning from others, and trying to find the right people at the best time. Andy and I valued Darren's opinion as highly as anyone's out there, and so when he suggested Ivan to us, we were going to take that seriously, especially as he knew both Andy and Ivan.'

This wasn't a quick courtship; nine months passed from the news stories about Lendl's interest in Murray to the announcement on New Year's Eve 2011 that they had decided to work together. Why did it take so long for Murray and Lendl to agree on a partnership? One reason was that Murray wasn't especially unhappy with the coaching arrangements since he had discarded Miles Maclagan after the 2010 Wimbledon Championships. He was receiving guidance and encouragement, albeit on a part-time as well as a restricted basis, from the very man who would end up selling Lendl to him.

Cahill was one of the perks of Murray's clothing endorsement deal, with Killer part of a touring posse of coaches who were offered as consultants to players who were contracted to wear Adidas kit. It was a far from ideal set-up; if Murray ever found himself playing an opponent who also wore the three stripes of Adidas, Cahill was not allowed to be involved. Also, during the grand slams, Cahill often wouldn't be available because he would be in a television studio working for an American broadcaster.

In addition to Cahill, Murray was working with Dani Vallverdu, an old friend. 'Andy continued with what he was doing until the end of the season. He was working quite happily with Darren at that time. And, actually, we looked into trying to get Darren to work with Andy on a semi-permanent basis,' Judy Murray recalled. 'But Darren had too many other commitments and a young family.' So Cahill set about helping Murray to find a full-time coach. 'I wanted to find Andy a good coach, and to mix the personalities together, and to make sure that it wasn't just a quick coaching job, but a long-term arrangement with a future in it,' Cahill told me.

Don't imagine that Murray only ever considered Cahill and Lendl for the job. According to Cahill, Murray had been 'extremely diligent' and had spoken to a great many people about filling his coaching vacancy. Still, the more people Murray spoke to, perhaps the more he would have realised how limited his options were. Professional tennis, the sport that touches almost every major city in the world, is essentially a hamlet at the elite level. There are a lot of coaches out there, and a good number of them would have made contact with Murray and his management company, but he would have taken only a small number of them seriously. 'Believe me, there were offers coming from everywhere,' Murray has noted. 'I suppose I could have been flattered by all the offers, but I couldn't understand why some people came forward. There was absolutely no way they could help.' One coach who did intrigue Murray was the Australian Bob Brett, who had previously worked with Boris Becker and Goran Ivanišević, but Brett wasn't interested in the role. There would, however, be a strong alternative to Lendl in Roger Rasheed, another Australian coach who had worked with Hewitt and Frenchman Gaël Monfils. 'Roger and I always got on well together. I knew he would work me hard, that he had a great appreciation for the game,' Murray wrote in his book, *Seventy-Seven: My Road to Wimbledon Glory*. 'I enjoyed our talks. I thought it could be a good fit because I really, really like and respect him.'

There was the growing body of opinion in tennis that what Murray needed was to buy in some expertise from one of the coaching grandees, someone who had either won a slam himself, or who had tutored another player to glory at the majors. If Murray was to take that advice, that would count against Rasheed, since Hewitt's two grand slam titles, at the 2001 US Open and the 2002 Wimbledon Championships, had come before they had started working together, and Rasheed himself hadn't made much of an impact as a player. From the spring of 2011, when Murray ended his association with Spaniard Alex Corretja, a former world number two and French Open finalist who had had the role of assistant coach, the Scot had sometimes gone into matches armed only with the expertise and guidance of Vallverdu. They had been friends since meeting as teenagers at Barcelona's Sanchez-Casal Academy. While Murray had gone on to compete at the highest level, Vallverdu's own singles career hadn't been quite so successful, with the Venezuelan's ranking peaking just outside the world's top 700. Though Murray wanted to keep Vallverdu on, he recognised that someone of gravitas and experience could help him to make the best of himself.

Maybe Lendl would be the coach who could help Murray realise his ambitions. 'You have to think about what you need. Andy didn't need somebody to teach him how to play the game,' Judy Murray said. 'Andy needed someone who could help him prepare better for bigger occasions and those tough situations at the back end of majors. He needed someone in his team who had been there and done it. There were similarities between the two, with Ivan losing all those finals before he won a slam. It was about having someone in Andy's team who had been in those tight situations, because there wasn't anyone else in Andy's team who had played or coached at that level. You have to find the right people at the right time. I wouldn't say that there was an expectation about what might happen if Andy worked with Ivan. You just hope that you are doing the right thing by bringing in some expertise that hadn't previously been there, as Ivan obviously had a wealth of experience, albeit from years ago.'

Nothing Cahill ever did for Murray was as significant as helping to broker the deal with Lendl, with Killer making a preliminary phone call to Lendl, asking whether he 'would be interested in having a chat to Andy, not knowing where it was going to lead, just to talk a little bit about tennis, and he jumped at it, which we were excited about'.

As Judy Murray observed, starting a new relationship with a coach in the middle of that season could have been disruptive for her youngest son, so it was agreed that Murray and Lendl would wait until the off-season before meeting to discuss the possibility of working together. Nothing would happen until the end of the 2011 tennis year. 'There are certain times of the year when it makes sense to engage a new coach, and there are other times when it doesn't make sense to upset the apple cart by bringing someone new in. Also, I guess, when you're possibly bringing in someone who is high profile, you would need time for that to settle down before you start competing. If you brought in a high-profile, celebrity coach in the middle of the season, that would potentially have been a huge distraction, with so much interest from the media. Ivan's got a huge number of fans around the world. I see that the whole time at tournaments now, with people stopping him. He's very popular. Hiring a celebrity coach is always going to attract a lot of attention. So there wasn't any direct contact between Andy and Ivan until the off-season.'

It has been said you can read something into the fact that Lendl didn't travel to Miami, where Murray has his second home, for the first meeting. Instead, arrangements were made for Murray, along with Cahill and Vallverdu, to meet further up the coast at Boca Raton. Justin Gimelstob, the former American player who in retirement joined the board of the ATP, saw that as Lendl demonstrating his powerful position in the negotiations, and so the power in any mooted coaching relationship.

Over lunch, Lendl spoke about his past experiences and the story of his career – it's impossible to imagine that he and Murray didn't end up discussing Wimbledon, the one grand slam Lendl didn't win, and the only tournament with the power to completely transform Murray's life. Lendl also expressed some views on Murray's era. Clearly, much had changed since Lendl's retirement. Lendl regarded Murray's generation as being better trained, better fed and better coached than his – twenty-first-century players had more shots, more power and a greater ability to withstand power. Lendl was astonished by the effect that string technology had had on tennis.

So Lendl had been taking a general interest in the modern game. And yet, as Murray would have been aware, there were gaps in Lendl's tennis knowledge. Lendl didn't know *everything* about the modern game. How could he? Even for someone with a tennis brain like Lendl's, there's only so much you can discover with a remote control in your hand, when you learned almost everything you know about the sport from watching it on television.

During his time away from the sport, Lendl hadn't been following every cough, spit and forehand winner of modern tennis. As recently as 2010, he was saying 'tennis tournaments aren't interesting'; only when there was a grand slam being played, and only when the players were at the business end of the fortnight, with just the semi-finals and finals left to play, did he bother to pick up his television zapper and flick channels over to watch Murray's generation. Even then his attention wasn't guaranteed; tennis's great obsessive, a man who had dedicated himself to the sport like no one before him, just watched 'most of the time'. Some of the second- and third-tier competitors on the men's tour would have been largely unknown to Lendl. But was this ignorance such a problem? Murray hardly needed Lendl's help to negotiate the first few rounds of a slam. What mattered was whether Murray believed Lendl could assist with his encounters against Federer, Rafa Nadal and Novak Djokovic at the crucial stages of grand slams. Lendl shared a few thoughts with Murray about how he might go about beating some of his rivals and even – this story comes via Greg Rusedski – sketched out some of his thought on a napkin. 'Andy was firing away with questions about the current game, and Ivan was all over it,' Cahill told the *New York Times*. 'He was all over Rafa, all over Novak, all over Roger. Obviously, there were going to be some players out there that Ivan hadn't seen that often, but, by and large, Andy was concerned by the top guys, as those were the ones he would have to overcome if he wanted to win a major tournament.'

In the course of the conversation it became apparent that Lendl had been taking a particular interest in Murray's career. This wasn't the first time that he had encountered Murray; years earlier, he had been impressed by him when they met briefly at Nick Bollettieri's academy in Florida. Lendl had watched a couple of Murray's practice sessions with Brad Gilbert, his coach at the time, and he liked the young man's work ethic; then they were introduced and Lendl appreciated Murray's manners. More recently, even though Lendl had only been watching tennis from afar, he had seen enough of the Scot to form the opinion that he needed to be more aggressive on court, even if that meant 'adjusting his personality a little bit to get out of [his] comfort zone'. If Murray went for his shots when he had opportunities, Lendl thought, he would win his 'fair share' of slams. Watching on television, it also hadn't escaped Lendl's notice how Murray carried himself on the big occasion. For all Murray's abilities, and his achievements, his body language didn't exactly project confidence when he was competing against Federer, Nadal and Djokovic. Around the table, you couldn't miss Lendl's enthusiasm for the project. Cahill recalled that Lendl had been inspiring to listen to. 'I had thought Ivan would be good for Andy as they had travelled down similar paths,' Cahill told me. 'And Ivan recognised that what he went through was eerily similar to what Andy went through, and so he wanted to help. He wanted to make a difference to Andy's life and to his career. You can't buy that.'

At the same time as exploring the possibility of hiring Lendl, Murray had also been speaking to Rasheed about how they could work together, with Rasheed even offering to fly in from Australia for some trial training sessions in Florida. Murray decided he wanted to see Lendl again. 'When they met for lunch, they seemed to get on fine, and so Ivan and Andy met up for a few days and did some work on court, and that seemed to go really well, too,' Judy Murray said. Lendl wanted more than one encounter before deciding whether he could possibly work with Murray. 'We met a few times in Florida and that was one thing I asked for, a few meetings, so we could see how everyone got on,' Lendl has said. It was those practice sessions that convinced Murray to opt for Lendl over Rasheed. As Lendl has put it, once he knew Murray was keen he had to think about it from his end. For Mats Wilander, the moment he believed that Lendl had a good heart was when he heard that his old rival was working with Murray. 'When he made that move, I just thought, "Wow, he's doing something to help someone else, that's amazing". He obviously knows the game and loves the game – we all do – but he was taking that step to help someone, and I thought that was really something.' All that was left to do was to agree the deal.

It was clear to everyone that Lendl's return to tennis would be big news in the sport. It was bound to cause even more turmoil and commotion around Murray's efforts to win a first grand slam title. Murray knew that, and Lendl knew that

Murray knew that. And that appealed to Lendl: 'Andy knew we would not go unnoticed. It upped the ante a little bit, and I liked that. It showed he wasn't scared of anything.'

There's now an almost irresistible temptation to romanticise that Italian restaurant off Interstate 95, and to look back at that lunch with hindsight, and to believe there was some kind of historical inevitability that this Lendl–Murray partnership would work out, that they were somehow destined to win grand slams and Olympic glory together. That's not quite how Murray or Lendl would have seen it; each would have been aware of the risks they would be taking in any partnership. And almost as soon as they agreed to work together, and made the announcement on New Year's Eve 2011, there were those in tennis wondering whether the arrangement could even last the 2012 season. Murray knew this: he was 'conscious that some people were saying it was a lousy fit'.

The first to employ a former star of the eighties as a coach, Murray started a locker-room craze. Before Murray, before Lendl, there was no proof this could work. At the 2014 Australian Open, it wasn't hard to spot the trend; indeed, anyone strolling around backstage at the Melbourne Park would have seen visible evidence of it. It was the 1980s all over again, just carrying a bit more weight and wearing longer shorts. Roger Federer had hired one of his boyhood idols, Stefan Edberg, while Novak Djokovic had turned to Boris Becker, and Japanese player Kei Nishikori was working with Michael Chang. In addition, Marin Čilić was being mentored by his fellow Croatian Goran Ivanišević, and France's Richard Gasquet had just hooked up with Spain's Sergi Bruguera. Suddenly, there was nothing more fashionable in men's tennis than a coach from the 1980s, and it would have been pointless to have argued that this was somehow coincidental. Others in the locker-room had looked at what Murray and Lendl had achieved together, and thought that hiring a name and a voice from the 1980s was something worth copying.

Even before the 2014 season, however, there had been signs that the locker-room was looking to copy Lendl and Murray. When Djokovic took the bold move of linking up with Becker, he had already tried to gain an insight into what Lendl was doing for Murray – for a brief period in 2013, which included that year's US Open, the Serbian hired Lendl's old coach, Wojtek Fibak, as a consultant. Fibak told me that was partly because Djokovic wanted an insider's view on the Lendl–Murray dynamic, as if he were some kind of 'counterpunch'. However, as Murray didn't reach a projected semi-final meeting with Djokovic, as the seedings suggested he would, Djokovic probably didn't gain as much from employing Fibak as he might have imagined. At the time of the 2014 Australian Open, Nadal was the only one of the leading four of men's tennis not to have a 1980s mentor, and perhaps if he hadn't a blood-bond with his coach, his uncle Toni, he too would have been leafing through old tennis magazines, picking out a leg-end from yesteryear as if he were mail-order shopping.

There was one influential voice in the tennis debating chamber who didn't accept that current players hiring former champions from past generations was a new phenomenon, and that voice had a Slavic accent with a touch of America in it. This wasn't Lendl being contrary – though you can be sure he'd be happy to espouse something other than mainstream opinion – just him speaking from experience. If Becker, Edberg and Chang were regarded as super- or celebrity coaches, what about Tony Roche, the Australian who had won a grand slam during his own playing career, and had then coached Lendl to seven of his eight majors? And, after Lendl's retirement, Roche had continued working in the tennis elite, going on to work with three other players who had topped the rankings, in Pat Rafter, Federer and Lleyton Hewitt.

But it's not quite true that the new gang of coaches was following in Roche's footsteps. Roche's grand slam success had come in the pre-modern, or wooden age, when rackets were kept in head-presses and the players were strictly amateur. Tennis in the 1960s and tennis in the twenty-first century were essentially two different sports. But there wasn't such a gap between Lendl's time and Murray's era; as we have seen, much of what happens today – the sports science and the power-baseline game – can be traced back to Lendl's own racket arm. And there is another powerful reason why Roche shouldn't be seen as the forerunner of the 1980s players who went on to become coaches; while Roche won a grand slam only once, Becker and Edberg did so on six occasions each and Lendl on eight. Roche was a fine player but he wasn't in the same stratosphere.

There wasn't exactly a crowded field of former champions who had found a second life for themselves in tennis as brilliant coaches. Perhaps most had taken heed of the cautionary tale that was Jimmy Connors' dalliance in coaching. Connors' partnership with Andy Roddick was never as fruitful as they had hoped it would be, and then in the summer of 2013 Connors lasted just one match as Maria Sharapova's coach before she fired him. If Connors' fiasco with Sharapova should have taught tennis anything, it was that a catalogue of achievement as a player was no guarantee of a glorious future as a coach. A second lesson was that coaching failures could potentially damage the aura and the legend that these greats had built up over years of glory as a player.

For Lendl and Murray, lunch in that strip mall turned out to be the start of a project that carried with it both great risks and rewards. Could Lendl become the first former playing great also to become a coaching great? Or was this a project that was going to explode in everybody's faces?

It's undeniable that there's a structural tension and power struggle in almost every player–coach relationship – while the coach is ostensibly the one in charge and giving directions, he's also an employee who can be fired at a moment's notice. For a relationship to have the best chance of working, both player and coach have to both understand and accept where the balance of power lies. That's down to the status, ego and needs of both parties; generally, the more successful a player is, the more power he has in his relationship with his coach. Still, Lendl wasn't an ordinary coach; he had already achieved enough to be given special status and standing. There's also the financial consideration – unlike your career coach, who needs the pay cheque, Lendl, while appreciative of any money he would be paid, wasn't motivated by financial rewards. He would be well paid – it has been said his contract contained clauses about the possibility of substantial bonuses – but he certainly wouldn't be doing this for the cash. And even if Lendl had been looking for ways to earn more money, he could have potentially generated as much from playing a few exhibitions than from spending half the year on the road with Murray. Lendl would never be beholden to Murray.

There had been much for Lendl to consider before committing to coaching Murray, a role which would include reacquainting himself with his old obsession of seeking glory on the Wimbledon grass. And, a couple of years later, Becker and Edberg would also pause before they came piling back into tennis. While a super-coach has a status above that of a career coach, he is still a member of staff; even with all those grand slam titles in your cabinet, there's still a degree of subordination. There would be fun, excitement and gratification from being involved at the highest level again, and the position would give you a greater media profile, but you had to be sure that you could cope with the possibility of your needs and status being very much secondary to those of your player and employer. Who could be sure how the relationship would play out? Some thought there was a danger in hiring a former superstar as a coach, as they would be too self-absorbed and too self-centred to do the job properly; rather than focusing on what the player wanted, they would for ever be drawing the conversation back to themselves and their achievements. Wasn't there also a risk that a top player toiling away on the court wouldn't appreciate being upstaged by the legend sitting in the corner of the stadium? Wouldn't they rather have someone a little more biddable? Where would the balance of power lie with these players and their megastar coaches? Clearly, there was more to this than simply plucking someone out of the tennis vault.

With Murray and Lendl, it was plain that the Scot needed the relationship to work more than his new coach did. He needed help in his quest to become the first British man for more than seventy years to win Wimbledon, or indeed to become the first British man since the 1930s to win any of the grand slam tournaments. While Lendl was willing to assist, he wasn't desperate for the job. And if he didn't think this was quite right, he could easily have walked away and returned to the life he had built for himself away from tennis.

The greatest risk of all was that Andy Murray would be entrusting his career to a coaching novice, to someone who had been off the circuit for several tennis generations. Never mind that Ivan Lendl had recently opened a tennis academy. Coaching aspiring American kids on Hilton Head Island in South Carolina wasn't the same as trying to guide Murray to a first grand slam title. For the best part of twenty years, Lendl had been a stranger to elite tennis. Some players barely bother to pause or even shower between playing their final match and joining the other talking heads in the TV commentary box. Alternatively, they almost immediately go into coaching, or they find some other role in the tennis industry. Anything to fill the void. Tennis sees almost as much of John McEnroe now as it did when he was competing on the regular tour. That wasn't how Lendl had played it after announcing in 1994 that, at the age of thirty-four, and constrained by a chronic back problem, he was retiring from his first life on the tennis tour.

At first, Lendl's plan had been to continue beyond 1994, for as long as he was taking some pleasure from his time on court. While others had started to regard him as a sad figure, he has said he had come to like playing without 'the pressure to produce'. Still, there wasn't much to like about his 1993 grand slam year – he lost in the opening round of the Australian, French and US Opens, while at Wimbledon he survived only one round before being bumped off the lawns in round two. At least in 1994 he went a little deeper, making the fourth round of that year's Australian Open, but he would never be a grand slam quarter-finalist again, and it had been a long three years since his last appearance in a major final, when he had been the runner-up at the 1991 Australian Open. During the rest of the 1994 grand slam year, Lendl was hardly a contender, losing in the opening round of the French Open, missing Wimbledon and going out early again at the US Open. Everything he tried – including an operation he has described as 'a root canal for your back' – hadn't stopped the terrible spasms, which were never worse than when he was running around on his once favoured concrete. Lendl appreciated that his opponents were no longer afraid of him. Fatigue must have got to him: all those years of perfectionism, all the time, energy and emotion he had put into improving his body and mind, must have been mentally and physically exhausting. So some might suggest that John McEnroe had been right when he had predicted that Lendl's approach would lead to burnout, but it wasn't as if Lendl's career was cut short with premature retirement. Lendl had carried on until his mid-thirties, with his last competitive appearance an aborted second-round match at that year's US Open against a German opponent called Bernd Karbacher. Lendl retired because of the pain, and then a paying crowd didn't see him swinging a racket again until 2010, the year he turned fifty.

When Lendl suddenly re-emerged in tennis as Murray's coach, there would be a theory about the timing of his return, one that would be aired on one of Australia's national television networks during the 2012 Australian Open, Lendl and Murray's first grand slam tournament together. A former world number one and a multiple grand slam champion – so someone whose opinion carries some weight in the sport – Jim Courier articulated his theory that the timing of Lendl's return had essentially been governed by the terms of a disability payout he had received because of the back condition that had ended his tennis career. Courier didn't doubt that Lendl's back problem had been genuine when he retired. What he did imply, though, was that it wasn't a coincidence that Lendl had suddenly rediscovered an interest in tennis, the suggestion being that he had been waiting for the restrictive period – when he wasn't allowed to make a living from the sport – to pass. On hearing this, Lendl immediately told Courier he didn't know what he was talking about; he also felt it wasn't a subject the American should have been debating on television.

It was true that an insurance company had paid out on the policy, but that same company hadn't barred him from going near a tennis court; it was his body that did that. For a fourteen-year period that began with his retirement in 1994 and ended when he had a successful procedure in 2008, his body simply wouldn't allow him to play the sport regularly, or play it with any vigour. Lendl wasn't suffering from just a back problem: he had a torn disc, torn ligaments and arthritis. While he would occasionally feed some tennis balls to his daughters, that was hardly playing. When he attempted even short hitting sessions for around half an hour, his back would react so angrily to the impact from the court that he would be very grumpy indeed the next day.

This enforced withdrawal from tennis was the second exile of Lendl's life, the first being his self-imposed exile from the country of his birth. So Lendl had that procedure and slowly he recovered, to the point where he found he was able to play without pain again. He hooked up in Vero Beach with Tom Fish, the father of Mardy, one of Murray's contemporaries on the tour. Playing regularly again – sometimes as often as three or four times a week – Lendl surprised himself by actually enjoying being on the court again, though after all those years without hitting a ball properly it took him a while to get his timing right. But the shots came back to him and soon he found himself 'pleasantly surprised' by what he was capable of. Though his body would sometimes ache the next day, Lendl wasn't alarmed by that – after all, he was fast approaching his fifties by then – and he was no longer in great pain or half crippled by the effort that had gone into chasing all those grand slams. Then Lendl started to work out more, shedding some thirty-five pounds of retirement weight. Part of Lendl's motivation for playing tennis again was to be able to hit with the juniors at his new academy, as he believed that, 'you have to show them, not just tell them'.

Lendl's tennis exile formally ended in the spring of 2010 when he played the Caesars Tennis Classic at Boardwalk Hall in Atlantic City, walking out to dry ice, pyrotechnics and actresses dressed as Cleopatra, to play a one-set exhibition against Mats Wilander. It was probably just as well that Lendl, according to an ESPN writer who attended the exhibition, 'felt detached from his former self, and so didn't feel as though he was competing with his own legacy', as he was beaten by Wilander. The Lendl of the 1980s and 1990s hated to lose even an exhibition. But Lendl no longer recognised the player he had once been. 'The guy who played a long time ago, to me, it's like somebody else. I'm so far removed from that. I went to such a different lifestyle immediately afterwards.'

So what had happened to Lendl during all those years away from tennis? For one thing, golf. During his tennis career, Lendl had had sporting interests away from the courts. His love of ice hockey was such that, if there was no live game on TV, he would sometimes call a sports line for half-hourly updates, but his real obsession away from tennis was golf.

During his playing days, Lendl had already been much more than some weekend hacker (there was a suspicion that he believed that being good at golf would somehow have made him more of a Connecticut Yankee). At the time, Lendl would sometimes remark that tennis was his business and golf his passion, which he would indulge as often as he could – it was said he even played nine holes on the day of his semi-final of the 1986 US Open, a tournament he would go on to win.

In retirement, Lendl could spend as much time with his five iron as he cared to, and what had been a passion could morph into an obsession. At the most golf-obsessed stage of his exile from tennis, Lendl was a member of at least four clubs, and was playing between 250 and 300 rounds a year. The most ambitious part of his golfing career came when he attempted to qualify for the US Open, though his 2008 challenge didn't go any further than the local elimination stage at the Wethersfield Country Club in Connecticut, with one golf writer who followed his round reporting that the former tennis player had a 'functional swing' and hadn't got off to the best of starts when he had bungled in the sand on the first hole, and on the second missed 'a tiddler' of a putt for par. He also made appearances on the European Tour, including at the Czech Open, where he missed the cut, and in America on the satellite or feeder tour below the main US PGA circuit. Though Lendl has said that he never finished last, that was only because others always dropped out.

Not everyone celebrates turning fifty, but for Lendl it meant he was eligible to compete in golf at the seniors' level, so then he had a go at qualifying for the US Seniors Open, but failed at that, too. In addition, Lendl has appeared in 'a bunch of senior golf tournaments', and a fair number of celebrity pro-am tournaments, and, at times, his handicap has been plus two.

To McEnroe's mind, 'Lendl deluded himself into thinking he was going to be a golfer – that was a bit like me deciding I wanted to be a rock star', and it would be to Murray's benefit that Lendl didn't have more success on the golf course. But it would be wrong to sneer at this as a vanity project, or to cast Lendl as a narcissist of the fairways, to believe that he was doing this simply for glory and pleasure. Rather, golf allowed him to keep on experiencing the agonies, nerves and tension of competitive sport. Golf allowed him to keep on suffering.

We know that because Lendl, who plays golf left-handed, feels as nervous standing on the first tee before playing in a club championship as he used to before leaving the locker-room for a grand slam final. In addition to competition, golf also helped to satisfy his lust for self-improvement. Having pursued perfection across the tennis map, he could now do the same at the country clubs of Connecticut, green and pleasant places to torture himself. 'My attitude was to see how good I could get,' Lendl once disclosed. 'Golf gave me something that tennis couldn't give me any more. I need to compete. I had been trained to compete all my life and I couldn't just walk away from that.' Without golf, Lendl has suggested, he would have ended up biting one of his German shepherds. Sometimes, while playing a match-play tournament – the format of the game he favoured – he would stare down his opponent. If there was a downside to his return to the tennis court in 2008 it was that it wasn't doing his golf swing any favours, as he would sometimes arrive at the course feeling stiff from playing tennis the day before; being right-handed on the tennis court and left-handed on the golf course also complicated matters.

Roller-blading, he had discovered, was a good way of getting into shape for golf. Lendl being Lendl, he took it to the extreme. As roller-blading was much gentler on the knees than running, he could do up to fifteen miles a day, six days a week. There, was, however, always the danger of crashing and damaging his wrist, and on the occasions he did wipe out, 'it wasn't pretty'.

With his golf, his five girls and his German shepherds, Lendl had a full life; there was more than enough to occupy his time without adding the task of trying to turn Murray into a grand slam champion. A family man he undoubtedly was, with the tribe wintering in Florida and summering in Connecticut, and retirement meant he no longer had to be an absent father; as a child, the boy Ivan had been upset on those occasions when his own father didn't have the time to play table football or read books with him, and now Lendl could be there for his daughters – the eldest, Marika, the twins, Isabelle and Caroline, Daniela and Nikki – whether or not they always wanted their father to be around.

In this tennis after-life, Lendl would also have more time for his wife, Samantha, who, during his playing days, had been viewed with pity by some as being a pliant wife who had submitted herself to her husband's needs and demands on the tour. From the beginning, people imagined that Lendl had been the one in total control in that relationship – after all, when they had met he had been an established tennis star in his twenties and Samantha a schoolgirl in her mid-teens.

Before Samantha came on the scene, Lendl could be awkward – fearful, even – around girls, something that could possibly be traced back to a time at high school when he had caught his foot in his partner's dress, ripping the material. On moving to America, Lendl and his agent would, according to Peter Bodo, 'cruise Bloomingdale's for girls'. But that's not to say that Lendl was a smooth operator. During those difficult early years in the United States, he would, according to *Sports Illustrated*, have his friends chat up potential dates on his behalf: 'He preferred women who were very young, very pretty and very unlikely to challenge him. If a woman interested him, he sent someone he knew to risk the opening line. He didn't trust his English, his face or his crooked teeth.' That's not how he met Samantha Frankel, a teenage schoolgirl who was being educated at a private school in New York City; they were formally introduced. The introduction was made during that stage of Lendl's life when Wojtek Fibak had huge influence over him, and the Pole, thinking that Lendl and Samantha would make a fine couple, brought them together. To encourage friendship and then romance, Fibak invited Lendl and Samantha, who was a family friend, to spend weekends at his house, the idea being that it would be a relaxed environment. Lendl and Samantha also spent some time together at La Samanna, a beach resort on the Caribbean island of Saint Martin that her father owned.

While it was true that Samantha was young when the relationship started – which resulted in some unwelcome publicity in some of the British newspapers, including one under the tabloid headline 'Lusty Love Games of Ivan the Terrible' – she didn't want anyone thinking Lendl had acted in an ungentlemanly manner. One summer during Wimbledon, she addressed suggestions that she had been thirteen when they had first met. 'I was fifteen at the time, not thirteen as has been reported. It's important to get that straight, otherwise it makes Ivan sound like some kind of pervert.'

There was speculation on both sides of the Atlantic about the age at which Samantha had started their romantic life, with the *New York Times* suggesting that she had actually been fourteen when she met Lendl. And it wasn't the only occasion that allegations of sexual impropriety were unfairly levelled at Lendl. One British tabloid accused him of having assignations with Pamella Bordes, a society call girl and former Miss India who had had affairs with British MPs. It was alleged that they had met at the cosmetics counter at Bloomingdale's before he had installed her in a Madison Avenue apartment, and that the relationship had only ended when she tried to buy a Porsche on his credit card. However, the newspaper, the now defunct *Today*, later admitted there had been no truth in the story; it would ultimately pay him an undisclosed but substantial settlement, as well as his legal costs.

In time, Samantha, who was attending the Spence School in Manhattan, moved into Lendl's Connecticut house. Her parents were divorced, and she had been splitting her time between New York with her French mother and the Caribbean with her father. 'My father had a talk with Ivan and they agreed that I could live at his house in Connecticut until I finished school. He was on tour most of the time, but he had a live-in couple who looked after me,' she has said. 'In the beginning I found it hard to travel with him. We'd be introduced to people and they would say hello to me but after that it was as though I wasn't even there.' Only when it became clear that the relationship was 'serious' did people in tennis stop ignoring her. Around six years after they met, and just a few days after he had lost to Boris Becker in the final of the 1989 US Open, Lendl and Samantha married at their home in Connecticut. Within a couple of days – there was no fortnight-long honeymoon – he was back to the tennis grind. The wedding was on a Friday and they spent that night in a rural inn in Connecticut, watched an ice hockey match together on the Saturday and on Sunday set off on a business trip as Lendl had exhibitions and tournaments to play in Europe.

For Lendl, some things hadn't changed after the wedding. Before and after they were married, Samantha knew that her husband liked her to watch all his matches, from the first ball to the last. There had been one unfortunate occasion when Samantha felt so unwell that she couldn't stay in her seat a moment longer, and so retreated to the loo; the first thing Lendl said to her afterwards was to ask where she had disappeared to. That would be the last time she abandoned one of his matches. His needs would have to come before hers; that was just the way it was when he was chasing grand slams, and he had to save his energies for the match and practice court. If she wanted to go dancing, and he was tired from a match, and was playing again the next day, he was never afraid to say no. If their children were ill, and he was playing a tournament, she would have to look after them. Lendl knew that it wasn't always easy for Samantha being a tennis spouse, especially in America, 'where being a career woman is so popular', and when he had to try to shut out domestic concerns, such as a baby's tears, if he was to be in the best possible shape to compete.

Samantha has remarked that her husband had 'a monster personality', that he could be 'difficult, demanding and short-tempered'. She described herself as 'very easygoing', and since she didn't like to argue she would often just 'take the brunt of it when he's upset'. If there was something annoying her, she wouldn't bring it up during a tournament, for fear of starting an argument and distracting him from his tennis. 'I have no trouble expressing my desires or opinions,' Lendl once said, 'but I have a hard time expressing my feelings.' Samantha knew how to deal with him: she liked to think that she was one of the reasons why, towards the end of his career, he seemed a bit more personable. Don't see Samantha as a pushover. While Lendl would say Samantha's greatest strength was her flexibility, that wasn't, as some might have supposed, 'a nice way to say that I [could] push her around'. Peter Bodo described her as 'the closest thing I've ever encountered to a Hitchcock blonde; she didn't even need that hair color. Samantha struck me as a very smart, secure, independent-minded young woman who knew exactly what she was getting into, from the get-go. Or perhaps she realized what she had gotten into, and resolved to deal with it. And isn't that what marriage is all about?'

No doubt it was beneficial that Mrs Lendl had her own interest and area of expertise – horses – and that her husband wasn't about to encroach on her paddock. As horses weren't as easy to train as German shepherds, he wasn't interested.

Some have said that you can't be both a good tennis player and a good father, and that travelling around the world with young children, and trying to win grand slams, is bound to end in failure. Lendl's views on being a tennis father while still on the tour changed. Before Lendl fathered any children, he once looked at McEnroe trying to combine being a father and a tennis player, and thought he would hate to be in that position as 'the moment you have kids it can't work because either you cheat your tennis or you cheat your kids'. But then Samantha fell pregnant, with their first child due in 1990, and Lendl resolved to split himself between career and family. But he never would win a grand slam title as a father. His last major came at the 1990 Australian Open, when he beat Stefan Edberg, and Marika was born in the spring. Still, it would be ridiculous to say that fathering a child neutered Lendl at the slams, as by 1990 he was thirty and few players in the 1980s and 1990s were winning majors as thirty-somethings. Lendl's problem wasn't that his prospects had disappeared in a pile of dirty nappies, but that he had the futile task of trying to defeat that tennis invincible, Father Time.

Just because Lendl would in time find himself surrounded by six women, as well as his German shepherd bitches, don't suppose that in his retirement he became a kind of super-feminised version of himself, an Ivana Lendlova. 'Ivan is a pretty macho guy,' Samantha has said. 'I wouldn't exactly say he is one of those people who has a feminine side.' Perhaps it was to thwart the oestrogen; most probably it was because he was just being himself and couldn't remember how to behave any other way, but there were times in this domestic world when he still acted like an alpha male. 'When the kids were crawling, he would say, "Okay, who can get to the top of the stairs first?" And he would sort of push them, and they went up the stairs,' Samantha has recalled. To further encourage a competitive spirit among his girls, he required that they all picked a sport and then committed themselves to it, while pressing home the message that there was nothing worse than losing. 'I always rewarded achievement and winning – that's good for sports and life,' he disclosed in an email to the *Palm*

Beach Post. 'It would benefit any athlete. It teaches you to take pride and ownership in your work.'

Some of the methods that Lendl would use when coaching Murray, including not showing any emotion with his facial muscles, he had developed while on the range or the golf course with his daughters. 'I've never shown any emotion as it can transfer to the players,' Lendl once said. 'It served me well with my daughters and I don't see this [coaching Murray] as being any different. Yes, Murray's a man and they were just children and this is a higher level, but I think the principle is just the same.' There was something paternal, fatherly, about the way Lendl would behave towards Murray, and also Murray's assistant coach, Dani Vallverdu. Doubtless, Lendl would have been delighted that three of his girls – Marika, Isabelle and Daniela – chose golf, and some of his happiest moments in retirement came when sitting on a five-dollar fold-up plastic chair from Wal-Mart, watching his daughters compete on the course. Being part of the Lendl clan, they didn't turn out to be hackers either, with the Lendl girls ending up attending a finishing school for golfers, the David Leadbetter Golf Academy in Florida. Marika and Isabelle went on to play golf for the University of Florida, while Daniela, known to her family as Crash, after an incident involving a tree, a dog and a golf cart, played for the University of Alabama. Like their mother, Caroline and Nikki would become accomplished horsewomen.

Only very rarely have Lendl's girls seen recordings of his tennis matches, and then only in part, not the full-length baseline feature. Not wanting to bore his children – nor feeling the need to impress them – he also hasn't made them sit through countless heroic tales from yesteryear.

At one stage, Marika showed some promise as a tennis player and at the age of eleven, her father remembers, she was ranked second or third in New England at under-twelve level. The problem was, Lendl has recalled, 'people were a pain in the butt' about any child of his playing competitive tennis, and her presence on court attracted the occasional heckler who would lean against the wire fence during the warm-up and call out: 'Are you going to be as good as your dad?' Understandably, that aggravated Lendl: 'I mean, what kind of person says that? To me, that was just uncalled for.' The other difficulty for Marika was that she was repeatedly picking up injuries, and her father concluded that her build wasn't right for tennis. 'The doctors were saying, "Growth plate this, growth plate that", but that was all baloney to me. To me something in that sport wasn't right for that kid and for that body type,' Lendl has recalled. There was also the realisation, when Marika and her team-mates travelled to a competition in Cincinnati 'and got their butts kicked by everybody else', that being highly ranked in New England didn't really count for much.

So Marika quit tennis and for a while she didn't play any sport, which, as her father described it, had them 'butting heads'. To persuade his eldest to take up golf, Lendl resorted to bribery, promising her a puppy if she played six days a week for three months, 'and then she got hooked'. Isabelle also tried swinging a racket rather than a golf club, but her father soon informed her she was 'too slow and clumsy' for tennis.

Wanting to help with his daughters' golf training, Lendl once noted which of their rivals had been long off the tee, and then went to chat up the parents, to learn which sports they were playing as well as golf. Hearing that most seemed to be ice-skating or playing football, Lendl advised his golfing children to take up roller-blading, as building up that strength in your legs clearly gave you a few extra yards with your driver. And when Lendl's daughters made a mental error – such as the time Marika teed the ball up in the wrong spot – he spoke to them afterwards to help them to learn from their mistakes.

However, there was no danger of Lendl becoming a pushy golf dad, living every one of his brood's drives, approaches and putts; he admired how Tiger Woods' father, Earl, had known when to pull back. 'I don't need to live my life vicariously through anyone. I live, have lived, a great life already,' Lendl said in an interview with the *Guardian* in 2008. 'Tiger's father, Earl, was the perfect example. Thousands of parents get it wrong, but he is the one who did it perfectly, as he knew exactly the right time to step away.'

Such was the competition between those girls, it wasn't unusual for whichever sister had lost to start sobbing on the eighteenth green. They were also competitive with Dad, the *Palm Beach Post* reporting that, after Isabelle, who 'had been working relentlessly to defeat her father, finally succeeded, she said he refused to acknowledge it'. On another occasion, when Lendl had beaten Isabelle, she 'was so furious that she refused to ride home with him and called her mother to pick her up'. Lendl has acknowledged how horrified his wife was when she heard how he had challenged Isabelle, who was then just ten, to her place in the club ladder, and had then beaten her in a sudden-death finish. 'My wife finds these stories upsetting,' Lendl has said, 'but I think they're funny.' Isabelle has said that while outsiders might regard the intensity of the sister-versus-sister and parent-against-child competition to have bordered on the weird, that was just the way they had been brought up, and the way they were: 'A lot of people aren't used to it, but in my family it's completely normal. If you lose to somebody and you're not upset, what's wrong with you?'

When his girls were young, Lendl thought about introducing them to the Eastern Bloc, to the world outside cosseted East Coast America. But what he didn't want was for his children to feel guilty about their privileged upbringing. Their childhoods were always going to be very different from the way he had been raised. While Lendl was never going to be as fierce a parent as his own mother had been, he was sufficiently authoritarian with his children that Samantha had to make what Americans might describe as an intervention. On top of any homework from school, Lendl had set his girls an additional weekly assignment of studying one of the rules of golf, and then writing him a report. In addition, he had told them that all their mobile telephones and laptops had to be left by the back door before they went to bed, and he set a nightly curfew of 9 p.m. Worried that the girls might end up despising their father, Samantha told him in no uncertain terms, 'You're going to make them hate you', after which he relaxed some of the house rules, including pushing the curfew back by an hour. Sometimes, Samantha has said, the girls have 'ganged up' against their father, as part of what was an 'ongoing battle' for control in the household: 'They're trying to take it, and he's trying to maintain it.'

Naturally, there was still scope for a few acts of teenage rebellion – in the Lendl household that didn't just mean slammed doors, but giving up golf for a month, as Marika did in protest at her father's perceived interference in her sporting life: 'I was sick of my dad riding my back on everything. I was rebelling against him.' So she told him that, unless she asked him directly, she didn't care for his advice. In time, though, she returned to the clubs and seeking her father's counsel.

Would Lendl cut back on his golf and his time with his family to dedicate himself to helping Murray? There was no chance of him ever giving up golf to coach Murray; the Scot simply wasn't that important to him. In any case, it would still be possible to squeeze in nine or eighteen holes, whether early in the morning or after he had completed his duties for the day. On Lendl's calendar there are few more important days than the Sunday of the Augusta Masters, and there have been suggestions that there was a clause in Lendl's contract that meant he would always be allowed to watch that final round, wherever he and Murray were scheduled to be.

How would coaching Murray fit in with Lendl's family life? As Lendl had discovered, a former tennis player can no longer get away with being selfish. As he once told the *Sunday Times*, 'life clearly changes after retirement – you have to readjust your values and learn very quickly that it's not about you all the time. If you don't, you're going to have problems.' Lendl had learned to readjust, and you have to imagine that the dynamic between husband and wife would have changed. Samantha Lendl could conceivably have blocked Project Murray. There would be long absences again, and Lendl had no great love for life on the tour. But this wasn't bad timing for Lendl. If he and his wife weren't quite empty-nesters yet, their girls were growing up and moving out.

CHAPTER EIGHT
MR LENDL

Andy Murray is never going to be properly Zen. That's not his on-court personality. Even so, with Ivan Lendl in his corner there were sudden changes to Murray's behaviour in the opening weeks of the 2012 season, evident at their first tournament together, in Brisbane, and then at their first grand slam, the Australian Open. It was as if the previously uncouth Murray, who had been in the habit of raging, spewing and cussing in the direction of his previous coaches, had swallowed a leather-bound copy of *Debrett's*. It wasn't as if he had stopped swearing altogether – the microphones at the back of the court confirmed that – just that he wasn't going to be using any colourful language with Lendl.

During their first few days together on the road, with Murray winning the title in Brisbane, it became apparent that the Scot had taken to calling his new coach 'Mr Lendl', which wasn't far off giving him an honorary knighthood and addressing him as 'sir'. There was no chance of Murray giving Lendl the

Brad Gilbert treatment – quite simply, he didn't dare heckle Lendl during matches as he had abused Gilbert. So tennis was never treated to the spectacle of Murray swivelling to face Lendl and telling him, 'You're giving me nothing out here', or coating him with a throatful of abuse, insults, stars and asterisks. 'We all knew that Lendl wasn't going to take any shit from Andy, so Andy was going to have to bite his tongue, and to stop behaving like a baby in some of his matches,' Pat Cash told me. 'Lendl didn't need the job. The message to Andy would have been, "Listen, start swearing at me and that's it, I'm walking out of here. You can yell and scream at me a bit, but don't push your luck, mate. And if I walk out of here that could be your last chance to win a grand slam title. We can win it together if you listen to me and act professionally".'

There was also a rapid improvement in Murray's body language – no longer was he bloodying his knuckles by smashing clenched fists into his strings, or grabbing at his clothes like the tennis version of the Incredible Hulk, or hitting his legs and feet with the frame of his racket. In short, he was no longer regularly telegraphing his emotional distress to his opponent. There would be the occasional relapse, but that tended to be when Lendl wasn't there – after a few months, it became clear that Murray's behaviour on court was significantly better when Lendl was around than when he wasn't. And Lendl would always be around when it mattered, which was at the grand slams. 'I think the thing that made the biggest difference with Ivan was the resetting of the focus, and Ivan getting Andy to understand that you play your best tennis when you're emotionally calm,' Judy Murray told me. 'It's important that Andy doesn't get too up or too down, so doesn't waste energy celebrating something or get distracted by something that has already gone, something he can't do anything about. It's about resetting your focus and getting on with the next point.'

For all the getting-to-know-you discussions, and lunches in Florida malls, that they might have had, it's only when a player and coach are a few tournaments into their partnership that they can be sure they are going to get along. Would their relationship survive even a season? Would this be an unhappy collision of personalities? Or would this be a success?

Murray was doing everything in his power to make it work. Indeed, so keen was he to impress 'Mr Lendl' during those early days, he didn't just cut out the on-court obscenities and start carrying himself a bit better, he even felt that rare sensation before a practice session: nerves. Murray has gone so far as to liken that initial wooing period with Lendl to the first weeks of his relationship with his girlfriend Kim Sears. You can be sure that he wouldn't have felt the tension before walking on to a practice session with some of his former coaches. For the first time, Murray had a coach who was much more successful than him, so someone for whom he had a great respect, someone he was going to listen to. 'I was surprised to see Lendl back in tennis, as he had been out of the game for years. It was unusual to see Lendl there, but it made sense,' Cash told me. 'Their personalities aren't that similar, even though they both have a dark sense of humour. But from the beginning, I thought it might work.' John McEnroe had his initial reservations – on first hearing the news, he thought Murray hiring Lendl was 'a left-field shot, sort of desperate' – but he would soon come around to the view that the partnership could be successful.

Like Murray, Lendl also worked hard at the relationship. This was a man from an era of shameless egomaniacs, from an age when the leading players behaved as though they were, as Boris Becker put it, getting close to God. And yet here he was being extraordinarily accommodating and flexible, in his conversations and dealings with Murray and also with the other members of Murray's entourage. This wasn't Lendl being humble for the sake of being humble; this was all part of Lendl trying to be the best possible coach he could be.

Lendl's great knowledge of tennis, and his personal experience of turning his career around after four defeats in grand slam finals, would have essentially been useless to Murray if he hadn't found the right way of speaking to his employer. As Paul Annacone, who has coached Roger Federer, Pete Sampras and Tim Henman, told me: 'Ivan's been there so his historical perspective is terrific – and that must have been a terrific asset – but really it's about the message and how you communicate it.'

Central to Murray and Lendl's relationship was that they were open and honest with each other from the start; player and coach felt as though they could unburden themselves, and their trust in the other was absolute. This relationship went far deeper than Murray's previous coaching arrangements; this was about much more than forehands and backhands, and perhaps for the first time in his tennis life Murray would have felt as though the coach in his corner fully understood him. There was no 'bullshitting' with Lendl, Murray has said. Working with Lendl was a pleasure, he has further disclosed, because Lendl was very clear with his aims; he wanted to be the best possible coach he could be, he wanted Murray to be the best possible player he could be, and they were going to work hard to achieve that. Lendl wasn't going to hold his tongue for fear he was going to lose his job. To Lendl's mind, there would have been no point even starting the job if he was going to feed Murray half-truths and platitudes. If Lendl felt Murray needed it, he would give him brutal, ugly honesty. If he ever felt disappointed about Murray's contribution, if he thought the Scot hadn't been applying himself properly, he would say so. 'I don't think every coach is great at being completely honest and open,' Murray has said. 'Sometimes guys want to protect their job.'

So Lendl was open, and he wanted Murray to be, too, encouraging his new charge to tell him anything, to share all his doubts, fears and insecurities. Lendl's view is that a tennis coach is bound to the same code of confidentiality as a priest, a doctor or a lawyer, and so he said to Murray: 'Tell me anything you want and it won't go anywhere – no one will know about it.' Tennis is a leaky place – a secret is something you only tell two other people – but Murray knew that didn't apply to his conversations with Lendl. All that Lendl has said on the subject is that, having asked Murray to 'tell me things that would help me to work with him', the responses went 'very, very, very deep'. You can imagine that those conversations would have touched on subjects such as Murray's self-image after his defeats in grand slam finals, how he thought he was a 'loser', as well as his relationship with the public. One exchange we are privy to – this came from Murray – had the Scot sharing his concern with Lendl that becoming a grand slam champion could change his life for the worse by turning him into public property. Relax, Lendl said, telling Murray that all that changed for him after winning a slam was that he was offered free rounds of golf and the best tables in restaurants. In addition to opening up about his doubts, Lendl wanted Murray to tell him immediately if he didn't want him around any more. Lendl didn't 'give a flip', saying to Murray: 'The moment you're tired of me, tell me, and I'll immediately go back to playing golf.'

Like Lendl, Murray had been denigrated for being grouchy, for never smiling. As one satirical site reported after Murray and Lendl had started working together, 'Murray has appointed a new misery coach.' Murray, after feeling he had been burned by the media for making a joke about football, and by a few other early dealings with the fourth estate, went from 'being very open and excitable to less open to rather closed off – that was a hard transition for me'. It seemed as though Murray was both influenced and impressed by how Tim Henman had covered up his 'real personality'. That was pre-Lendl, but there was something very Lendlesque about that. Still, Murray would eventually open up again, which was something that Lendl never really tried.

They rallied back and forth with questions for each other. Lendl invited Murray to ask him anything, and Lendl answered them all. 'Sometimes he surprised me with his questions, because they seemed to have come out of nowhere, so obviously it had been something he had been thinking about,' Lendl has said. 'The more questions he asked, the happier I was, because it showed that he wanted to learn. I never liked to push things on him unless I had to – which I had to at times. He could pluck what he wanted from this closet, that closet or this closet. I really didn't know at times which was the best one for him – or whether any of them were right. Only he knew what he was struggling with inside.' When Lendl answered Murray's questions, it wasn't just a demonstration of the knowledge he had acquired over his hard years of learning on the tour; it was also a display of his warm-hearted nature.

But, and this further showed Lendl's sensitivity and flexibility, this wasn't one-way questioning, as there were sessions when it was Lendl putting questions to Murray. And that impressed Murray, who believed that many other former players would have been much more dictatorial in that position, and would have been saying, 'this is what I would have done in that situation' or 'that's how I would have played'. But that wouldn't have achieved much apart from allowing the former player to go ego-tripping back to yesteryear. Lendl isn't so insecure that he needs to keep being reminded of the 1980s. And, anyway, Lendl was interested in discovering more about Murray. So, rather than being dictatorial, he asked Murray about why he chose a certain shot at a particular time. Every time they spoke, Lendl was adding to his bank of information. Criticised for his arrogance as a player, there was a humility to Lendl as a coach; he accepted that there was plenty he, too, needed to learn.

No longer did Murray feel so alone on the tennis court; he now had a coach he could trust to share everything with him. 'You could see that Lendl's relationship with Murray was very good,' Boris Becker told me. 'Lendl is one of the all-time greats. He knows what it takes. Lendl played and lost in four grand slam finals before he won one, so he and Murray have a common history, but above that you could see that they had a strong relationship.' Suddenly, Murray was learning much more from his losses than he ever had in the past. So Lendl was honest, but that didn't mean he was hugely critical or negative; sometimes after a defeat Lendl would tell Murray how proud he was of his performance. That signalled to Murray that he was on the right path – he might have lost, but he had lost in the right way. One example of that was the debrief that followed Murray's five-set defeat to Novak Djokovic in the semi-finals of the 2012 Australian Open. This was the first grand slam of his new partnership with Lendl, and clearly Murray was sore that, having led by two sets to one, he hadn't gone on to beat the Serb. Lendl and Murray met the next day to discuss the match, and the constructive comments from his coach would help Murray to take the most from that disappointment. Looking back, that match was key for Murray – though he had lost, he had played just as he should have done, with some positive and attacking tennis. It was important that Murray didn't feel discouraged. He thought that Lendl handled a 'delicate situation' with great sensitivity. One of the central messages from Lendl, a man who said he hated losing, was how you could take pride in defeats – so Lendl stressed he was proud of Murray before discussing what he needed to work on.

But not every conversation they had touched Murray's soul. One of Lendl's talents was knowing when the time was ripe for a deep and personal conversation, and when it was time to lighten the mood. It is strange to consider that Lendl's off-colour, perverse and luridly unpleasant jokes, so useful for unsettling his rivals during the 1980s and 1990s, were now helping him to settle Murray, to stop the Scot from becoming too consumed by stress, anxiety and pre-match tension. So he would launch tennis balls at Murray, or tell some outrageous joke. 'Ivan had a perfect manner for Andy as he could lighten things up with humour,' Mark Petchey told me. 'That's something that Andy needed at times because he was puting so much pressure on himself to excel. So Andy had someone there who could keep it intense but who wasn't going to take it over the edge. That's important, and Ivan was very skilled at doing that.'

You could go so far as to say that bad jokes are at the centre of this story. No one has ever accused Lendl and Murray of being among tennis's great entertainers. Lendl was supposedly the grumpiest player of his generation, and Murray of his. But these two dark princes of the courts would never have formed a bond between them if they hadn't laughed at the same things. 'Andy and Ivan worked incredibly hard together, they're driven people, but they also share a scarily similar sense of humour, and laughed at the same jokes,' Judy Murray told me. 'Some of the things they laughed at are terrible. Ivan is so far away from that persona he had during his playing days, it's just not true. He was always sending through little YouTube clips or rude jokes. I remember a time at the US Open one year when we were in the player box, and Greg Rusedski was right underneath us, standing on the court doing a live pre-match chat for television. Ivan got out his bottle of water, took the cap off and started squeezing the bottle so it was firing water into the back of Greg's head. It was so childish, but it was so funny. Lendl has a wicked sense of humour. So Ivan and Andy got on well off the court as well as on the court, and that was the important for their player–coach relationship. It was important that they were able to enjoy each other's company.'

Lendl's perspective is that Murray's sense of humour is 'almost as sick as mine and that helped our relationship – you didn't have to tiptoe around if you want to tell a bad joke'. Inevitably, the disclosure that Murray and Lendl shared a sense of humour has been the subject of some mockery, with one Australian newspaper columnist saying it 'evoked visions of coach and player rolling around on the floor at the sight of a drowning puppy'. Where Murray was concerned, Lendl was using physical comedy to show affection; the more tennis balls he smacked at him in practice, the fonder he was becoming of this Scot. It was perfectly possible that Lendl's personality, humour and methods wouldn't have worked with another player, but they worked with Murray.

All this silliness and laughter – one prank was to come off the practice court, his shirt wet with perspiration, and find someone to hug so they could be a sweaty mess, too – enabled Lendl to make new friends in Murray's entourage. 'I bumped into Ivan recently and the first thing he did was to pull out his mobile phone and show me a practical joke he had played on Jez Green, Murray's trainer,' Cash told me. 'He had beaten Jez in a challenge on the Versa-Climber fitness machine, and as a forfeit Jez had to stand up in one of Murray's press conferences and say a few words. Lendl told me how he had beaten Jez. He said that the first thing he did after the challenge was made was to go out and buy a Versa-Climber. And he trained on it every day. That's the sort of thing that Lendl does. So there was a video on YouTube of Jez standing up in the press conference, and Lendl took great pleasure in that, putting somebody though an embarrassing moment.' The message that Green had to deliver at the news conference was to declare publicly: 'Ivan is a far superior physical specimen to myself.'

There was also the time when Murray and Vallverdu were having their body-fat percentage checked by submerging themselves in a tank of water, exhaling and then waiting for the signal to resurface. When it was Vallverdu's turn, Lendl held on to the technician's hand so she couldn't tap on the glass to tell Vallverdu that the test was complete and he could surface. 'Dani comes up twenty seconds later panicking, ha ha,' Lendl has said. 'Guess what he called me? It wasn't pretty.' Vallverdu would have his revenge; if Lendl was ever changing his shirt on court, so revealing any middle-aged spread, the South American would have something to say. Such is Lendl's nature, if anything untoward happened in Murray's circle, if someone had been the victim of a prank or practical joke, it was the coach who was blamed first. But he didn't mind being suspect number one, so long as it lightened the mood. 'It was all right, as long as it kept them loose, it was all good,' he has said. So Lendl wanted to work hard, but he wanted to laugh hard, too, and that was a combination that Murray liked in a coach.

Lendl also knew the importance of not swamping Murray. It wouldn't have escaped Lendl's notice that Murray's relationship with Brad Gilbert hadn't been helped by the amount of time they spent together. All those who think of Murray and Lendl as the odd couple of tennis should consider that Murray and Gilbert were a far stranger pairing, and the two of them spent a lot of time together, down to having breakfast, lunch and dinner in each other's company. However insightful and useful a coach is, there's only so much a player can take of him in any one day. So Murray and Lendl wouldn't have dinner together every night. And, before and after practice sessions, or after they had completed a post-match debrief, Lendl would sometimes disappear, to play a round, half a round, of golf, or sometimes just to hit a few balls on a range. 'When Ivan was on the road with Andy, he played golf every day. He fitted the golf in around the tennis sessions,' Judy Murray said. 'He played golf every single day. He's very disciplined like that. If Andy was practising at ten in the morning, Ivan would get up at six to play golf. A player needs his own space. Ivan and Andy spent plenty of time together around the courts, and the two of them occasionally went for dinner together, but any player will tell you that they don't want the coach in their pocket all day long.'

In Murray's own words, he and Lendl weren't 'in each other's faces the whole time'. 'He was happy to do his own thing and we would have the occasional lunch or dinner together. He was very easily pleased,' Murray told *The Times*. 'It wasn't a stressful relationship at all.' There were times on the tour, Murray's mother has said, when her son needed to get away from his coach and the rest of the team, and to talk about something other than tennis. Lendl, who has never enjoyed life on the road, supported anything that made Murray happier, especially during the grand slam tournaments. 'If Andy's at a slam and Kim is with him, he will stay with Kim and the team will stay somewhere else. So when Andy's work is done, he has time to switch off. And that's really important,' Judy Murray said. 'You shouldn't underestimate the need for emotional support, and having your friends and family around you and having different conversations. Otherwise it's just work, work, work, the whole time. The tennis calendar is packed, and there's pressure on top players to always perform, and on top of hitting the ball and competing, they've got all their other duties, such as responsibilities to the tournament and to the media. It's exhausting. Having emotional support is so important – you need friends and family around to keep that balance.'

It was also important, Lendl considered, to keep it simple. Tennis is a simple sport, Lendl has long thought, and he has accused others – the media especially – of overcomplicating and overanalysing this game, or business, of trying to win seven matches in a grand slam fortnight. There are some things, Lendl appeared to have been suggesting, that tennis's chattering classes simply can't intellectualise, and the clarity and simplicity of his tennis instruction made life a lot easier for Murray. The Scot has an excellent tennis brain, and has more variety in his racket arm than all but a few others in the game, so in the past it had appeared as though he had had too many thoughts in his head. Lendl, though, just gave him a few areas to consider before going on to the match court. 'Ivan tried to keep things fairly simple and not overcompli-cate. That's something that I think especially at the beginning of my career I struggled with. I had a lot of variety but I didn't know how to use it,' Murray has said. 'I think I've started to use it a bit better now.'

So when Murray called Lendl 'a pretty simple person', he meant it as a compliment. Lendl's past would help to define him as a coach. To avoid confusing Murray, Lendl used a trick he had picked up from his old coach Tony Roche, who had shown it was possible to 'work on certain things without the player knowing you're working on it, so you don't clog up his mind, but it just kind of happens for him'. And Lendl didn't feel the urge to prattle on during practice sessions. Indeed, the more time they spent on the practice court, the less Lendl felt the need to say anything. At the beginning, Lendl had opened his mouth a little more, but over time it reached the point where he would keep quiet throughout a practice set, and only when that set was over would he share a thought or two. Then Murray would resume training, and at the end of the session he and Lendl would discuss what they had been pleased with, and what hadn't been so great, as well as looking ahead to what they would work on at practice the next day.

Lendl didn't just have to consider Murray; he also had to think about those around him. When Lendl arrived on the scene, the rest of Murray's staff – including his fitness trainers Matt Little and Jez Green, his hitting partner Dani Vallverdu and his physiotherapist Andy Ireland – had been *in situ* for some time, and Lendl knew not to unsettle them. The first time that he and the rest of Murray's entourage were all together was in Melbourne just before the 2012 Australian Open; Murray was half expecting Lendl to suggest that they mark the occasion with dinner at Nobu or somewhere similarly expensive. But yet again, just as he had done with that lunch in Florida, Lendl proposed somewhere modest; they ate in the 'food court' area of a casino. Murray has never enjoyed a plate of 'awful' food as much as he did that night.

Clearly, Lendl wasn't much of a fine diner. 'Ivan doesn't really taste anything. He told me that if he could he would eat all of his meals in a shake form. So if he could put his steak in a smoothie-maker, he would drink it,' Murray told the *Wall Street Journal.* 'He just can't be bothered.' Murray was appreciative of how accommodating Lendl was being; he believed that one of the signs of a great coach was the ability to 'relate to everyone', to be flexible and to be able to adapt to what the player required. As much as Murray respected Lendl for everything he had achieved in tennis, he also looked up to him for the way he behaved towards others. As a coach, Lendl was many things, but one thing he wasn't was self-absorbed. Coaching Murray clearly wasn't an ego trip.

Very quickly, there was a sense of unity about Lendl and the rest of Murray's staff. Lendl had made sure of that. 'As a player, you have to have everyone around you on the same track, and Ivan was very good at making sure that happens,'

Judy Murray told me. 'Ivan obviously had an unbelievable work ethic, and he was an unbelievable competitor, and also he's older, and all that gave him the authority to lead the team, and that meant that everybody was looking at everything in exactly the same way.' After losing to Djokovic in the semi-finals of the 2012 Australian Open, Murray had to wait to do a post-match drugs test, and at Lendl's suggestion the whole team sat with the player. That was also noted by Murray.

Given his own expertise, and his personal experiences of transforming his body and his life by hiring nutritionist Robert Haas, Lendl could have been dictatorial about how Murray ought to be preparing for his matches. Still, after a few initial discussions with Murray's team, or as Jez Green described them, 'a few little battles about my philosophy and Ivan's philosophy', Lendl was happy essentially to let them carry on as they had before. 'I found that Ivan listens,' Green has said. As Lendl would have come to appreciate, Murray and his team hadn't exactly been using outdated methods. As a junior, and then as a young player new to the tour, Murray wasn't as strong or as explosive or as fit as he could have been, but he had since turned himself into one of the best athletes on the tour. Just like Lendl thirty years earlier, Murray has exercised great self-denial and self-discipline to improve his physical capabilities. And just as Lendl had found, Murray has discovered that strengthening your body also strengthens your mind. Still, Lendl hadn't been hired as a fitness consultant, to stand over Murray and make him do press-ups.

As a player, Lendl had made sure everyone was aware of the great shape he was in. Several tennis generations later, Murray wasn't exactly publicising every bench press of his off-season on Instagram, but he was one of those players who didn't mind people knowing how hard he was working on his physique. Perhaps this was in the spirit of openness, but more likely it was a reaction to accusations in the early days that he had been unfit. And when Murray linked up with Lendl, his coach wasn't going to stop him from speaking about his regime; as Murray prepared for the 2013 season, the Scot invited a group of British journalists to run along the Miami sands with him.

Away from matches, Lendl's domain was more the practice court than the gym, the track or the Bikram yoga studio. But even there, he was never totally dominant, knowing that it would have been inappropriate to destroy Vallverdu.

Of course, Lendl made some changes to Murray's practice court world. Soon after he arrived in Murray's life, that game of tennis-football – kicking and heading a ball back and forth over a net – no longer seemed so central to Murray's routine. For years, you knew that if you went to watch Murray on the practice court, at some point in the session you would see him heading tennis balls, and later you would probably overhear him discussing the forfeit that the winners would impose on the losers (these varied from wearing a pink velour tracksuit, selecting a Hannah Montana film as your next inflight movie, or wearing a cricket helmet to training). But Lendl wanted to introduce a new intensity to Murray's practice sessions. 'Lendl trained really hard as a player, and he would have made sure that they would have changed the intensity,' said Cash. 'One of the things that disappeared was doing the soccer stuff, all that kicking a ball around. I'm sure Lendl would have said, "Look, listen, do that for five minutes, but if you're on the practice court, you're on the practice court, and there's no mucking about. You have to be professional and intense on the practice court. You can't do it on the match court unless you do it on the practice court. It's always about business, that's the way to do it". You learn from the guys who've done it, and Lendl clearly had done.'

One way of raising the intensity was to outnumber Murray on the practice court, giving him two hitting partners at the same time instead of one, as a result of which he would have to keep running and hitting almost to the point of exhaustion. This was something Lendl had picked up from his time with Wojtek Fibak. 'Ivan told me that he was using the same methods with Andy that I used with him,' Fibak disclosed. 'He told me that one of the first things he did with Andy was to take him to Florida and to put two juniors on the other side of the net, and to tell the juniors to play cross-court. Andy was supposed to play down the line. After two minutes, Andy couldn't breathe. And so they stopped for a few minutes, and then started again, and again after two minutes Andy couldn't breathe. And so they stopped again. A few days later, Andy could carry on for a few more minutes. A few days after that, he could carry on for a bit longer. And then, after two weeks, he was really fit. I remember when I did the same with Ivan, he hated it.'

It wasn't unusual for Lendl to borrow training methods from his past. As well as copying Fibak's drill of doubling his hitting partners, and Roche's techniques for working on a certain shot or strategy without the player being aware of it, Lendl was also hot on repeating plays on the practice court. 'Ivan was into repetition, because that was the way he was trained,' Judy Murray told me. 'A lot of the things he tended to have Andy doing were things that he would have done when he was playing. So there was a lot of repetition to get the consistency. Ivan was also very good at putting particular tactics into training, tactics that Andy would need when play-ing particular opponents. So Ivan might have been trying to get things into Andy's head before he played a particular opponent further down the line in a tournament, so he was introducing those tactics into training and getting Andy to focus on those.'

In the early days on the practice court, Lendl was taken aback at how cleanly Murray struck the ball; a mishit off the frame, even a shot that didn't connect with the G-spot on the strings, was a rarity. Lendl has recalled an occasion at the 2012 Australian Open when he was strolling around the prac-tice court, 'and all of a sudden, I heard a mishit, so I looked at Andy and said, "What happened?" That's how rare it is.' Another of Lendl's practice court tweaks was to suggest to Murray that he didn't serve basket after basket of balls in train-ing during a grand slam; why not save his arm for matches? After all, he would be serving enough balls in matches to maintain his rhythm.

So there was change. But there was no reason for Lendl to push Vallverdu out of the entourage. Although Lendl hadn't forgotten how to smack a forehand, and was in decent shape, he wasn't young or strong enough to have given Murray the workout he needed. For that, Murray needed Vallverdu or a fellow competitor on the tour. Often during practice ses-sions, Lendl would be found at the back, on Murray's side; he wanted to see the court as Murray would see it. And all the time he would be encouraging Murray to look for, and then expose, weakness on the other side of the court. So Vallverdu was useful as a hitting partner. But it wasn't simply the case that Vallverdu would provide the ground strokes and Lendl the overview; Vallverdu's contributions went beyond that.

The story goes that Murray and Vallverdu practised together on Murray's first day at the Sanchez-Casal Academy in Barcelona, and the South American found himself thinking: 'Oh my God, who's this kid? He's very good.' Murray has recalled that Vallverdu gave him 'attitude' that day, and wasn't very friendly, but that's not how Vallverdu remembers it. Vallverdu may not have made it as a professional tennis player but he did stay part of Murray's life, and then he became ever more important to his friend's career; he graduated from sometime doubles partner and occasional hitting partner to a full-time member of staff. They tend not to hand out business cards at the practice courts, so Vallverdu's full job title has never been made official, and perhaps that's because it wouldn't fit on the card – as well as being a hitting partner and assistant coach, he has also been an executive assistant, confidant, counsellor and cheerleader-in-chief. You won't find a more excitable presence in Murray's entourage during a match. Maybe Judy Murray is the loudest of the group – you can sometimes hear her voice on the other side of the stadium – but Vallverdu is definitely the one who can't sit still in his seat. It was quite a contrast when he was sitting next to Lendl. During tight matches, Vallverdu was up and down out of his seat so much that Lendl was genuinely concerned lest he toppled over the low wall in front of him and landed on the court.

When Lendl started his new job, he was the coaching rookie; it was Vallverdu who could speak from experience about preparing players to compete at the slams. Probably more than anyone, Vallverdu knew how to get the most out of Murray on the practice court. He knew what would work and what wouldn't. And when Murray and Lendl were still new to each other, Vallverdu would have helped, where possible, to ensure everything ran smoothly.

Among Vallverdu's responsibilities was to hold the show together when Lendl wasn't around. From the outset, Lendl, who doesn't much enjoy life on the road, had made it plain that he didn't intend to flog himself around the circuit to every tournament; he would be building his diary around the four peaks of the slams. It was a measure of Lendl's commitment to Murray that in 2012 he spent around twenty-five weeks with the Scot, which exceeded the figure they had agreed on. But even then Lendl didn't attend a number of the tournaments that Murray played that season. In 2013, with Murray missing the French Open because of a back problem, Lendl spent fewer weeks on circuit. It was when Lendl wasn't at a tournament that Vallverdu would prove to be particularly valuable. He was skilled at making sure that, in Lendl's absence, Murray would still practise and prepare for matches in the way his head coach would have wanted. Vallverdu gave this project continuity and consistency.

It was plain that Lendl valued Vallverdu's opinion. In pre-match discussions it was often Murray who started the conversation, with Vallverdu chipping in. Only if Lendl 'noticed something about an opponent, or what's going on' did he contribute to the conversation, and that didn't happen often as 'the boys have it covered pretty well'. There was no egotistical bun fight, no voices or opinions vying for attention.

Serial defeat at the slams wasn't all that Murray and Lendl had in common; the former world number one Mats Wilander has observed that the two also both had 'a heavily involved mother', and Murray's partnership with his coach wouldn't have worked so well if Lendl didn't get on with Murray's mother. Their similarity in age did help. 'I'm almost the same age as Ivan, although I'm six months older than him, which he kept reminding me about,' she told me. 'That seemed to be an important point to him, but not to me.' Lendl teased Judy about her vocal support for her son when he was on court – he told her after one match that she would have to bring him earplugs if she ever wanted to sit behind him again. There was also the occasion when Judy, who had recently had her hair coloured, sat at the top of the stands watching her son practise with his coach. On espying Judy, Lendl called out: 'Hey, granny, what happened to your hair?'

'Confidence is everything', one leading coach on the men's tour has said of life in the tennis stratosphere, and that is something Lendl agrees with. If Lendl's partnership with Murray was to be successful, he would have to have Murray playing with belief again, and not questioning himself as the Scot had done in the dark weeks that followed his defeat to Novak Djokovic in the final of the 2011 Australian Open, his last slam final before teaming up with Lendl. Lendl could tinker with Murray's strategies all he wanted, and he could tell Murray all the dirty jokes he knew, but there would have been little point if he didn't first have Murray believing in himself, and trusting in his talent. Lendl knew from his own experience that confidence comes from playing well, that playing well gives you confidence, and that it wasn't always easy to start that virtuous circle. But Lendl did what he was hired to do, which was to transform's Murray's mentality for competition, to take away his fear.

Rafa Nadal's uncle and coach, Toni, told me that the greatest improvement he had noticed in Murray since the onset of the Lendl era was mental: 'The talent and the shots, they have always been there, but Lendl definitely helped Murray with the mental side, so in the important moments, Murray could be much calmer on court, much more tranquil.' And, according to Paul Annacone, Lendl had made Murray much more mentally resilient. 'I'm not sure how to measure how Ivan improved Murray, but Andy matured and learned to win more with his average level, so perhaps Ivan helped him with his resiliency, but Andy is a resilient kid,' Annacone told me.

No doubt Murray's improved behaviour on court helped to give him more poise and purpose; cutting out the negative behaviour meant that he no longer thought about tennis in the way he once had. But there was much more to this than Lendl helping Murray to reset his focus before a match; this was about him looking assured and confident, and Boris Becker offered the opinion that Murray no longer looked so anxious on the big occasion, which would have been because of Lendl's guidance, encouragement and presence: 'Mentally, Murray looked different in grand slam finals during his time working with Lendl. He didn't look as nervous. He was composed, poised and ready to play. From a mental point of view, Murray played the way he had to play.' Pat Cash observed that Lendl had helped Murray to improve his concentration, and to banish negative thoughts from his head. Darren Cahill, the man who had put Lendl and Murray together, observed: 'Andy was already a great player. But he needed that extra bit of belief when you step on the courts against guys like Federer, Nadal and Djokovic.'

Perhaps Murray had had too much respect for his rivals, both personally and professionally, which certainly wasn't something that ever held Lendl back. But Lendl knew from his own experience that you could boost your self-belief by knowing that you had done everything in your power to prepare your body for competition. Just like Lendl, Murray was never knowingly underprepared for matches. Lendl didn't have to beg Murray to work hard, just to remind him of the psychological and mental benefits of every bench press or burpee. And just having Lendl around would have confirmed in Murray's mind that he was following the right path. 'Mentally and psychologically, it was great for Andy having someone in his corner who has been through exactly the same things,' Tim Henman told me. 'Just having Lendl there would have given Andy the confidence that he was working on the right things. That must have been very reassuring.'

In addition, Murray could also take confidence simply from having Lendl in his corner – just looking over at his coach was a reminder that he was on the right path. He could be calmed, encouraged and emboldened by Lendl's stillness during matches, his coach sitting with his chin in his upturned hand. It was tempting to look at Lendl's impassive face and to think there was nothing behind it, but the reality was that this nothingness was what was keeping Murray calm. When Lendl had played junior tennis, his parents' faces had never shown any expression, but this was different. Olga and Jiří had deliberately done this because they didn't want to encourage their son to turn to them repeatedly during matches, thinking that made him appear needy, weak and vulnerable. Lendl, though, didn't mind Murray looking at him between points, but he believed that staying calm and collected would help Murray to be that way, too.

So open and direct were they with each other that during those off-court conversations Lendl was now communicating to Murray by doing nothing, or almost nothing. And maybe Murray had learned how to differentiate between one nothing look and another. 'Ivan is so poker-faced, so stoic and he never claps,' Chris Evert, the former world number one and a winner of eighteen women's grand slam singles titles, told me. 'Ivan's intense, but in a low-key way. Andy used to get so down on himself, and that was having an impact on his tennis. Ivan stopped that. He had Andy mentally balanced. If Andy played a good shot and looked over at Ivan at the side of the court, Ivan looked back in a way that said, "Okay, but keep going". If Andy was down, Ivan was saying to him, "You can get out of this". Ivan's message to Andy was "Don't get so heated or emotional – just chill".' According to Michael Chang, Lendl liked the fact that, even as a coach, people found it hard to know what he was thinking and feeling. 'I don't think he likes to be read. He's not the sort of person who likes a lot of attention. When Andy won anything, you didn't see him jumping for joy, or going nuts or anything like that, and that's just his personality. I'm sure that off the court, he was really excited and happy for Andy.'

Conventional wisdom had it that Lendl was completely quiet during Murray's matches, but that was not the case. According to Judy Murray, 'Ivan hardly moved at all – sometimes he would get up and go to the loo between the third and fourth sets – but he talked quite a bit behind his hand, and he was talking to Dani. But you didn't see that because he was covering his mouth with his hand.'

But Lendl didn't transform Murray's mental approach on his own. Once again, Lendl was plundering his own back story; for assistance, he turned to Alexis Castorri, the psychologist who had helped him in the 1980s. Murray hasn't always been keen on sports psychologists. He wouldn't have had fond memories of a previous occasion a coach had urged him to talk to a psychologist – former coach Brad Gilbert had thought the Scot was depressed and should see someone. But Murray was willing to see the lady who had transformed Lendl's tennis life, in part by the 'visualisation' mental exercises that involved describing everyday objects for five minutes without pause. When Castorri watched footage of some of Murray's early adventures on the tour, she noted that he had once played with 'happiness, excitement and zest'; where had that gone? How could she help Murray to regain the sense of fun he had once had on court? 'Andy is a creative genius, a tactical and technical genius, so he needed to reconnect with his inner strengths. It's natural that someone puts their heart and soul into what they're doing, and then sometimes forgets how much enjoyment they once took from it. Andy has lofty goals and he is hard on himself,' she told the *Daily Telegraph*. 'In that situation, you need to remember that you love the battle, that's why you are out there.'

That was a message reinforced by Lendl, suggesting to Murray he should be taking more pleasure from the fight. Sometimes your opponent was going to be better, and you just had to accept that. That was the theory anyway. 'You have to have fun,' Lendl has said. 'Once you work hard and do everything you can, the result is irrelevant. The key is to have the conviction that what you're doing is the right thing.' And Murray knew, from speaking to Lendl, that it was perfectly normal to feel nerves before a match; indeed, Lendl disclosed to Murray that he had experienced butterflies before each of his nineteen grand slam finals, and that made the Scot feel a little better. As Murray said: 'Everyone gets nervous – and he got more nervous than most people, and he knew how to deal with it.' Lendl once observed that you have to live through the fear you feel on a big occasion: 'You have to get to the point where you can say to yourself, "This is just a game, this is just a kind of exercise".'

If Murray was to enjoy his tennis and play with belief, he would have to change his tactical approach. 'If you're going to lose,' Lendl said to Murray, 'go down swinging, don't go with your ass against the back fence.' For years, Murray's problem had been that he had become so accomplished as a defensive player, at scrambling and scuffling around the court, and waiting for an opponent to make a mistake, that he hadn't attacked the ball enough. What Lendl was asking him to do was to be more proactive, to dictate traffic in a rally. You don't win many slams by just hanging about in rallies; to become a grand slam champion you had to embrace risk, go for your shots. You could reach grand slam semi-finals, even finals, but making that last step – winning a final – required something more than great defence. There could be no more diffidence, no more taking the easy and safe option. 'Ivan encouraged Andy to be more aggressive at the right times, particularly with the forehand,' Judy Murray told me. 'Ivan wanted Andy to be looking to use the forehand from the backhand side of the court. Andy's backhand is very good, but when he makes the commitment to go around to play a forehand on the backhand side, he's obviously moving his feet more, and he always plays his best when he's moving well. Sometimes, Andy can get a little bit edgy, and then he doesn't move so much. Ivan also helped Andy to be more aggressive with his second serve.'

In truth, wanting Murray to stand firm on the baseline, or to step inside and take a swing, rather than playing his shots in line with the ball kids and the line judges, wasn't an original piece of thinking from Lendl. This was colour-fully put by Lendl, but essentially what he was calling for was the same advice that all of Murray's previous coaches – plus assorted others in tennis – had been asking the Scot to do for years. Miles Maclagan, for all his abilities as a coach, had had a modest career as a player – he is probably best known for having held, but not converted, match points when play-ing Becker in the first round of Wimbledon one summer. As Maclagan said to me: 'What Ivan Lendl said to Andy might be the same as what I used to say to Andy, but it carries more weight when you've got eight grand slam titles in your tro-phy cabinet.' Mark Petchey agreed with that analysis: 'Ivan brought something which very few people on this planet are capable of. Ivan has been there, done that, and he can say, "This is what happened, and this is how I dealt with it, and this is what I feel you are capable of, and what you should do in these situations". And when someone with his experience says that, you're going to listen to it.'

If Murray had heard all this before, now he had the pio-neer of the power-baseline game, someone who had won multiple majors by throwing his racket at the ball, telling him the same. Finally, Murray was going to listen to the advice. 'The most important thing is that Murray respected and lis-tened to Lendl,' Cash told me. 'We always knew that Andy had the talent, though he just had to improve in a few areas here and there, such as being more attacking and less defen-sive. People had been saying that for years, but he needed someone he would listen to. He hadn't listened to coaches like Petchey and Maclagan, but he did listen to Lendl.'

You don't hire a legend of the sport to tell you how to grip a racket, or to make any great technical changes to your game. Anyone near the top of the sport is unlikely to have many technical flaws in his game. And, as Murray has noted, just because a great from the past had been highly success- ful during his own playing career didn't mean he would be any good at teaching someone the technical stuff, where he would be useful would be in discussing the psychological, mental and tactical aspects of the sport. That legend would be able to discuss how to behave on the big occasion, and lead conversations about how to cope at certain moments, because he would have already been through those matches and moments himself. This was true of Murray and Lendl. There weren't any great technical upheavals – it would have been rash for Lendl to dismantle Murray's game and then rebuild him. As Judy Murray observed: 'How you grip a racket didn't come into it.' And as Henman noted: 'Technically, I don't think that Lendl changed much, but he helped with Andy's game style and with getting the right balance between being proactive and reactive, and making sure he's looking to dictate. Plus, making sure that Andy stays on his forehand and doesn't spin off on his forehand. Those were very minor adjustments, but, at this level, those very small things can make all the difference.'

Thanks to Lendl, Murray had become a better tennis player. 'With Lendl as his coach, Murray began to play bet- ter tennis,' Becker told me. 'His positioning on the court was different, his forehand different, too. You could see that his whole approach towards matches had become much more positive. That was because he had improved, and he had improved because of Lendl.'

CHAPTER NINE

OBSESSION

Golden, and topped with a pineapple, it does sound as if the object of Ivan Lendl's desires could have been a cocktail in a beach bar or in some kitsch nightclub. But let's not trivialise this: nothing made Ivan Lendl more human than his failure to win the men's singles trophy at Wimbledon. Or, as he called it, 'Vimbledon'.

That's not to say that Lendl ever became, in that great Vimbledon or Wimbledon tradition, a lovable loser or glorious failure – rather, his inability to win the Championships, the only major missing from his collection of grand slam titles, made him appear weak, inadequate, mortal. Inevitably, there were plenty who took pleasure in that – this most modern, manufactured and scientific of tennis professionals was unable to win a tournament played on the sport's original surface, one that hadn't changed since nineteenth-century ladies in corsets were flashing a bit of ankle. Every time Lendl lost on the lawns of the All England Club, you would hear this again from his critics and their three-ring circuses of relish: the Machine had broken down on the grass. So each summer Lendl took Concorde back over the Atlantic, and he looked just that little bit smaller. 'Obsession by Ivan Lendl is rivalling *The Mousetrap* as a long runner', the *Guardian* noted in the summer of 1990. 'Both plays have wooden characterisation and a far too predictable plot.' Still, as the paper thought the only other alternative at the time was 'Bored to Death: the Stefan Edberg Story', they resigned themselves to Lendl's being the strongest narrative out there on the grass.

You wouldn't imagine that a man who won eight grand slam titles, and who held the number one ranking for 270 weeks, would be remembered anywhere on the tennis map as a failure. Indeed, had Lendl been the Wimbledon champion he would have finished his career with membership of the most elite club in tennis, as one of the very few to have won all four grand slams at least once each (at the time, the only members were America's Don Budge, Britain's Fred Perry, and the two Australians Rod Laver and Roy Emerson). And yet for the British public, for whom tennis has always been refracted through a green and purple prism, Lendl wasn't a success – he was the man who couldn't win the one tournament that obsessed him.

It's not as if Lendl wasn't the only great player from modern times who had found that winning one of the majors was beyond him. Hadn't John McEnroe – who came closest to victory when he led Lendl by two sets to love in the 1984 French Open final – never conquered the clay of Roland Garros? And what of Pete Sampras, who won every slam apart from the French Open? Or how about Boris Becker, a champion at the other grand slams, but a failure in Paris, or Mats

Wilander, who won every major apart from the Wimbledon Championships, or Björn Borg who, for all his success at Roland Garros and Wimbledon, never won the US Open? Becker has an interesting perspective on this, telling me that Lendl's serial failure at Wimbledon would have taught him some humility: 'It's very difficult for players to win all four grand slams, but maybe it's a good thing that a group of us didn't win everything, as otherwise Lendl, and the likes of McEnroe and myself, would have ended up believing – we were confident guys anyway – that we were close to God.'

There isn't just one theory as to why Ivan Lendl didn't win that golden pot, as to why as a player he never wore a tux and a dickie-bow to the Champions' Dinner. There's a whole racket bag crammed full of these theories, and some of them appear, at least on first reading, to be contradictory.

The sport's sages say that tennis often comes down to who wants it more – well, if that were so, Lendl would have won ten Wimbledons. If Lendl appeared to have one insurmountable problem, it was that he cared too much, that he had turned himself into a Wimbledon fanatic. So consumed was he by the pursuit of glory at the All England Club, it would be no surprise if he admitted to being consumed night and day by the dream of winning Wimbledon. Lendl couldn't help caring so much; what he could help was how open he chose to be about his ambitions to win, as Americans sometimes called it, 'The Big W'. Was it really so smart of Lendl, who didn't win a set in his two Wimbledon finals, against Boris Becker in 1986 and Pat Cash in 1987, to have been so indiscreet about his ambitions? Broadcasting the extent of his Wimbledon obsession had two effects – it meant that, for the British, and for many other tennis enthusiasts around the world, Lendl would be defined by his success, or otherwise, on Centre Court. That's why Lendl's failure at Wimbledon appeared to be on a far grander scale than any other player's thwarted ambitions to win a slam. The other consequence of Lendl's honesty was that there was additional pressure on him every summer. Putting everything into winning one tournament – even skipping the French Open on a couple of occasions to give himself more grass-court preparation before Wimbledon – was hardly going to allow him to play with greater freedom on the lawns. Fail on the grass and there was a danger that the entire season, even if it yielded grand slam success elsewhere, could be viewed as a disappointment. 'Everyone knew that winning Wimbledon was Lendl's obsession,' Becker told me, 'and that hurt him. These days, maybe he's thinking to himself, "I wish I hadn't been so open and maybe then I would have won Wimbledon".'

Not that Lendl liked to talk of having an obsession, saying to a journalist one summer, 'that's your word, not mine'. Nor did he call it a fixation or a monomania, using instead a Czech word, *zazrany*. 'That means very much into it, stubborn almost. But make sure you get it right when you say it because it sounds like another word, which is a dirty word.'

Obsessed, fixated, stubborn, Lendl perhaps couldn't help himself, perhaps he couldn't do anything other than speak openly and honestly about his grass-court ambitions. He had also said he wanted to win other slams, and that had worked out for him. 'That's who Lendl was – he fought with an open shield,' Becker told me. 'Lendl wasn't hiding the fact he wanted to be a Wimbledon champion, just as he hadn't hidden how he wanted to win the other grand slams and to be the world number one. So maybe at the time he thought he was doing the right thing. Winning Wimbledon, though, is a bit more mental than the other slams, and a bit less about the physical side of things and your technique. It's about how you mentally approach the game. So maybe in the Wimbledon finals he played, he was more uptight than his opponent because he regarded it as being so important. A Wimbledon final is always a nerve-racking moment – it was important for me in 1986, and it was important for Cash in 1987 – but when you talk so openly about the importance of it, maybe it's a bit more.'

By doing everything in his power to prime himself for the All England Club, by removing all possible excuses for not winning the title, Lendl was setting himself up for the crushing thought that he simply didn't have the talent to be a Wimbledon champion. Lose, and there wouldn't be any rationale to shelter behind. He would just be left with his imperfections, that and a blank against his name. There was courage in taking such an approach; he wasn't just leaving himself open to others' comments, but also to the critic in his own head. Perhaps subconsciously other players would have wanted to compromise on part of their preparations – at least then they would have had an excuse for the failings. That wasn't, however, the Lendl way. Hence, some years, Lendl started his preparations for Wimbledon as early as April; at a time of year when his contemporaries would have been raising orange-red dust clouds on European clay courts, he was on the other side of the world, practising on Australian grass. Lendl and Tony Roche would host what they called 'Wimbledon Day', with Roche inviting some of his Australian buddies, players such as Ken Rosewall and John Newcombe, along to help prepare the Czech for that summer's Championships.

Between them, those Aussies could have told Lendl everything he possibly wanted to know about Centre Court despair – Roche had lost in one Wimbledon final, against Rod Laver in 1968, while Rosewall had been the runner-up on four occasions in a twenty-year period between 1954 and 1974. And Newcombe could speak about Wimbledon glory, having won the tournament three times.

Lendl was certainly more interested in what that gang of Australians had to say than in what his parents were advising – it used to amuse and frustrate him that, although his mother and father didn't exactly have a depth of grass-court experience, they still thought they could coach him by long-distance phone calls how to become a Wimbledon champion. Some seasons, such as in 1986, Lendl practised on the grass of Forest Hills in New York, training so hard that they were in danger of running out of balls. That was the season the All England Club made the switch from white to yellow balls, and in preparation Roche had had 300 yellow Slazengers shipped out to America for the pre-Wimbledon boot camp, but even that wasn't enough – he had to request an additional six dozen.

Lendl wasn't afraid to be bold in his pursuit of a Wimbledon title. But was missing the French Open, not once but twice, actually counter-productive? This upped the ante; this was Lendl telling tennis he cared so much about winning Wimbledon that he was willing to relinquish the chance to add to the three titles he had already won at Roland Garros. By skipping the French Open in 1990 and again in 1991, Lendl would also be forfeiting the points that could have kept him at the top of the rankings. 'By missing the French Open, Lendl was putting more pressure on himself,' Becker observed. Lendl's own coach wasn't sure that the Czech was being wise – Roche advised Lendl to consider seriously whether he was making the right choice by skipping Roland Garros. 'I told Ivan that it was one hell of a gamble, that he would really be putting all his eggs in one basket,' Roche has said. 'It would cost him the number one ranking because of all the tournaments he missed and it would certainly add pressure at Wimbledon. I didn't say, "Don't do it". I just said, "Give it some thought".'

Lendl, though, was clear in his mind – not winning Wimbledon would leave a void in his life, and he wanted to be able to look back in his retirement either with the satisfaction of having been the champion or of having given his all. One of the qualities that Cash used to admire in Lendl – though he wouldn't have been so open about his admiration at the time – was his ability to travel the world, switching from one surface to another, and to adapt quickly. 'We played on a real variety of courts then, from really lightning fast all the way to really slow clay courts, and he could move from one surface to the next with ease. I admired that a lot. I didn't know how he did that. It used to take me four or five days to get used to a court; but he used to walk off a plane and get right into it.' However, that didn't extend to grass courts. With just a fortnight between the French Open and Wimbledon, there wasn't a great deal of time for players to make the toughest transition of the season, going from a high, looping bounce on clay to a quick, skidding one on grass. Suddenly, from hitting shots from up around your ears on one side of the Channel, you're dealing with balls shooting through at ankle height.

Presumably, Lendl's plan didn't involve defeat to Stefan Edberg in the semi-finals of the 1990 Championships, and his wife fleeing the court in tears, telling journalists, 'I don't want to talk about this,' It is worth noting that Lendl's preparations for that Wimbledon were complicated slightly by the birth of his first child in May, as he wanted to be there to support his wife. That summer, they reportedly rented a three-storey house in Wimbledon Village, with Lendl installed on the third floor, the baby on the first and Samantha apparently 'shuttling back and forth'. But becoming a father wasn't going to be an excuse for any defeat, with Lendl saying at the time: 'I know this sounds terrible but at least until Wimbledon is over, I need to get my sleep. When we get home, I will help more.' And then the following summer, at the 1991 Championships, he endured a third-round defeat against America's David Wheaton, his earliest departure from the tournament for a decade. In mitigation, it should be remembered that Lendl's hand was causing him problems during that season, as it was swollen up, and there was also a growth on the webbing between his thumb and forefinger that was said to have resembled a baby forefinger.

Another theory about Lendl's failures is that, as a young man, he hadn't cared enough about the sport's history, and winning the most traditional of the slams, and the result was that he didn't get a good grass-court education. And how eccentric these English are, he used to think on his first few visits to the All England Club, that they break off for tea at four o'clock every afternoon, aborting a match that was only halfway through. It was hardly surprising that someone who had grown up behind the Iron Curtain, and who was caricatured by Londoners as a Cold War villain, would experience such cultural confusion and unease when confronted with cream teas. Perhaps Lendl was also displaying an Eastern European's natural suspicion of grass courts. You would have thought that Lendl's exposure to Wimbledon as a teenager, when he won the junior title, would have opened him to the appeal of the All England Club. Some thought, and still think, that as a young man, Lendl didn't take the tournament quite as seriously as he should have done – this would catch up with him a few years later when he was a contender for the title, and perhaps hadn't banked enough Wimbledon experience. At least one observer who watched Lendl at the 1981 Championships, when he lost in the first round to Australia's Charlie Fancutt, thought he was just going through the motions, and then the following summer he didn't even bother with Wimbledon, only to then turn up on a golf course, competing in a pro-am competition at the Westchester Country Club to promote something called the Manufacturers Hanover Westchester Classic. Lendl's explanation was that he was missing Wimbledon because he was allergic to grass, that running about on a lawn made him sneeze a lot. On the course that day, Lendl asked nobody in particular: 'Has Wimbledon started yet?' But, as someone who saw him there that day pointed out, the Country Club had considerably more grass than Wimbledon. In time, Lendl's attitude towards Wimbledon would change, but that summer his indifference could hardly have been in greater contrast to the mania of the British public, who hadn't had a male British champion since the 1930s.

But there was more to Lendl's absence than his runny nose, since he also suggested he had missed Wimbledon to dedicate himself to playing clay-court tournaments – at the time, clay was the most productive surface for him, to the extent that he thought concentrating on the dirt would propel him to the number one ranking. Why go to the bother of playing Wimbledon, when that would leave him feeling 'dead', and so not in the best possible shape for scuffling around in the clay the rest of the season? Exhausted and disappointed after the 1982 French Open, where he had lost in the fourth round to Mats Wilander, Lendl thought he needed a rest from tennis. He had scheduled a holiday for the same time as the Wimbledon fortnight and he wasn't going to be changing his vacation plans for something as inconsequential as the grass-court grand slam. During the tournament, Lendl found himself reading a newspaper report of the rain delays and backlog of matches at the All England Club, and he imagined the players sitting around in the locker-room fretting about when they might go on court. And he smiled to himself; he was where he wanted to be, sitting in Miami drinking Coca-Cola.

It would have made sense if Lendl's feelings towards the slams had been coloured by living among Americans. The four grand slams are supposedly all equal – few players ever admit to having a favourite major, just as parents seldom admit to having a favourite child – but moving to the United States as a young man had clearly had an impact on Lendl's view of the tennis world. For a while, it seemed as though one slam was more important than all the others and that was the hard-court US Open. In time, Lendl would change his views. There's little doubt that he would have been influenced by the views of coach Roche, one of the great Wimbledon heads. But you also have to imagine that, after winning a first French Open in 1984 and then a first US Open in 1985, Lendl would have started to look around a bit more and perhaps have developed a greater appreciation of what else out there was worth coveting. And then, after winning a first Australian

Open in 1989, the career grand slam was on – he was just a Wimbledon title away from the full set. With each year that passed, the more foolish it must have seemed not to have been totally serious about Wimbledon in his youth. Certainly, towards the end of his career, he was no longer disturbed by the English crowds breaking off for tea during matches. But he couldn't go back in time and retrospectively add to his tennis education. 'I now realise,' Lendl once said, 'that if I had played Wimbledon that year [1982] it would have helped me to learn to cope with grass quicker.'

In the summer of 1986, teenage girls in London screamed for Becker. 'Boom Boom versus Gloom Gloom' was how the English press had billed the climax of that summer's Championships, and afterwards Lendl was pulling another of his sad faces – he couldn't stop Becker from retaining the title he had won the previous summer at the age of seventeen. With John McEnroe missing the tournament, the pre-Championships consensus had been that there might never have been a better chance for Lendl to win Wimbledon. It wasn't to be. 'I always felt good on grass, I always liked playing against Lendl on grass, and I had a good day,' Becker told me. Becker has recalled that Lendl wasn't his usual provocative and talkative self in the locker-room; rather, he had been silent, frightened and transfixed. Becker, though, had dreamed of victory the night before, and was sure he would beat Lendl. All afternoon, Becker kept stepping in and taking big swings at Lendl's second serve, which made life very awkward for the Eastern European. Lendl wasn't quite sure how to counter Becker's aggressive returning, which was putting great pressure on his first serve, and he also couldn't do the same back to Becker as the German was serving so well. This was Becker showing the world that it hadn't been a fluke the summer before – he was also capable of winning Wimbledon at eighteen. There was a moment in the match when Becker looked over and thought he could see something in his opponent's face: Lendl didn't know what to do; he simply didn't know how to respond.

The following summer, at the 1987 Championships, Becker lost early, with a second-round defeat against Australia's Peter Doohan. In the after-shock of that result, a nineteen-year-old Becker had to remind some at the All England Club that no one had died. With Becker out, there was a growing body of people who thought that Lendl could win the tournament. Lendl would indeed reach that year's final. Yet, once again, it was a fairly one-sided match. One tabloid headline read: 'Hard Cash bounces blank Czech'. Some of the most excruciating moments of Lendl's tennis life came in the moments after the completion of that match. He couldn't retreat into the locker-room; rather, he had to stick around on Centre Court, watching as the Wimbledon committee brought out the table smothered in a Union flag, plus the prizes and the royalty, and as Cash, a descendant of a Tasmanian bandit, ignored the protocol about waiting by the umpire's chair, and instead bounced up the stands to embrace his friends and family. You'll never see a man looking as despondent after a tennis match as Lendl did that day. Lendl thought he should have been allowed to leave. Trapped on the court, he stood to the side, a sad and pitiful figure.

Almost thirty years have passed since that day, but anyone sitting down with Cash at a café near London's Carnaby Street, expecting to hear him express any regret for what he put Lendl through that afternoon would be disappointed. But you have to wonder whether Lendl would have given himself a better chance of winning Wimbledon if he had been a bit more pleasant to be around in the locker-room and on the tour. It's plain that personal animosity played some part in the 1987 Wimbledon final; after all, at the time Cash had always regarded Lendl as being too unfunny for words, and so wouldn't have minded at all that he had made his rival suffer. 'Often people say to me, "How do you feel about beating Lendl at Wimbledon and stopping him from winning the one tournament he really wanted to win?" And I say, "Well, he won everything else, and I only won one grand slam". So, no, I don't feel sorry for him, not one iota. If I had lost to Lendl in the Wimbledon final, it would have been painful. I would have lost a Wimbledon final and, to make it worse, I would have lost to him. That would have really upset me. But I didn't really think about losing. I knew if I played my best tennis, I would beat him.'

Throughout Lendl's career, mainstream tennis opinion had been that you volleyed your way to a Wimbledon title. Primarily, that was because grass played so fast – the ball came so quickly on to your racket that it was generally thought to be a better option to move into the court and play a shot before the ball bounced. In addition, during Lendl's time, the grass would become scarred, scuffed up and churned up; deeper into the fortnight, little patches of bare earth would start to appear, and if the ball landed on one of those you couldn't be sure about the trueness of the bounce. This was quite unlike the New York cement, where you could swing away with confidence knowing that the ball would be exactly where you thought it would be. Much of the analysis about the Wimbledon Championships in the 1980s, even into the early 1990s, comes down to gardening. If Lendl replicated the Arthur Ashe Stadium playing surface in his backyard, he couldn't ever do the same with the Centre Court grass – every lawn has its idiosyncrasies, its own dead patches and peculiar bounces. For a man who loathed surprises and unpredictability, and who craved control, the bounces on a grass court were the ultimate challenge. And even at the start of the Wimbledon fortnight, when you were more likely to get a true bounce, Lendl didn't always look comfortable – in the first couple of rounds, the grass would be greener and therefore slicker, which would mean that the ball would shoot on to his racket at even greater speeds.

So Lendl was for ever hearing that, if he wanted to win Wimbledon, he couldn't possibly stay back – he would have to be at net whenever possible, just like Edberg, Becker and McEnroe. Let's not underestimate what a wrench it must have been for Lendl, who had presided for so long on the baseline, to have attempted to transform himself into a serve and volleyer every summer. One of the reasons why Lendl had been drawn to Roche in the first place was that he thought the Australian could improve his volley; even so, actually going ahead and becoming a serve and volleyer wasn't going to be an easy process. So, each summer, Lendl would have to unlearn his usual game from the back of the court. All the while knowing that, after Wimbledon was over, he would have to rebuild his normal baseline game. Some years, in the days leading up to Wimbledon, Lendl would even struggle to live with Roche on the practice courts. 'By the end of the Wimbledon fortnight, I would finally get the timing of playing on grass, but then all of a sudden the tournament would be over, and I would go back home and I had nothing again, because I had lost my ground strokes. Then I had to work twice as hard to get back to my regular game, so every year it was a difficult time for me,' Lendl has said. His view has long been that his record was something to be proud of, that appearing in two finals at the All England Club, and reaching the semi-finals at five other Wimbledons, was much more of an accomplishment for him than featuring in eight successive US Open finals.

'Huge credit to Ivan – you don't see anyone in this era having to change their game so dramatically for one tournament to try to be so successful, and the guy did a great job at almost winning it,' Mark Petchey told me. 'Sometimes that is lost in the whole discussion about Ivan not winning Wimbledon. Boy, did he work hard to change a game that was a winning game on all other surfaces – for years he was crunching people on other surfaces. He almost got there. I'm sure Andy has looked at Ivan's Wimbledon record in that kind of detail, and that would have increased the respect he has for the guy.'

Lendl's rackets had been set up for serve and volleying, not for blasting away from the baseline. It had taken a good while, and lots of experimenting, for Lendl and his racket technician Warren Bosworth to settle on what they believed to be the right tension for his rackets – eventually they committed to fifty-five pounds, which was seventeen and a half pounds lower than the seventy-two and a half pounds he played with on other surfaces. On grass, Lendl had thought his usual tension had felt too 'boardy' when he was trying to jab at the ball after getting a rotten bounce; by dropping the tension, he had more life in his returns, plus he also found it helped his serve and his volley. That was all well and good, but having his rackets strung at such a low tension meant Lendl couldn't change his mind in the middle of a match and decide to stay back.

Of course, in Lendl's playing days you couldn't have missed the news that he had committed to a new grass-court game, that he had been working hard with Roche at adding variety to his tennis, chipping and charging, chasing in after his serve, volleying. Roche was teaching Lendl all about the geometry of a tennis court, showing him that you could win a point by using angles rather than brute power. Those were all the skills, both player and coach thought, that could have Lendl winning Wimbledon. But Cash didn't buy into that. He told me that Lendl never did enough work on his net game, that he never truly committed to becoming a serve and volleyer. 'The strange thing was that Lendl really thought about the game, the tactics, and how to become a better player, but he would only serve and volley for one month a year. It was always a great relief to me when I saw him playing at a hard-court tournament – for example, some tournament in February that didn't really matter – and never going to net. Not once, never. I would think, "great", because there's no way you can become a great volleyer in just a week or so before Wimbledon. He should have been coming to the net for six months a year. If he had served and volleyed consistently over the course of the year, he would have won Wimbledon. But he didn't do it. There might have been a reason why he didn't try that. It's quite possible that he didn't want to experiment during the year, as he didn't want to lose his ranking, as there was money involved. But it was a big mistake.'

Cash isn't the only voice in tennis who thinks that Lendl should have been more committed to serve and volleying. It was a view that Martina Navratilova – one Czech émigré whose Wimbledon obsession resulted in great success, with nine women's singles titles – articulated after yet another of Lendl's grass-court disappointments. Navratilova went even further than Cash, suggesting that Lendl should have played a serve and volley game *all year*. Word reached Lendl, and he couldn't agree with that assessment: 'It's just not possible for me to serve and volley all the time. I still have to stick to my strengths and it would be silly for me to throw the whole year away. I sacrificed three months for Wimbledon. You have to draw the line somewhere.'

That wasn't the only weakness Cash detected in Lendl's grass-court game: 'I've discussed this with Becker – Lendl didn't have a powerful blocked return. He had a chipped forehand return and he had a big wind-up return. And on the backhand, he had a slice and then a big, powerful backhand. But he didn't have anything in between and he needed that. What he needed was almost like a punch return, a doubles player's kind of return, which would have allowed him to punch the ball down to his opponent's feet. For whatever reason, he didn't have that, and that was probably because he didn't feel comfortable on the grass. But again, for a guy I had seen as being really professional, that wasn't very professional,' Cash said. And Lendl's failings made Cash look at the Czech in a new light. 'I realised I had stepped it up, and leapfrogged him in terms of training and professionalism – doing all those things gave me great confidence, and had me thinking to myself, "Hey, I've overtaken you – you think you're the fittest guy in the world, but you're not". He believed he had thought about the game, but I could outattack and outplay him. It was probably about a year before the 1987 final that I thought to myself, "Nah, you're not improving as much as you need to if you're going to win Wimbledon". There must have been a reason he didn't fix up his return. He didn't have a bad return. It just didn't work on grass.'

While Lendl won titles at the pre-Wimbledon grass-court tournament at London's Queen's Club, there's a world of difference between going through a draw-sheet in West Kensington, and then doing the same a few miles away at the All England Club. For one thing, there appeared to be a difference between the lawns at the tournaments; Lendl observed that the bounce on the Wimbledon grass was appreciably lower than at Queen's: 'The court at Queen's was so true, it was like a hard court, with the bounce high, which suited a tall player like me.' Even after all the time he spent on grass courts, whether practising or competing, he couldn't shake off his awkwardness, with one British magazine, the *Spectator*, noting how the Czech 'played backhands from a constipated crouch'. Close to God? There was no tennis tournament where Lendl was degraded as he was at Wimbledon; there was a mocking line in the *Guardian* one summer noting that, 'though never better prepared for grass this year, he still has the uneasy look when he walks on court of someone who has inadvertently walked into the ladies'. Even on his favoured hard courts, Lendl's movement wasn't the strong part of his game, and that flaw was exposed on the Wimbledon greensward – Fred Perry watched Lendl and thought that the Eastern European didn't know how to run on grass: 'Normally Lendl runs to the ball and gives it a clout. On grass you run to the point where you can conveniently reach out and hit it. It's a different rhythm and I think he has trouble with that.' In addition, Perry saw fear in Lendl's eyes. Writing in the mid-1980s, Perry observed: 'I know Lendl is a big hitter with a crunching serve and a bomb of a forehand, but when he plays a shot he hesitates for just a fraction of a second to make sure he's hit it right. You cannot afford to wait in tennis and you cannot be deliberate on grass. Points must be put away with the killer thrust of a swordsman – and that's not Lendl.' To Perry's mind, Lendl was 'too deliberate, too regimented'.

Perhaps Lendl was unlucky at Wimbledon; at the 1989 Championships, he led Becker by two sets to one in their semi-final, and then the rain came, and Becker's coach, Bob Brett, could give his man a match-changing pep talk: 'I can live with losing. Anyone can lose a tennis match. But you've quit. You've given up. How can you do that? Are you really such a loser that you can walk out in a Wimbledon semi-final and quit?' On the resumption, Becker was the player in command, and he came back to win the match in five sets. 'Nothing is ever a sure thing,' Roche has said, 'but I think that if it hadn't rained Ivan would have won that match.' If the weather had stayed dry, Lendl certainly would have been well placed to make a third Wimbledon final, where he thought he would have had a very winnable match against Edberg. As it was, Becker went on to win his third Wimbledon title.

But what if Lendl could have made his own luck, and given himself a greater chance of winning Wimbledon, by playing his normal power-baseline game? Would Lendl have been better placed to win Wimbledon if, instead of attempting to become a serve and volleyer, and chip and charging dur-ing return games, he had focused his energies on becoming an even better baseline player? As the great Lew Hoad said of Lendl: 'He was trying to turn himself into something he could never be.' Jack Kramer said that Lendl's decision to try to win Wimbledon as a serve and volleyer, rather than with his own game, was 'the tragedy of his career'.

There's a group of tennis thinkers who argue that, if Lendl had played on today's grass courts, he would have won Wimbledon. Certainly the twenty-first-century grass would have been much more favourable than the stuff he played on. The general slowing of the conditions at Wimbledon, as well as a more even and consistent bounce, has all but killed off the serve and volleyers and those who attack at every opportunity. But what if, even in the 1980s and early 1990s, Lendl could potentially have won Wimbledon from the baseline? After all, Björn Borg, a man not known for the quality of his volley, had won five Wimbledons with a game built around his ground strokes, showing that it was possible to succeed from the baseline. And just a few years on from Borg's time, no one was more effective from the back of the court than Lendl. The year that Lendl did win Wimbledon – alas, it was only the junior title, in the summer of 1978 – he did so by serve and volleying. But that wasn't because he had adapted his game for the grass. That was just how he played back then, as attacking the net helped to cover up all the problems in his game, such as a weak serve and a soft, inoffensive backhand. But, by the mid-1980s, he was a committed baseliner; that was his game, so why not stick with that strategy?

True, Borg sometimes followed in after his serve to avoid becoming predictable, but he never tried totally to transform himself, for one slam only, from baseliner to committed serve and volleyer. Key to Borg's Wimbledon triumphs was that he was so adept at coping when his opponent struck the ball deep and then galloped towards the net; pushed back, the Swede would either respond aggressively with a passing shot down the line or cross-court, or he would whip a topspin lob up and over the man at net – on such a wicked parabola – for a winner.

There was no reason why Lendl couldn't have developed Borg-like skills in that situation; indeed, he was already capable of hitting excellent passing shots. If there was one shot in Lendl's game that needed work, a few thought, it was the topspin lob. As they sat in Centre Court watching another Lendl flame-out, some observers couldn't help but think to themselves: if only he had improved his lob, and other parts of his baseline game, he could have won the tournament he coveted above all others. It's not that Lendl never thought about Borg's victories at Wimbledon – all in a row, from 1976 to 1980. Lendl once considered that Borg was 'limited talent-wise, and he won Wimbledon five times, and that's a mystery to me, a tremendous achievement, but a mystery'. Was there really something so mysterious about sticking to your strengths?

Becker is right with his analysis – more than the other majors, Wimbledon is a slam contested in the mind. On the Wimbledon grass courts of the 1980s, you had to think about your strategy much more than you ever did on Melbourne and New York's hard courts or on Parisian clay. In addition, one of Lendl's great strengths, and a source of much of his confidence, was nullified on the lawns; he may well have been the fittest man on the tour, he may well have had a greater capacity for pain and suffering than anyone else, but on grass, when the points were so much shorter, there wasn't much of a premium on physical fitness and the ability to keep on running. 'I don't think Lendl liked grass.' Cash told me. 'I find this hard to believe but he said that sometimes he felt as though he couldn't play on grass at all, and he had no confidence at all.' On any other surface, Lendl pretty much had any fears and insecurities under control, but on grass, the self-doubt came flooding back into his mind.

On grass, you were at a great disadvantage if you couldn't improvise. For all Lendl's preparations, he was still, in the words of his psychologist Alexis Castorri, a 'structured thinker'. This meant he had a mental block over improvisation, and that was a problem on Wimbledon's courts, which rewarded free-thinking players. How Lendl could have done with having a more creative and nimble mind, a mind like Murray's, with the Scot never suffering from a similar grass-court block. For the best example of Lendl's inability to deal with the unexpected, cross the Channel to Roland Garros in the spring of 1989. Two hundred years on from the birth of the French Republic, there was a clay-court insurrection with Lendl beaten in the fourth round of the French Open by seventeen-year-old Michael Chang, and on the surface it remains one of the most shocking and puzzling occasions in grand slam history. There was a good explanation for Lendl's defeat, and how he was unable to cope with a teenager who, because of cramp, was barely able to walk, and who took to serving underarm. There was nothing in Lendl's files about this, and he had never been in this situation before, so was it really that surprising that he looked totally bamboozled by Chang's tactics? This was about Lendl's lack of spontaneity. Why didn't Lendl have Chang regularly running wide outside the single sidelines? Why didn't he bring Chang into net with the occasional dropshot, or take the ball early and hit behind the teenager? Why wasn't he trying to wrong-foot his opponent? One statistical analysis of the match showed that Lendl played just one semi-dropshot, and made just one voluntary visit to the net. This was an astonishing spectacle: Lendl simply allowed Chang to keep on looping the ball back into play, with the rally often carrying on in that way until Lendl played the ball short, and Chang then took a big swing and went for a winner. This wasn't information that Lendl could process.

'The situation was kind of shocking for Ivan,' Chang told me. 'He was such a professional, and worked so incredibly hard, but that situation was something he had never had to experience before, and it certainly wasn't something you would ever train for. You wouldn't ever tell anybody, "Hey, you've got to be careful because one day you're going to be playing against a seventeen-year-old kid with cramp". That's not something that happens every day. Those circumstances were very shocking for him. It was Andre Agassi who first showed me how effective an underarm serve could be, and how you could unsettle an opponent. He used to do that in junior matches in the twelve-and-unders and the fourteen-and-unders. It was a spur-of-the-moment decision, really, to hit that underarm serve against Ivan in Paris. I just thought to myself: "I could hit a sixty-nine mph serve and that would give him something different to deal with". He was forced to come in, and he didn't like that. But, more than anything, I think that underarm serve changed the whole mentality of the match. After that, he became more frustrated that the match wasn't going his way.'

Lendl was serving when Chang reached match point. To further unsettle his opponent, Chang stood up to the service line to receive Lendl's second serve. 'You have to remember that I was just out of juniors, and this is what we did in the juniors, but it worked in men's tennis, too,' Chang recalled. 'I found that opponents either dropped the ball short, as they didn't want to double-fault on a big point, and then you had a great chance to win the point. Or they double-faulted, which was what Lendl did.' Castorri noted that, although Lendl had got better at 'taking a situation as it is, rather than how he would like it to be, this apparently was a constellation of events he just wasn't able to format in his mind, and as a result he lost control of the match'. As *New York* magazine noted in the 1980s: 'The one variable Lendl has not been able to eliminate is the fact he's still human. Even the most meticulous planning will not produce all the answers. When you count on being able to use logic to remain in control and then something illogical occurs, the computer can crash. The whole system can go haywire.'

Though perhaps never as graphically, or as obviously, as that humiliating loss to Chang, Lendl's structured, unimaginative thinking also hurt him in London. As *The Times* noted during one Wimbledon in the 1980s: 'He is no jazz musician – he prefers to have the sheet music in front of him.'

The Wimbledon public never learned to love Lendl; they learned to ignore him. Since Lendl appeared to regard Wimbledon's fans as the fairest and most knowledgeable of all tennis crowds, he would perhaps have expected some more love from London, or at least a greater respect and understanding. Any other character would have become the sentimental choice for the title; Lendl never acquired that status. At times, it sounded as though he was trying to change the argument. So Rosewall had lost four Wimbledon finals, but had that stopped 'Muscles', who won all the other grand slams, from being regarded as one of the greats? And what of Ilie Nastase, twice a beaten finalist at Wimbledon, but a French Open and US Open champion? Was he not a great player? By 1992, the Wimbledon narrative had moved on; by then the public were more interested in Andre Agassi's cycling shorts than they were in Lendl's long, slow Wimbledon death; it didn't happen for him that year either, with a fourth-round defeat to Goran Ivanišević. The following summer, you couldn't find a single preview feature about Lendl in the British newspapers; how quickly he had become the forgotten man of grass-court tennis. The 1993 Championships were a sad experience for that select bunch – those who cared deeply about Lendl at Wimbledon. After his second-round defeat to Frenchman Arnaud Boetsch, he immediately departed the scene, skipping the customary post-match news conference to catch the first Concorde home. Ordinarily, a player would have been fined for not showing up, but the All England Club didn't enforce the rule, almost as if they felt sorry for Lendl. As someone there at the All England Club that day said of Lendl's defeat, this was a moment that begged for poignancy, but Lendl 'has always been as poignant as a garden tool'.

CHAPTER TEN
THE ENDGAME

Ivan Lendl thought he knew about playing in the white heat of Wimbledon. He thought he knew what it was like, as one of the top seeds, to have every aspect of your game, your character and your off-court life picked over. He thought he knew about the pressures of the garden party (as someone said of Centre Court, it's a lovely place where horrible things happen). And then, in the summer of 2012, during his first Championships in Andy Murray's corner, he had to reset a lot of what he thought he knew about Wimbledon.

The place – this most traditional of tennis venues, this faux-Victorian idyll – now looked so fresh to Lendl. Back for the first time since the early 1990s, Lendl saw how the All England Club had reinvented itself with new courts and buildings, as well as improvements and additions to the existing structures, such as a retractable roof for Centre Court. And these weren't the lawns that Lendl remembered. He noted how the over-all quality of the grass had been raised to the extent that the lawns at the practice courts were superior, he thought, to the turf on the show courts during his career. Most of all, though, Lendl was taken aback by the scrutiny of the Scot, as well as how much national expectation was loaded up into Murray's racket bag as he walked past the quotation from Kipling's *If* – 'If you can meet with triumph and disaster and treat those two impostors just the same' – and out on to Centre Court. How different this was to when Lendl had been competing. Yes, Lendl's character used to be assassinated in London every summer, along with his volley. But the only person in the city who would have been truly obsessed by the Czech's quest for a Wimbledon title would have been Lendl himself; for everyone else in London, Lendl's obsession would have been a passing summer fascination, nothing more. The same couldn't be said for Murray's efforts at Wimbledon; not when Britain goes through a two-week tennis hysteria every summer. Over the summer of 2012, Lendl would come to understand why every summer Murray's mouth would break out in ulcers in the days leading up to that year's Wimbledon Championships. No other tournament has such a physical effect on Murray.

Lendl has no love for the modern media's critical analysis of everything a public figure says or does, so he wouldn't have appreciated the level of scrutiny of Murray during the grass-court swing in England. 'Things have got out of hand recently,' he has said. 'Twenty years ago I said things which, if I said them today, I would be apologising for the next twenty years.' The media was a potential distraction for Murray before and during Wimbledon. Ideally, Lendl didn't want Murray picking up any newspapers he might find lying around on the benches of the locker-room or in the competitors' restaurant. Or for him to be watching himself on the television news. Still, Murray was aware that, though Lendl would be telling him to ignore the media, his coach would have been consuming a fair amount of it and so would have known 'what every journalist and pundit had said'. Lendl was reading, listening and watching so Murray wouldn't have to. And on occasion, Lendl would step in to make himself the pre-match preview, not Murray. It's true that Lendl's presence in Murray's entourage added to the interest and air of expectation, but there's also no denying that having Lendl around to occasionally feed the media beast also helped Murray to focus on his tennis.

But it wasn't just the press's attention on Murray that flabbergasted Lendl; he was also shocked by the interest and expectation from the public. If Lendl went to a restaurant, tennis fans would often approach him, introduce themselves and ask whether Murray was going to win Wimbledon. 'It got to the point where I couldn't go out to have dinner without people swarming all over, so can you imagine what it was like for him [Murray]?' And, according to Murray, Lendl was 'getting bothered by it all'. 'Ivan had experienced pressure playing at Wimbledon, but I don't think he experienced anything like this,' Murray has observed, and it sounded as though, when it came to this particular aspect of the Wimbledon fortnight – dealing with the hoopla – Murray was tutoring Lendl as much as Lendl was advising Murray.

One of the gaps in Lendl's tennis expertise was that he couldn't tell Murray what it was like to win Wimbledon. Another was that he didn't have a great deal of experience of playing in front of an expectant home crowd, and none at all of performing in front of an expectant home crowd at a grand slam. It's true that Lendl was part of the Czechoslovakian team that won the Davis Cup in 1980, so that was one occasion he excelled on the big occasion in front of his country's tennis enthusiasts, but there weren't many others, since he had made himself unavailable to represent the CSSR from the mid-1980s onwards.

And the suspicion had always been that he didn't always look at ease competing in front of a home crowd. With a house in Connecticut, the closest thing that Lendl had to a home crowd at a slam was when he commuted into the US Open, but the spectators at Flushing Meadows never treated him as one of their own. How different from Murray's experiences – the Scot could hardly hit a forehand at the All England Club without someone throwing a Union flag over his shoulders.

Tennis is an individual sport, and Murray was clear he was primarily playing for himself, but that didn't stop everyone on Centre Court, on Henman Hill, or watching at home, from repeatedly invoking Fred Perry's 1936 victory, and the seventy-plus years of British grass-court inadequacy that had followed. Until the summer of 2012, the last tennis player to have lost to a British opponent in a Wimbledon semi-final would die of his wounds at the Battle of Stalingrad. That was Germany's Henner Henkel, who lost to Bunny Austin in the last four of the 1938 Championships, and who then served on the Eastern Front. Murray hadn't had any problems reaching Wimbledon semi-finals, but his ambitions kept on being pulped in the last four, with defeats to Andy Roddick in 2009, and to Rafa Nadal in 2010 and 2011. In 2012, Murray beat Jo-Wilfried Tsonga to at last go through to a Wimbledon final.

Murray's loss to Federer – the Scot's fourth defeat in a grand slam final – shouldn't just be lumped together with the previous three occasions on which he had finished as a runner-up.

This may have been another disappointment, but for the first time there was some life and ambition and endeavour about Murray in a grand slam final. Rather than look inhibited by the thought of playing for a slam title, he appeared invigorated, and there's a decent chance he would have won if the day had been dry. When Centre Court's retractable roof was open, Murray was the better player, and took the opening set, the first he had ever won in a slam final. The moment the match changed was when someone pressed the giant red button to close the roof, to shut out the great British summer. Federer, even classier indoors than out, came back to win in four sets. But there had been plenty to like about Murray's tennis. In his first three slam finals, he hadn't played anything like his best tennis, being too tentative and too passive, but on this occasion he had been a different animal, playing with verve and ambition, and going for his shots. This was the first grand slam final that Murray had featured in since hiring Lendl, and the coach's influence was there for all to see; just as Lendl had urged him to, Murray was being bold. So Murray had lost again, but there was no shame in this defeat – he had lost to the finest grass-court player of all time. And this was how Murray needed to play if he was to win Wimbledon at some point in the future. Every modern player has to make adjustments when playing on the lawns, but Murray didn't have to reinvent himself for grass, as Lendl had had to. He just had to be a little more adventurous.

'That was the match that set the standard for how Andy has played since,' Darren Cahill told me. 'That was when we saw the new Andy Murray in a slam final, who was willing to rip shots and not wait for the game to come to him. The big thing was that Andy showed that he wasn't just going to play set parts of the court any more. He showed he was willing to hit his forehand down the line earlier in the point, and the same on the backhand side. That match was a big turning point for Andy, even though he lost the final to Federer, as it was the first time he was able to step off a grand slam final and say, "You know what, I played on my terms. Yes, I lost the match, but at least the final was played on my terms". I like Andy a lot – he's a great friend – but when it comes to the slams, you earn everything, nothing is a given. So I loved the fact that Andy was going out there and being more positive and aggressive, and going after it and not waiting for it to come to him.'

Still, in the hours and days that followed that final, Murray wasn't exactly in the sunniest of moods. Federer's victory gave him parity with Pete Sampras – now he, too, had seven Wimbledon titles. At the same time, Murray's defeat meant he was now level with Lendl with four defeats from his first four slam finals. One of the first great tests of Lendl's partnership with Murray came in the aftermath of that final, with the Scot so distraught he sobbed through most of his post-match interview with the BBC's Sue Barker, and then, on returning home, couldn't even find comfort in the company of his two Border Terriers, Maggie May and Rusty. It could take Murray a while to recover from a defeat in a grand slam final. True, he wasn't completely distraught after losing to Federer at the 2008 US Open, as there would have been a certain feeling of accomplishment at just having reached a first slam final. But after the 2010 Australian Open, when he was runner-up to Federer, and then after the 2011 Australian Open, when he lost to Novak Djokovic, it took him weeks, perhaps even months, to find his mojo again. So now Murray had lost to

Federer in the final of a major for a third time, and, at that moment in his career, on one of the saddest days of his tennis life, he couldn't have had better counsel. He was now just one of two players in the modern era to have lost their first four major finals, and the other man was his coach.

Clearly, the Olympics were a great help during Murray's post-Wimbledon recovery period; since the players were all to return to the All England Club for a second time that summer, for the tennis event of the London Games, there simply wasn't much time for moping. However, the key was how Lendl built Murray up again; Murray couldn't have done this on his own. The first of their restorative conversations came almost immediately after the match, backstage in the Wimbledon locker-room, with Lendl telling Murray how proud he was of his performance. During Murray's on-court interview, he had said through the tears: 'I'm getting closer.' Backstage, Lendl agreed, telling him he would be stronger next time. And he was right. Just a few weeks later, Murray was victorious on Wimbledon's Centre Court. There was glory in Murray's Olympic success, and hearing 'God Save the Queen' being played on Centre Court, and, for Lendl, the manner of Murray's success would have been enormously satisfying – in the last two rounds, against Djokovic in the semi-final, and then opposite Federer in the gold medal match, the Scot had played punchy, positive tennis. 'When Andy won the Olympics with Ivan as his coach, that was the signal to me, and to all of us, that Andy would go on to win a grand slam,' Lendl's old coach, Wojtek Fibak, told me.

Who would have imagined that clapping could help make tennis history? Lendl made some key interventions later that summer at the 2012 US Open, as Murray became the first

British man for seventy-six years, since Fred Perry's victory at the same event, to win a grand slam. But the most significant numbers were these: Murray had won his first major on his fifth appearance in a grand slam final, just as Lendl had done. Perhaps it was fitting that Murray's breakthrough came at the US Open, a tournament that Lendl had won three times from eight appearances in the final. To help his player over the line in that epic five-setter against Djokovic, Lendl showed he could sometimes deviate from his protocol of silence and restraint, of projecting a stillness and an authority during the chaos of a slam final. Any other coach clapping when their player appeared in a grand slam final wouldn't be news; it wouldn't even be close to being news. But there was a story breaking in Murray's support box in the Arthur Ashe Stadium, with Lendl putting his hands together. There had been times during the match – Murray scored the first couple of sets, Djokovic then gathered the next two to take the match into a one-set shoot-out – when Murray had thought his coach looked thoroughly bored by proceedings. Of course, Lendl wasn't, but if a bored face was what Murray had come to expect from his coach, you can begin to understand how the Scot would have been emboldened by the sound of Lendl signalling his approval. Even in a stadium filled with more than 20,000 New Yorkers, and with music being played around the stadium, could Murray still hear Lendl clapping? Coaches aren't supposed to give their players any instruction during matches but what Lendl was doing was telling Murray that he liked the big and bold forehands he was playing. 'Andy started hitting better forehands, and I tried to show him, "That's the way". It was a war out there and he needed every bit of encouragement,' Lendl would later disclose, though he has also said that he hadn't been too alarmed by Djokovic levelling the match, as he thought the Serb would be tired in the fifth set. Behind the scenes, behind a closed bathroom door, Murray gave himself the pep talk that changed his life. On leaving the loo, and walking back into the stadium, Murray turned to his guest box, and just looking at his coach galvanised him more for that fifth set.

So, in the swirl and the chaos of a windy New York City, Murray won his first grand slam, and afterwards he was greeted backstage by Lendl, who was smiling like an air stewardess. This was all new. Murray had never had sight of Lendl's American smile for as long as he did that night. Then Lendl was saying how proud he was of Murray, how the Scot had turned in a brilliant, bloody-minded performance. 'That was exactly what I wanted to hear,' Murray would later disclose. You get the sense that Murray took almost as much pleasure from the post-match praise he received from his coach as he did from the initial on-court thrill of finally turning the Big Three and a Half of the men's game into the Big Four. This was their fourth grand slam together, Lendl and Murray were just over nine months into their working relationship, but still one of Murray's motivations was trying to impress his coach. By then, it was also becoming increasingly clear that Lendl was having a good time. Though Lendl had no great love for being on the road, Murray sensed that his coach was enjoying being back on the scene. Still, joshing with old friends in tennis, as well as making new ones, was nothing when set against the pleasure and satisfaction Lendl would have felt from helping Murray to become a grand slam champion.

There was no triumphalism from Lendl that night. He didn't join Murray and the rest of the party at a Chinese restaurant in Manhattan. No one had to tell Lendl that these supposed breakthroughs at the slams sometimes don't turn out to be breakthroughs at all. Winning the 1984 French Open, for his first grand slam title, hadn't been the great turning point in Lendl's life. Indeed, he lost a couple more slam finals after that, giving him a record at that point of just one victory from seven appearances in major finals. Murray's victory in New York certainly wasn't the culmination of Lendl's second act in tennis; he knew that to relax would be to risk the possibility of Murray also struggling to win a second major. Murray would have to keep on toiling. As Cahill put it, there was constant improvement in Murray under Lendl's guidance. 'When Lendl started, he set certain standards for Andy to live up to, and you don't hit those standards straight away, as it takes a bit of time. You're looking for a one or two per cent improvement over the course of time,' the Australian told me. 'Andy has kept on getting better, and that's because he had to. Everybody has to keep on improving because, once you stagnate, you lose touch with the rest of the field. You have to keep tweaking your game and looking for improvement, and to keep practising to make sure you're working on your strengths. It's just small things in many parts of your game.'

For the great majority of the British tennis public, Wimbledon was all that mattered. So Lendl was a failure because, despite everything else he achieved in tennis, he didn't win Wimbledon. Murray's victory at Flushing Meadows was only the second occasion in more than seven years, starting at the 2005 French Open, when someone other than Federer, Nadal or Djokovic had won a slam, with the only other time being Juan Martín del Potro's victory at the 2009 US Open. And yet, for all the applause that followed Murray's achievement, that hadn't satisfied the picnickers on Henman Hill. Winning a grand slam was fine, they were saying, but they weren't going to be happy until Murray had held up a golden pot on Centre Court. Like Lendl, Murray would be defined, in the eyes of the British tennis public, by whether or not he won a title at the All England Club.

So Murray, who finished as the runner-up to Djokovic at the 2013 Australian Open, for what was his fifth defeat from his first six grand slam finals, skipped the French Open to prepare for that summer's Wimbledon Championships, just as his coach had done a couple of times in the early 1990s. But don't imagine for one moment that the Scot's absence from Roland Garros was because of some Lendlesque reasoning that missing the clay-court grand slam would give him the extra grass-court practice he needed. Murray was forced into missing Paris, with a back problem causing him more pain and discomfort when sliding around on clay than when competing on grass. Even so, missing the French Open did wonders for Murray's preparations, as he arrived at the All England Club much fresher than if he had been toiling on French clay just a few days earlier. He also went into Wimbledon having won a tournament at Queen's Club, with that title coming on the same Sunday that he slammed a forehand into his coach's flesh.

Just over a week later, we were into Wimbledon, or, as some American commentators started calling it, 'Wimble-geddon', after some unexpected results, including Rafa Nadal and Roger Federer losing uncommonly early. Nadal's departure came on the opening day – never before had he lost in the first round of a grand slam – when he was beaten by Belgium's Steve Darcis. Then Federer lost in the second round to Ukraine's Sergiy Stakhovsky. And Murray would have some dramas of his own before the final. In all the history and hysteria that followed the tournament, it is easy to forget how Murray came extremely close to going out of the Championships in the quarter-finals when he found himself trailing Spain's Fernando Verdasco by two sets to love. It was plain that Murray hadn't quite adjusted to playing a left-hander for the first time all year, and perhaps if Verdasco, a former top-ten player who had fallen down the rankings, had had more matches in his legs and in his head, he could have closed it out, and the 2013 Wimbledon narrative would have been very different.

But let's not downplay how Murray swung his way out of trouble. At two sets down, he sat down in his chair and started talking to himself. For a moment or two, this was alarming – this looked like a return of one of his pre-Lendl habits, the Murray Monologues. And perhaps the old Murray, the one untouched by Lendl, would have disappeared into some Centre Court vortex, some black hole of despair where he would have met the ghosts of Lendl's Wimbledons past. But this was the new Murray; he dealt with the negative emotions, gathered himself, steadied himself, and then went on to make the semi-finals once again. There was great excitement at the All England Club when Murray shared a few details of his post-match conversation with Sir Alex Ferguson, and how the former manager of Manchester United had spoken to him about the importance of concentration ahead of his semi-final against Poland's Jerzy Janowicz. But even those who have to see everything through the prism of football should be able to accept that Ferguson's pep talk wasn't going to be life-changing. How could it be when he had Lendl in his corner?

Behind the scenes, the pressures of Murray competing for

the Wimbledon title were getting to Lendl. To escape the grass-court frat house, Lendl would turn to his golf clubs. In all, he was in England for more than a month during the summer of 2013 – there was the warm-up tournament at Queen's Club, then the preparation week before Wimbledon, followed by the fortnight at the All England Club – and he has estimated he played golf on twenty-five of those days. Sometimes, he didn't just play a full round, maybe just the last five or six holes, whatever he could fit in before the sun went down: 'I'd just go hit balls to clear my head.'

In the heat and the haze of the All England Club – the referee's office would later disclose that the temperature on Centre Court had touched fifty degrees Celsius – Lendl had hoped to stay composed as he prepared Murray for the final against Novak Djokovic. But that wasn't possible; while Murray didn't feel as much stress before his second Wimbledon final as he had done ahead of his first, as this time he had previous experience of the emotions and the choreography, Lendl somehow seemed more anxious. Throughout the 2013 Championships, Murray had favoured Practice Court Fifteen at Aorangi Park, the training facility inside the Wimbledon grounds, and on the second Sunday of the fortnight he returned to the same court for a late-morning session. As usual, assistant coach Dani Vallverdu was hitting the balls, and Lendl was overseeing the practice, standing at the back of the court. But it was a long way from being a regular practice session. If ever there was confirmation of how much the tender-hearted Lendl cared about Murray's career, it came at Aorangi Park that morning. Immediately, Murray knew that Lendl was nervous because he was 'talking total nonsense – about the colour of the grass, about how the mud on the court is like part of this golf course he had played recently. Anything.' It was a moot point who was more tense – Vallverdu, who was 'framing' shots during practice, or Lendl? Only a Wimbledon final could do this to Lendl, although he has since claimed he was talking rubbish on purpose 'to get Andy out of being nervous'. For Lendl, this was the fourth occasion he had been involved in a Wimbledon final; twice he had suffered defeat as a player, and then he had experienced another failure as a coach; this time, would a title-match finally go his way on Centre Court? The practice session ended with Murray smoking a backhand cross-court winner, a shot that brought, just for a moment or two, a relaxed and contented look to Lendl's face; that soon faded.

In the hours leading up to the match, Lendl gave Murray some final guidance and encouragement. He spoke to Murray about the importance of fighting for every ball against the world number one, while also telling the Briton, 'That's your court, your fans are going to be behind you, just bring the title home.' Lendl told the media, and you can be certain that his message to Murray would have been very similar: 'When you play Djokovic, we all know it's going to be war out there. In a final against somebody ranked nine or ten in the world, the match could be a blowout. Against somebody like Novak, it's very unlikely to end up that way. You know at some stage it comes down to who wants it more, who is tougher and who can execute under extreme pressure. I'm not saying it to sound dramatic – it is war.' But Murray needed to do so much more than show his spirit and resilience; he also had to play the type of tennis that Lendl had always encouraged him to; if he slipped back into his old, pre-Lendl habits of being diffident and reactive rather than proactive, the Serbian was bound to dictate the rallies and would almost certainly win the match.

'Andy has to be focused, and he has to go in with the game-plan discussed with Lendl and execute it,' Tim Henman was saying before play began just after 2 p.m.

Even when the match started, before a British audience of 17.3 million viewers, and tens of millions more around the globe, there was no release of tension for Lendl. It has become one of the Lendl clichés to say that he doesn't ever move during matches, that he shows all the life and animation of the Fred Perry statue, that he only has one pose, chin on upturned palm, and that he only has one expression: blank. That may have been true in some of the earlier rounds, but it wasn't true towards the business end of this tournament. Even in the middle of trying to beat Djokovic, Murray allowed himself to enjoy the sight of seeing Lendl look so 'agitated' during a match. Stoic? Unmoving? The man couldn't sit still all day. 'I had never seen Lendl like that before,' said Boris Becker, who was inside Centre Court. 'So he is human after all.' Whenever Murray looked over at his corner – whether in the moments between points, or while sitting on his chair during a change-over, when there was more time to observe – he invariably saw that Lendl was out of his seat. The clap-count was very high; Lendl possibly clapped his hands together more during that final than he had done during all of the previous matches he had watched as Murray's coach. This went way beyond Lendl's clapping during the 2012 US Open final. And Lendl wasn't silent either. Instead, he was for ever talking to Vallverdu.

Though Murray had taken much from Lendl's usual calmness, there were occasions, such as when he was playing for a grand slam title, when he appreciated seeing just a little more emotion from his coach. 'I could tell he was nervous. It was nice for me to see that because he had been there and done everything,' Murray observed in his book, *Seventy-Seven.* 'I could see how important it was to him. For the first few rounds he didn't move, but this was the Wimbledon final, a stage he had reached himself as a player. This was why he wanted to come back to tennis. He wanted to be the best coach he could be and it was nice to see him in a bit of a state in the final. I liked that.' Still, it wasn't just Lendl: almost everyone inside Centre Court that afternoon was in 'a bit of a state' as Murray served for a straight sets victory that would make him the first British man to win Wimbledon for seventy-seven years. From leading forty-love, Murray then went through the stress of having to fend off three breakpoints for Djokovic, before then taking his fourth Championship point when the Serb fired a backhand into the net.

Judy Murray once described the experience of watching her son play tennis as a mixture of 'nausea and heart-attack', and you can imagine that, after this final, that would have been a description that Lendl would have agreed with. One former Wimbledon champion, Dutchman Richard Krajicek, observed that someone who hadn't watched the final could have looked at the scoreline – a 6-4, 7-5, 6-4 victory for Murray – and concluded that it must have been a straightforward affair. The reality, as Lendl would have appreciated, was that much hung on that tenth game of the third set; had Djokovic broken Murray as the Briton served for the Championships, there would have been such a giant swing in momentum that the Serbian would have been well-placed to go on to win the title. Had Murray finished as the runner-up, his record in grand slam finals would have been just one victory from his first seven appearances, but, more significant than that is that he would have lost a Wimbledon final after holding match points. That would have been hard to recover from, even for someone who had been toughened up and Lendl-ised. And, for Lendl, the second Sunday of a Wimbledon fortnight would have brought him even more pain. As it was, Murray had held it all together.

It was after Pat Cash defeated Lendl in a final that he pioneered the post-match celebration of climbing up the Centre Court seating to hug, kiss and high-five friends, family, lovers, employees and anyone else within range. Since then, most players have done the same or something similar after winning Wimbledon, and Murray wasn't going to break with what has become the new protocol. It wasn't the case, as he made his ascent towards his own section of Centre Court, that he had already decided he would hug his coach first; it just turned out that way, because of where Lendl was standing. 'But it was fitting,' Murray would later observe, 'that Ivan was the first person I saw.' Not for the last time that day, there was a smile on Lendl's face. 'I'm just glad I could be part of it,' Lendl said later. Once again, part of Murray's motivation had been wanting to please and impress his coach. 'This one is for Ivan because I know he did everything to try to win it when he was playing,' Murray disclosed, 'so I'm glad I could help him out when he was coaching.'

There's a theory, and one I put to Boris Becker, that Andy Murray won the 2013 Wimbledon Championships because of Ivan Lendl, that the Scot couldn't have scored the tournament that summer without Lendl in his corner. Becker didn't disagree. 'It's difficult to prove otherwise,' was his response. 'Since Lendl came on board, Murray has gained an extra ten per cent. Their record together speaks for itself. Before working with Lendl, Murray hadn't won a grand slam. And then suddenly in their first couple of years together, Murray won an Olympic title, and then a couple of slams, the US Open and then Wimbledon. A lot of that has to be because of the coach.'

There is a range of opinions on this subject. Paul Annacone, who has coached two of the greatest players of all time, Roger Federer and Pete Sampras, took a different view. 'Absolutely Murray could have won Wimbledon without Lendl,' Annacone told me. 'I have never thought that the coach is the reason a player wins a tournament – we are ingredients, some more valuable and impactful than others – but ultimately the player is driving the bus, so to speak. Andy is a great player and I never doubted he would be a grand slam champion – it was more a question of when it would happen.' Maybe the best way of looking at this is to suggest that Lendl accelerated the process. Perhaps, if Murray had never employed Lendl, he would still have ended up becoming a Wimbledon champion during his career, but would he have won the title in 2013 if he hadn't had Lendl in his entourage? There has to be considerable doubt over whether a Murray without Lendl could have closed out that straight-sets victory over Djokovic. And it's universally agreed that Lendl has transformed Murray. 'A coach is only as good as a player, and Andy is a phenomenal player, so I don't think you can say that Andy won the 2013 Wimbledon Championships just because of Lendl,' Tim Henman told me. 'But has Lendl had an impact on Andy? In my opinion, absolutely he's had an impact.' Murray himself has described hooking up with Lendl as the best decision he ever made.

Maybe we shouldn't be looking at how Lendl inspired,

encouraged and shaped Murray, but how he intimidated Murray's opponent; perhaps that was where Lendl had the greatest effect on events. It's the view of Lendl's old coach, Wojtek Fibak, that it was Lendl's presence in Murray's support box that enabled the Briton to win his first Wimbledon title. The 2013 Wimbledon final was pre-Becker: Murray had a former legend in his corner, and Djokovic didn't. And maybe the Serb felt a touch underpowered without a grandee on his staff. 'I told Djokovic that he lost the Wimbledon to Murray in the locker-room. And that was because of Ivan,' Fibak told me. 'It was the same the year before in the 2012 US Open. Djokovic also lost that match because Ivan was there. Andy believed that he could win those two matches, at the US Open and at Wimbledon. I'm not taking anything away from Novak's team, but that team had been there for a long time, and the fact that Ivan was there, with Andy, that changed the mental momentum. It went Murray's way. Of course, Murray could have lost to Verdasco earlier in the 2013 Wimbledon Championships, but because Ivan was there, Murray knew that he couldn't lose, even when he was two sets down. Against Verdasco in the quarter-finals and then against Janowicz in the semi-finals, and against Djokovic in the final, Murray believed because he had Ivan sitting there in his corner.'

But what had Murray done for Lendl? Lendl has said that in his retirement he didn't spend too much time thinking about his past disappointments at the All England Club. Lendl's anxiety before and during the final showed just how much he cared about Murray realising his ambitions. Had Murray's victory somehow made up for the fact that Lendl never won Wimbledon in the 1980s? Cash didn't think so. 'I'm sure that Murray winning Wimbledon would have given Lendl great joy,' Cash told me, 'but that wouldn't have been the same for him as Lendl doing it himself.' Just recall what Lendl had said in the summer of 2012, on the subject of whether coaching Murray to a Wimbledon title would in any way make up for his disappointments as a player: 'You guys are overthinking everything. You are so far in left field, so far out of the ballpark, you just have no idea.'

It's not Lendl's style to overstate his role. As Lendl has said: 'It's about Andy, not me.' Still, just consider how Murray reacted after Lendl told him that he was proud of him for his Wimbledon victory: 'Coming from Ivan, that meant a lot. I mean, I think he believed in me when a lot of people didn't. He stuck by me through some tough losses the last couple of years. He's been very patient with me. I'm just happy I managed to do it for him.' If Murray won Wimbledon for himself, he also won it for his coach.

And coaching a Briton to the Wimbledon title had enabled Lendl to attain what had always been out of his reach during his first tennis life: popularity with the British public. Eight months after Murray won Wimbledon, Lendl found himself competing in front of a British crowd, facing Cash in a World Tennis Day nostalgia match at Earls Court Exhibition Centre in London. Looking at the demographic of the crowd, you have to imagine that a fair number of those in the audience that night would have been the same people who around thirty years earlier would have been deriding Lendl as a robotic failure; now they had paid to watch him relive one of his two failures in Wimbledon finals, and appeared to be enjoying every one of his creaky moves. The match was punctuated by loud cheers. And then, when Lendl gave a fine, funny performance during his post-match chat on court, the place exploded into laughter. That wasn't love he could hear all around him, but it was certainly affection.

While Lendl had skipped the evening celebrations that followed Murray's victory at the 2012 US Open, he wasn't going to miss the official function after the 2013 Wimbledon fortnight. So Lendl went to the Champions' Dinner, at a London hotel that night. He would be photographed wearing a tuxedo and a grin, and posing with the trophy. One spy at the dinner – where guests were served sea trout, crab and seared scallop, followed by halibut, flourless chocolate cake, and coffee and petits fours – told me that he had never seen Lendl smile so much. 'Ideally, Ivan would have won Wimbledon himself,' Murray has said, 'but I think this was the next best thing for him, and I'm being serious when I say that.' For Murray, winning Wimbledon was 'the pinnacle of tennis'. Look again at those photographs of Lendl with the golden, pineapple-topped cup. Squint hard. Now squint a little harder again. That's almost how Lendl would have looked as the Wimbledon champion.

EPILOGUE

I t was the tennis divorce that no one, not even Andy Murray as he made his way to a dinner with Ivan Lendl one Saturday evening in Miami, had been predicting. If it's highly irregular for a coach or employee to be the one who precipitates the end of a working relationship – almost every partnership ends with the player doing the ditching and the dumping – it's rarer still for a tennis couple to split up because they had been so successful.

Here was a break-up that can be traced back to Centre Court: the indications are that Lendl and Murray's collaboration would have continued beyond March 2014, so extending a relationship that had already given the Scot the best two years of his tennis life, if Murray hadn't won Wimbledon. Most tennis lives, and partnerships, end in failure; the Lendl–Murray project didn't. Officially, Lendl and Murray broke up during a springtime meeting in a Miami restaurant but, looking back, it would appear that the end had really come the previous summer – and an ocean away – on that glorious, near-mythical and sun-buttered July afternoon in London when the Scot defeated Novak Djokovic in the 2013 Wimbledon final. Maybe you can even trace it to a hug, to that moment during the wait for the prizegiving ceremony when Murray climbed up to his guest box and the first person he embraced was Lendl. By then, Murray had already won the Olympics and the US Open, but it was victory on the Wimbledon grass that had given the project a sense of completion. Had Murray been broken as he served for a straight-sets victory, and subsequently gone on to lose that final after holding match points, Lendl would have felt very differently about the work he had done with the Briton.

In the eight months between Murray and Lendl going to Wimbledon's Champions' Dinner and the partnership coming to a close, the Scot hadn't accomplished a great deal. For a couple of months after becoming Britain's first Wimbledon champion in shorts, Murray had felt, quite understandably, flat and lacking in inspiration, and then in September 2013 he had an operation to resolve his back problem and didn't play again that season. Between winning Wimbledon and finding himself without a head coach, Murray didn't reach another final of any category of tournament, let alone win another title. But even if he had it wouldn't have touched the heights of Wimbledon. The reality was that Murray and Lendl were never going to have another emotional high like the one they experienced together in the summer of 2013. They could have gone on to win another five Wimbledons together, but every time it wouldn't have felt as special or as cathartic as that first victory.

This break-up hadn't been trailed anywhere. To Murray's

mind, his time with Lendl had come to a premature end; and most would indeed contend there were gaps in their body of work. It was a pity that Lendl, who has great admiration for Rafa Nadal's work ethic and uncompromising approach to competition, never had the opportunity to prepare Murray tactically and psychologically for playing the Majorcan. Also missing from Murray's Lendl Years was a full-blooded challenge at Roland Garros – where his coach had won the title on three occasions – as Murray experienced back spasms during the 2012 tournament and then missed the 2013 event because of the discomfort caused by his back. Technically, Lendl coaching Murray to the French Open title, on the clay courts where the man from Dunblane had historically achieved weaker results than at the other slams, would have arguably been a greater feat than what they achieved together at Wimbledon, though of course it wouldn't have had anything like the same impact. But it wasn't to be. While Lendl and Murray hadn't conquered the world, they had achieved plenty. 'Ivan was brought in to help get me over the line in big events,' Murray would observe, 'and that's what he did.'

There was something fitting about the termination of this partnership; they ended as they had started. Lendl and Murray had astounded tennis when news broke on New Year's Eve 2011 that they would be working together, and then in the spring of 2014 they would shock the sport again. A partnership that began in one Florida restaurant would end in another. And however painful it would have been for Murray to hear over dinner, it was also appropriate, perhaps even inevitable, that it was Lendl who had triggered the breakup. For Murray, one of the attractions of hiring Lendl had been that this former champion didn't need the job, that he

wouldn't in any way be beholden to the Briton. That enabled Lendl to give Murray honest, direct opinions; that also
allowed Lendl to walk away from the job that had not only
transformed Murray's career, but had also changed how the
galleries saw Old Stone Face.

The way it was presented was in a statement that the protag-
onists had both signed off: Lendl and Murray had mutually
agreed to stop working together. And yet it would appear that
it was Lendl who precipitated the end, and not Murray, with
Lendl making it clear he couldn't give Murray the time he
wanted. For a few weeks before that Miami dinner, Murray
had been aware that there was a degree of uncertainty over his
future with Lendl; a couple of telephone conversations had
suggested that it 'wasn't impossible' that their player–coach
relationship could be dissolved between courses. However, he
certainly hadn't been expecting the partnership to end that
evening; that's evident from the pair speaking about other
matters for at least an hour before then turning to the subject
of how they could 'move forward' together.

One consequence of Lendl's highly successful second tennis life as a coach had been that it had brought a surge in
his value in the tennis marketplace; sitting in Murray's corner
had raised his profile and increased the public's appetite for
seeing this face from the 1980s competing in what some like
to call the 'old dudes circuit'. Thanks, in no small part, to
the exposure and recognition he was receiving for coaching
Murray, Lendl's diary was filling up with other commitments,
and Lendl was having a ball at those seniors' events. In the
weeks that preceded the split, Lendl had appeared at four
events in the United States – in Kansas City, Oklahoma City,
Nashville and Charlotte – as well as taking part in the World

Tennis Day exhibition in London. In addition, Lendl had been giving coaching clinics in the Canary Islands and promoting his own academy in South Carolina, though, of course, the best promotion that place ever had was when Lendl guided Murray to the Olympic, US Open and Wimbledon titles (even if Lendl hadn't been there in person during the 2012 London Games). The academy's website even ran a special discount of 10 per cent off the tuition fees if you called and mentioned Murray's name.

Throughout their time together, Lendl hadn't been one of those coaches who turns up at every stop on the calendar – that had never been the plan. Indeed, Murray's last tournament with Lendl on the payroll was a hard-court event at the Indian Wells Tennis Garden in the Californian desert, where the Scot played some soft tennis to lose in the fourth round to Canada's Milos Raonic, and that was played out in Lendl's absence. When, a few days later, they met for that Miami dinner, it was the first time they had seen each other since January's Australian Open – at what would turn out to be their last grand slam tournament as a duo, Murray had lost in the quarter-finals to Roger Federer. One of the tournaments that Murray had played between Melbourne and Miami was in Acapulco, and Lendl had been reliant on information from assistant coach Dani Vallverdu. And then in early March, towards the very end of his time as Murray's coach, Lendl disclosed that he hadn't had the chance to speak to his employer about the Scot's decision to break into his annual off-season training block in Miami to appear in an exhibition series in Asia. In the six months between Murray's September back operation and the March break-up, they hadn't spent much time in each other's company. Some would later wonder why Lendl and Murray couldn't have carried on, just with a reduced commitment. After all, Stefan Edberg and Federer had agreed to spend ten weeks together in 2014, and the Swede seemed to be having a positive impact on the Swiss's game. But such a part-time arrangement wouldn't have satisfied Lendl or Murray.

Over dinner, it became plain that Lendl didn't have enough space in his diary to give Murray what the Briton would regard as 'a decent amount of time together'. 'Ivan completely understands that as well, and that was why we decided to stop working together because it wasn't going to be of benefit to anyone doing the job half-baked. That's what Ivan's like,' Murray said in an interview with British newspapers. 'He will do things properly, he doesn't want to do it halfway.' It was plain from Lendl's comments that, having helped Murray, he now wanted to do other things with his time. 'Working with Andy over the last two years has been a fantastic experience for me. He is a first-class guy. Having helped him achieve his goal of winning major titles, I feel like it is time for me to concentrate on some of my own projects moving forward, including playing more events around the world, which I am really enjoying,' Lendl said. 'I will always be in Andy's corner and wish him nothing but great success as he goes into a new phase of his career.'

This was a new experience for Murray, with a coaching relationship ending before he had wanted it to. Mark Petchey, Brad Gilbert and Miles Maclagan hadn't broken up with him, which would have made it easier staying on friendly terms with those exes. But, for all the disappointment that Murray would have felt over Lendl's departure – this was already an unsettling time in his tennis life as he built himself up after his back operation – he didn't display any anger or resentment towards Lendl. This pair had introduced the idea of the modern generation coupling up with superstars from the 1980s, and here they were demonstrating that it was perfectly possible for superstar divorces to be amicable. The night of the Miami dinner, Murray would disclose, was 'tough'. 'The next couple of days on court weren't particularly fun. I was gutted but I still think the guy is great. It's not like anything has changed there,' Murray said. 'It's a tough one for me because he's been a big part of my life. He's been a big part of my team, and he made a huge difference to my tennis. So he's a very hard person to replace.'

That evening, and at all times, Murray would act with good grace, with the announcement of the break-up even being pushed out from the email account of the managing director of 77, the company that Murray had set up after winning Wimbledon to look after his business interests. Just days later, there was a very public display of friendship between Lendl and Murray, with Lendl making a three-hour journey from his home in Vero Beach to watch Murray play at Miami's Crandon Park, where he was hoping to retain his title. In some ways, this was a rather confusing spectacle, with Lendl sitting back in Murray's support box, as if the break-up had never happened. But, in other ways, this looked very different. In a departure from Lendl's past behaviour during Murray's competitive appearances, there were even a few grins (the first tournament of this post-Lendl phase of Murray's life would end in the quarter-finals with a defeat against Djokovic).

Above all, Murray was 'eternally grateful' for the time and energy that Lendl had invested in him. Even as Murray grieved for the relationship, he would surely already have started to appreciate that the process of being Lendl-ised would help him for the rest of his playing days. It wasn't as if all they had done together, all those conversations and practice sessions, all those matches and silly jokes, had suddenly been deleted. Lendl was gone, but you imagined Murray wouldn't be going back to his old ways. And whatever happens to Murray for the rest of his career, he will always have his Wimbledon title. As far as any coach can do this to a player, Ivan Lendl, that man from the Ostrava smokestacks, had future-proofed Andy Murray.

LENDL RETURNED JUNE 2016

ACKNOWLEDGMENTS

This wasn't a project that began in some crappy Italian restaurant in a shopping mall near a highway; we'll leave that to Ivan Lendl and Andy Murray, whose collaboration was sealed just off Interstate 95 in Florida. This started over a good cup of coffee in a private members' club in London's Soho: I'm grateful to Robin Harvie, my editor at Aurum, for not subjecting me to soggy pasta, but primarily for having the idea for this book and for asking me to write it. As well as for his guidance and encouragement along the way. I'm also indebted to all those who spoke to me on the record, including Lendl, Judy Murray, Boris Becker, Pat Cash, Mats Wilander, Wojtek Fibak, Tomas Smid, Jan Kodes, Darren Cahill, Michael Chang, Toni Nadal, Paul Annacone, Tim Henman, Mark Petchey, Miles Maclagan, Chris Evert and Marc Howard. And to everyone who gave me off-the-record background information.

Thanks is also due to Martin Prazak and his colleagues for

their help searching through the Security Services Archives, as well as to Mark Kramer, the Director of the Cold War Studies Programme at Harvard University, and Igor Lukes, a Professor in Boston University's International Relations Department, for their guidance, and to Veronika Milarova for translating the documents. Thanks also to Stefano Semeraro for his valuable insight into Ostrava's towerblocks, to Audrey Snell and Alan Little at the All England Club Library for the 1980s time travel, the hot drinks and biscuits, to Lisa Trampota at the George Bush Presidential Library, and to President George Bush Senior's official spokesman, Jim McGrath. A couple of new fathers, James Buddell and Simon Cambers, were extremely generous with their time, looking over the manuscript and making suggestions on how I could improve the text. Thanks also to David Luxton and Rebecca Winfield of David Luxton Associates, and to Robin's brilliant team at Aurum, including Lucy Warburton and Charlotte Coulthard.

INDEX